The Epistles of St. Peter and St. Jude Preached and Explained

Martin Luther

Alpha Editions

This edition published in 2021

ISBN : 9789354840074

Design and Setting By
Alpha Editions
www.alphaedis.com
Email - info@alphaedis.com

As per information held with us this book is in Public Domain.
This book is a reproduction of an important historical work. Alpha Editions
uses the best technology to reproduce historical work in the same manner
it was first published to preserve its original nature. Any marks or number
seen are left intentionally to preserve its true form.

Contents

PREFACE BY THE TRANSLATOR. — - 1 -

THE FIRST EPISTLE GENERAL OF ST. PETER — - 5 -

INTRODUCTION. — - 6 -

CHAPTER I. — - 8 -

CHAPTER II. — - 42 -

CHAPTER III. — - 75 -

CHAPTER IV. — - 100 -

CHAPTER V. — - 112 -

THE SECOND EPISTLE GENERAL OF ST. PETER — - 123 -

PREFACE. — - 124 -

CHAPTER I. — - 125 -

CHAPTER II. — - 139 -

CHAPTER III. — - 159 -

SAINT JUDE — - 165 -

PREFACE BY THE TRANSLATOR.

Several years ago, among the dusty piles of old pamphlets stored away upon the upper shelves of the Union Theological Seminary library, I met with several works of Luther, in the original editions, as they were issued during his lifetime from his press at Wittemberg. Among them were his Commentaries, or rather Lectures, on the Epistles of Peter and Jude.* The forbidding aspect of the page, with the obsolete spelling of its words, and its somewhat coarse typography, was rather an incitement to master it; for here was Luther, presenting himself to the eye of the reader just as, more than three hundred years ago, he presented himself to the eyes of thousands of his countrymen. Upon a partial perusal of the Commentary, I became satisfied that it would repay a more attentive study; and finding, upon investigation, that it had never been translated into English, I set myself to the task which had been so long neglected. The pleasing labor was accomplished, and the manuscript laid aside for several years. The conviction, confirmed by a re-perusal of it, that others besides myself would be interested in the work, has led me to determine on its publication.

> * Another copy of this same edition of Luther on Peter, belonging to a clergyman's library which was sold at auction in this city, four or five years since, brought an almost fabulous price.

Luther's Commentary on the Galatians, excellent as it is, is too voluminous and expensive to be very extensively circulated, while the phraseology of the early translation, which has not been modified, prevents its proper appreciation by modern readers. And yet any one that would truly know the man, and the secret of his power, must study these in his writings. The Commentary on the Epistles of Peter and Jude, presented in a literal but more modern style to the English reader, is not liable to these objections; and yet, in the variety of its themes, the clearness of its exposition, the stinging force of its rebukes, the simplicity and directness of its language, it is scarcely surpassed by any of Luther's other writings. On the great subject of justification by faith alone, he is here, as in his Commentary on the Epistle to the Galatians, full and emphatic. The relation of faith to works is clearly and carefully defined, while the subjects presented in the text afford full opportunity for discussing the great questions that concern the relative duties of civil and social life. The volume thus becomes at once a manual of doctrine and of duty. On the foundation of faith is reared the superstructure of a Christian life. Luther is seen to have fully apprehended the force of all the objections that could be urged against his teachings, and with convincing ability he vindicates them from every charge. Throughout the volume we have ever before us the earnest, devout spirit of the Reformer, for the most part unfolding in the simplest manner the great doctrines of the Gospel, but occasionally indulging in volcanic outbursts of indignation against the hierarchical corruptions of his day, and pouring out upon them the lava-tides of withering rebuke.

It may seem strange that this work of Luther's has never before been translated. But, unlike his Commentary on the Epistle to the Galatians, which he himself translated into Latin, that it might have a wider circulation among the learned of Europe, this was published by him only in the German language, which was little known in England, and hence it was deprived of that notoriety which would have drawn special attention to it, as well as of that Latin dress which would have facilitated an English translation. It is well known, moreover, that Luther formed a most humble estimate of his own writings, and was uniformly reluctant to collect his works in volumes, or bestow upon them any editorial care. He seemed perfectly willing to have them sink to oblivion, and could not be persuaded by the most urgent representations to do anything which might rescue them from such a fate. Besides, it is to be noted that a perusal of this volume especially would soon satisfy the reader, that after the accession of Queen Elizabeth to the throne, it stood little chance of securing the necessary approval or *imprimatur* of an English bishop.

Yet the work is one of no little historical as well as antiquarian interest. It has done its part in one of the greatest intellectual and religious conflicts of the world. It is the sword that a giant wielded, and that has done execution on a broad field. In the great armory of the Reformation-writings, scarcely another deserves a more conspicuous place. It presents those views of the relative spheres of Divine and human authority which became prevalent wherever the cause of Reform advanced. It unmasked popular errors, rebuked ecclesiastical corruption, and vindicated most effectively the simple doctrines of faith. Here, moreover, we see Luther clad in the armor with which he boldly challenged the Papacy to a lifelong combat. The man is before us, girded for the battle, and we see the weapons upon which he relies. If one of those cannon balls with which English valor won the battle of Cressy,—the first in which the efficiency of the new invention was tested,—could be picked up there now, and it could be ascertained that it did service in that famous battle, it would be an object of no small interest, at least to the antiquary; but in regard to this treatise of Luther, we know full well that Rome felt its visitation as something more terrible than a bombshell exploding beneath the dome of St. Peter's. Under the authority of Peter himself it demolished the very foundations of the throne upon which his pretended successors were seated, and gave a most effective impulse to the onward movement of reform.

Nor is this all. It is still capable of doing effective service. After all the rust and tarnish of three centuries, these words of Luther are remarkably fresh, and seem almost like a living utterance of to-day. Their critical value is not indeed great, although by no means contemptible, for the quick sagacity of the Reformer in detecting the meaning and the force of the Scriptural argument, is evident on every page, and is rarely at fault; but his clear views of the Gospel, his untrammeled freedom of thought, his strong good sense, and his most effective energy of application are everywhere conspicuous. His language is uniformly simple and direct. The exposition contained in this volume was first delivered from the pulpit. According to the title-page, it is Scripture "preached and explained," and in addressing it to the people, Luther did not fail to keep in view the object upon which he set so high an estimate, when he said, "I preach as simply as possible. I want the common people, and children, and servants, to understand me."

The care with which he fortifies his positions with Scriptural citations is likewise obvious. He rarely presents views upon any theme from which one who acknowledges the authority of Scripture will feel forced to dissent, unless, with some, the subject of baptism should an exception. In regard to this, he speaks like one who as yet sees "men as trees walking."

Considerable space is given up to an exposure of the errors and abuses of the Papacy, but the exposure is made uniformly by the light of Scripture. Vehement as are Luther's occasional bursts of indignation, he never wanders from the subject, and never ventures beyond where he is sustained by the clear warrant of the word of God.

In the purpose of presenting this translation to English readers, I have been encouraged by the prospect of affording to others the same opportunity of acquaintance with Luther's modes of thought and feeling which I have myself enjoyed. I believe, moreover, that his exposition has a high value, apart from the interest which attaches to it as the production of the great hero of the Reformation. Occasionally, the views presented have seemed to be such as required some explanatory note or correction, and in a few instances this has been appended, but the necessity has rarely occurred, and Luther is left throughout to speak for himself. The translation is strictly literal, and almost the only variations from the original are so marked, by being inclosed in parentheses. These will readily be distinguished from the passages or words included in parentheses of the original text, by their explanatory character.

It would have been a far easier task to have given a more liberal and polished rendering of Luther's language. But I think most readers would prefer to have me give them Luther, rather than—the translator. There are occasional roughnesses of expression, and some sentences which were evidently not very lucidly reported, but they are features of the book which presents Luther to us, and even the wart on the face must appear in the faithful portrait.

For assistance in the labor of revising some of the more difficult passages, I am indebted to Prof. ROBINSON, of the Union Theological Seminary, and to Rev. M. BUSHE, pastor of a German church in this city. By their aid, which I take this occasion gratefully to acknowledge, I feel confident that nearly every passage, in which the text of the original is not in fault, has been correctly rendered.

I had hoped, in this connection, to present an estimate of Luther's writings, from the pen of one of the most eminent German scholars which our country can boast. The permission to do so was kindly granted, but the limited space allowed for prefatory remark forbids it. I will only add the expression of my own conviction, that from the exceedingly voluminous works of Luther, other selections of high merit might be made, the translation and publication of which would be welcomed with grateful acknowledgment by a large class of American and English readers. I should be highly gratified if the encouragement afforded by my words or example should induce any one more competent than myself, or who can command more leisure for it, to prosecute the work which I have only just begun.

E. H. GILLETT.

HARLEM, March 8th, 1859.

THE FIRST EPISTLE GENERAL OF ST. PETER

INTRODUCTION.

Before we enter upon this Epistle of St. Peter, it is necessary to present a brief Introduction,* that it may be understood how this Epistle is to be ranked, and in order that a right apprehension of it may be attained.

 * Literally, *instruction*.

In the first place, it must be understood that all the Apostles present one and the same doctrine; and it is not correct to speak of* four Evangelists and four Gospels for all which the Apostles wrote is one Gospel. But *Gospel* means nothing but a proclamation and heralding of the grace and mercy of God through Jesus Christ, merited and procured through his death. And it is not properly that which is contained in books, and is comprehended in the letter, but rather an oral proclamation and living word, and a voice which echoes through the whole world, and is publicly uttered that it may universally be heard. Neither is it a book of laws, containing in itself many excellent doctrines, as has hitherto been held. For it does not bid us do works whereby we may become righteous, but proclaims to us the grace of God, bestowed freely, and apart from any merit of our own; and it tells how Christ has taken our place, and rendered satisfaction for our sins, and canceled them, and by His own works justifies and saves us.

 * Count.

Whoever sets forth this, by preaching or writing, *he* teaches the true Gospel, as all the Apostles did, especially St. Paul and St. Peter, in their Epistles. So that all, whatever it be, that sets forth Christ, is one and the same Gospel, although one may use a different method, and speak of it in different language from another, for it may perhaps be a brief or extended address, or a brief or extended writing. But yet, if it tends to this point, that Christ is our Saviour, and we through faith on Him, apart from works of our own, are justified and saved, it is still the same Word, and but one Gospel, just as there is also but one faith and one baptism in the whole Christian world.

So, also, one Apostle has written the same [Gospel] that is contained in another's writings; but they who insist most largely and emphatically on this, that faith on Christ alone justifies, are the best Evangelists. Therefore St. Paul's Epistles are more a Gospel than Matthew, Mark and Luke, for the latter give little more than the history of the works and miracles of Christ; but of the grace which we have through Christ, none write so emphatically as St. Paul, especially in his Epistle to the Romans. And yet, since more importance by far belongs to the word than to the works and deeds of Christ, and where we are to be deprived of one it were better that we should want the works and the history than the word and the doctrine; those books are to be most highly esteemed which most largely treat of the doctrine and words of the Lord Christ; for though the miracles of Christ had never been, and we had no knowledge of them, we should yet have had enough in the *word*, without which we could not have had life.

Thus this Epistle of St. Peter is one of the noblest books in the New Testament, and contains indeed the pure Gospel; for he takes the same course as St. Paul and all the Evangelists, in inculcating the true doctrine of faith,—as that Christ has been given us, who takes away our sin and saves us, as we shall hear.

Hence you may judge of all books and doctrines, what is Gospel or not; for what is not set forth or written of in this manner, you may safely decide to be false, however excellent in appearance. This power to decide is one that all Christians possess,—not the Pope or Councils, who boast that they only have the power to determine.—This is sufficient introduction and preface. Let us now listen to the Epistle.

CHAPTER I.

V. 1, 2. Peter an Apostle of Jesus Christ, to the strangers scattered abroad in Pontus, Galatia, Capadocia, Asia and Bithynia, elect according to the foreknowledge of God the Father, through sanctification of the Spirit, unto obedience and sprinkling of the blood of Jesus Christ.

That is the superscription and subscription. Here you quickly perceive that it is the Gospel. He calls himself an Apostle—that is, one sent to declare a message; therefore it is correctly rendered in Dutch, a messenger, or a twelfth-messenger,* because they were twelve. But since it is generally understood what Apostle (the Greek word) means, I have not rendered it in Dutch. But its peculiar meaning is, one who bears a message by word of mouth; not one who carries letters, but a capable man who presents a matter orally, and advocates it,—of the class that in the Latin are called *Oratores*. So he would now say, I am an Apostle of Jesus Christ,—that is, I have a command from Jesus Christ that I, from Christ, am to proclaim.

> * *Tswolffbott* in the original, for which we have no equivalent English word.

Observe, here, how promptly all those who teach human doctrine are excluded. For *he* is a messenger of Jesus Christ who presents that which Christ has commanded; should he preach otherwise, he is not a messenger of Christ, and therefore should not be listened to. But if he does this, it is just as important as though you heard Christ himself present.

To the strangers scattered abroad. This epistle was written to lands which were formerly Christian but are now subject to the Turk, yet it is possible some Christians might be found there even at this day. Pontus is a large, broad region, lying on the sea. Capadocia is in the same neighborhood, and borders on it. Galatia lies back of them. Asia and Bithynia border on the sea—extending eastward—and are extensive regions. Paul also preached in Galatia, and in Asia; whether in Bithynia also, I do not know. In the other two he did not preach. *Strangers* are such as we call foreigners. He names them so because they were Gentiles; and it is a thing to surprise us, that St. Peter, inasmuch as he was an Apostle to the Jews, should still write to the Gentiles. The Jews called these (of whom we speak) Proselytes,—that is, associated Jews, such as adopted their law, but were not of a Jewish family or the blood of Abraham. Thus he writes to those who had previously been heathen (of the Gentiles), but were now converted to the faith, and had joined the believing Jews, and he calls them *elect strangers*, who certainly are Christians, to whom alone he writes. This is a point worthy of observation, as we shall hear.

According to the foreknowledge of God the Father. They are elect, he says. How? Not of themselves, but according to God's purpose: for we should be unable to raise ourselves to heaven, or create faith within ourselves. God will not permit all men to enter heaven; those who are his own he will receive with all readiness. The human doctrine of free-will, and of our own ability, is futile. The matter does not lie in our wills, but in the will and election of God.

Through sanctification of the Spirit. God has predestinated us that we should be holy, and, moreover, that we should be spiritually holy. Those precious words, Holy and Spiritual, have been perverted for us through the greed of the preachers, in that they have denominated the state of priests and monks holy and spiritual, and have thus scandalously robbed us of these noble, precious words, as also of the word Church, since with *them* the Pope and Bishops are the Church, while they do according to their own pleasure whatever they choose, in virtue of the declaration, "The Church has forbidden it." Holiness is not that which consists in the estate of monks, priests and nuns,—the wearing of the tonsure and cowl; it is a spiritual word, meaning that there is an inward holiness in the spirit before God. And this is the reason specially why he said this, in order to show that there is nothing holy but that holiness which God produces within us.

For although the Jews had much outward or ceremonial holiness, there was yet in this no genuine holiness. Peter would say here, God has predestinated you to this end, that ye should be truly holy; as Paul also says, in Eph. iv., "In righteousness and true holiness"—that is, in a genuine and well-founded holiness,—for outward holiness, such as the Jews had, is of no value before God.

Thus the Scripture calls us holy, while we yet live on earth, if we believe. But the Papists have taken the name from us, and say, we are not to be holy; the saints in Heaven alone are holy. Thus we are compelled to reclaim the noble name. You must be holy, but you must also beware against imagining that you are holy through yourself or by your own merit, but only that you have God's word, that Heaven is yours, that you are truly pious and made holy by Christ.

This you must confess if you would be a Christian. For it would be the greatest affront and reviling of the name of Christ, if we took from the honor due to Christ's blood, in that it is this that washes away our sins, or from the faith that this blood sanctifies us.

Therefore, you must believe and confess if you would be holy; but by this blood, not by your own excellence must it be, insomuch that for it you would be willing to give up life and all that you possess, and endure whatever might come upon you.

To obedience and the sprinkling of the blood of Christ. Hereby, he says, are we made holy, if we are obedient, and believe the word of Christ, and are sprinkled with his blood. And here St. Peter speaks in a somewhat different manner from St. Paul. But it is in substance the same as when Paul says that we are saved through faith in Christ; for faith makes us obedient and submissive to Christ and his word. For to obey the word of God and the word of Christ is the same thing, and to be sprinkled by his blood is the same as to believe. For it is difficult to nature, hostile to it, and exceedingly humbling, to submit to Christ, give up all its own possessions, and account them contemptible and sinful. But yet it must be brought into subjection.

Of sprinkling, the Psalm *Miserere Domine* (li.) also speaks: "Sprinkle me with hyssop, and I shall be clean." It refers to the law of Moses, from which St. Peter has derived it, and he discloses Moses to our view, while he brings in the Scripture. When Moses had built the tabernacle, he took the blood of bullocks and sprinkled it over all the people.

But *this* sprinkling sanctifies not in the spirit, but only outwardly. Therefore there must be a spiritual purification, since an outward holiness, and one that pertains to the flesh, is of no avail before God. And so God, by this sprinkling, has typified the spiritual sprinkling. As though Peter had said, the Jews who were in that holiness which was outward were held as righteous, and persons of a pure life. But you are reputed base, yet you have a better sprinkling; you are sprinkled in the Spirit, that you may be pure from within. The Jews were sprinkled outwardly with the blood of bullocks, but we are sprinkled inwardly in the conscience, so that the heart is made pure and joyful.

Thus the Gentiles are Gentiles no longer. The righteous Jews, with their sprinkling, are no more righteous, but all is reversed. There must be a sprinkling which converts us and makes us spiritually minded.

To preach sprinkling is to preach that Christ has shed his blood, and for us has ascended to his Father, and intercedes, saying, "Beloved Father! behold my blood which I have shed for these sinners." If you believe this, you are sprinkled. Thus you see the right method of preaching. If all the popes, monks and priests were to fuse all the matter of their preaching into one mass, they would not even then teach and present as much as St. Peter here does in these few words.

Thus you have the subscription of the Epistle, wherein he manifests his office and what he preaches, as you have now heard. For this alone is the Gospel, and all else that does not accord with it is to be trodden under foot, and all other books are to be avoided in which you find some fine pretence of works and prayers and indulgence that does not teach similar doctrine, and is not confessedly grounded thereon. All Papal books have not a letter of this obedience, of this blood and sprinkling. Now follows the greeting to those to whom he writes.

Grace and peace be multiplied. Here St. Peter adopts the Apostle Paul's mode of greeting, although not to the same extent, and it is as much as though he had said, ye have now peace and grace, but yet not in perfection; therefore must ye continue to increase in them till the old Adam die. Grace is God's favor, which now begins in us, but which must continue to advance and grow even till death. Whoever confesses and believes that he has a gracious God, possesses it, while his heart gains peace also, and he is afraid neither of the world nor of the devil; for he knows that God, who controls all things, is his friend, and will deliver him from death, hell and all evil,—therefore his conscience has peace and joy. Such is the desire of St. Peter for those that believed, and it is a true Christian greeting with which all Christians might well greet one another.

Thus we have the superscription, with the greeting; now he begins the Epistle, and says:

V. 3-9. *Blessed be God and the Father of our Lord Jesus Christ, who, according to his abundant mercy, has begotten us again to a lively hope, through the resurrection of Jesus Christ from the dead, to an inheritance imperishable, and undefiled, and that fadeth not away, reserved in heaven for you, who are kept by the power of God through faith to salvation, ready to be revealed in the last time, wherein ye greatly rejoice, though now for a little time (if need be) ye are sad through manifold temptations; that the trial of your faith might be found more precious than the perishable gold (that is tried by fire), to praise, honor, and glory, when Jesus Christ shall be revealed, whom ye have not seen and yet love, in whom through ye believe and see him not, yet for your faith's sake ye rejoice with joy unspeakable and full of glory, receiving the end of your faith, even the salvation of your soul.*

In this preface you perceive a truly Apostolic address and introduction to the matters in hand, and as I have said already, this is the model of a noble Epistle. For he has already exhibited and made manifest what Christ is, and what we have attained through him, when he says, that God hath begotten us again to a lively hope through the resurrection of Christ.

Thus all good things are bestowed upon us by the Father, not for any desert of ours, but of pure mercy. These are true Gospel words which are to be preached, but how little—God save us—of this kind of preaching is to be met with in all sorts of books, even those that must be considered the best; how little agreement is there, as St. Jerome and St. Augustine have written, in this position,—that Jesus Christ is to be preached, that he died and rose again, and that he died and rose again that through such preaching men might believe on him and be saved. That is preaching the true Gospel. Whatever is not preached in this wise is not the Gospel, do it who will.

This is now the *summa summarum* of these words. Christ, through his resurrection, has brought us to the Father; and so, too, St. Peter would bring us to the Father by the Lord Christ, and he sets him forth as Mediator between God and us. Hitherto we have been taught that we should call upon the saints; that they are our intercessors with God, while, moreover, we have had recourse to our dear Virgin, and have set her up as Mediatress, and have let Christ go as an angry judge. This the Scripture does not do; it goes further, and exalts Christ; teaching that he is our Mediator, by whom we come to the Father. Oh! it is a blessing infinitely vast that is bestowed upon us through Christ, that we may go into the presence of the Father and claim the inheritance of which St. Peter here speaks.

These words also well exhibit the feelings which the Apostle had, as with the deepest reverence he begins to praise the Father, and would have us adore and bless Him for the sake of the infinite riches which He has bestowed upon us, in that He has begotten us again, and this, too, before we had desired or sought it; so that nothing is to be praised but pure mercy, in order that we may not make our boast of any works, but confess that we hold all that we have of God's compassion.

There is no more the law and vengeance before us, as heretofore, when He affrighted the Jews so that they were forced to flee, but dared not go toward the mount. He vexes and chastises us no more, but shows us the greatest friendship, creates us anew, and appoints us, not to do some work or works, but produces within us an entirely new birth and new being, that we should be something different from what we were before, when we were Adam's children,—namely, such as are transplanted from Adam's heritage into the heritage of God; so that God is our Father, we are His children, and thus also heirs of all the good which He possesses. Observe with what emphasis the scriptures present this matter; it is all a living, not a vain, matter in which we are concerned. Since we are thus begotten again the children and heirs of God, we are equal in honor and dignity with St. Paul, St. Peter, our blessed Virgin, and all the Saints. For we have the treasure and all good things from God just as richly as they; for it is just as necessary for them to be begotten again as for us,—therefore they have nothing more than all other Christians.

To a living hope. That we continue to live on earth is mainly to this end, that we should be of service to others. Otherwise, it were better that God should have taken away our breath and let us die as soon as we were baptized and had begun to believe. But He suffers us to live here in order that we may bring others also to believe, doing to them as He has done toward us. But while we remain on earth, we must live in hope; for although we are assured that through faith we have all the good things of God, (for faith brings along with it assuredly the new birth, the adoption, the inheritance, and makes them yours,) still you do not as yet behold them; but the matter exists in hope, while it is of but small importance that we may not see it with our eyes. This he calls *the hope of life;* that is, by a Hebrew phrase, as though for sinful man we should say, a man of sin. We call it a living hope; that is, one in which we certainly expect, and may be assured of, eternal life. But it is concealed, and a veil is drawn over it, that we see it not. It can only be apprehended in the heart and by faith, as St. John writes in his Epistle, 1 John v.: "We are now the children of God, and it doth not yet appear what we shall be; but we know that when it shall appear that we are like Him, we shall behold Him as He is." For *this* life, and *that,* cannot be commingled, cannot consist with one another, so that we should eat, drink, sleep, watch, and do other works of the flesh which this life renders necessary, and at the same time have our full salvation. Therefore we can never arrive at eternal life unless we die, and this present life passes away. Thus, as long as we are here we must stand in hope, until it be God's pleasure that we should behold the blessings that are ours.

But how do we attain to this living hope? By the resurrection of Christ from the dead, he says. I have often asserted that no one can believe on God except through a mediation, since we can none of us treat for ourselves before God, inasmuch as we are all children of wrath; but we must have another by whom we may come before God, who shall intercede for us and reconcile us to God. But there is no other mediator than the Lord Christ, who is the Son of God. Therefore that is not a true faith which is held by the Turks and Jews,— I believe that God has created heaven and earth. Just so does the devil, too, believe, but it does not help him. They venture to present themselves before God without having Christ as mediator. So St. Paul speaks in the fifth of Romans, "We have access to God by faith, not through ourselves, but through Christ." Therefore we must bring Christ with us, must come with

Him, must satisfy God by Him, and do all that we have to transact with God through Him, and in His name. That is the thought implied here by St. Peter, and he would also say, we surely expect this life, although we are still on earth. But all comes in no other way than through the resurrection of Christ, since He has arisen and ascended to heaven, and is seated at the right hand of God. For on this account He ascended, in order to bestow upon us His Spirit, that we might be born again, and now through Him might come to the Father and say, "Behold, I come before thee and pray, not because I rely on my own request, but because my Lord Christ has gone before me and is become my intercessor." These are all glowing words wherever there is a heart that believes; where there is not, all is cold and unimpressive.

Hence we may determine what genuine Christian doctrine or preaching is. If the Gospel is to be preached, it must concern the resurrection of Christ. Whoever does not preach this is no Apostle; for it is the head article of our faith. And those books are truly the noblest which teach and enforce such doctrine, as was said above. So that we may easily discover that the Epistle of James is no true Apostolic Epistle* for it contains scarcely a letter of these things in it, while the greatest importance belongs to this article of faith. For were there no such thing as the resurrection, we should have neither comfort nor hope, and all beside that Christ has endured or suffered would have been in vain.

> * The well-known views of Luther in regard to the Epistle of James, and the grounds upon which he rejected it from the canon of the New Testament, are presented in this passage. He was too impatient of the *seeming* contradiction between Paul and James upon the subject of faith, and too hastily concluded that they were irreconcilable. A careful consideration of the scope of the argument in the Epistle of James, removes the difficulty, as may be seen at large in later commentators. There is no historical reason for casting discredit upon the Epistle of James. The early Christian writers furnish very decided testimony in its favor. Clement of Rome has alluded to it twice. Hermas has not less than seven allusions to it, according to Lardner fully sufficient to prove its antiquity. Origen, Jerome, Athanasius, and most of the subsequent ecclesiastical writers quote from it, and it is found in all the catalogues of canonical books published by the general and provincial Councils. But an argument of still greater weight is, the fact that it is inserted in the Syriac version of the New Testament, executed at the close of the first, or early in the second century. None certainly would question that the Jewish believers to whom it was addressed

> would be the best judges of its genuineness and authenticity, and by them it was unhesitatingly accepted.

Therefore one should teach after this manner: You perceive that Christ has died for you, has taken upon Himself sin, death, and hell, and bowed Himself under them. But in no respect were they able to crush Him, for He was too strong for them; but He has risen up from beneath them, and has vanquished all, and brought them in subjection to Himself; and to this end, that you might be relieved from them, and made to triumph over them. If you believe, you possess this. All these things, by our own power, we could not effect; hence it was necessary that Christ should do it, otherwise He had never needed to come down from heaven. We can only conclude that if one preaches of our own works, *that* preaching does not agree and cannot consist with this. Oh, so thoroughly as we Christians should know this! so clear should the Epistle be to us!

V. 4. *To an imperishable and undefiled and unfading inheritance.* That is, we hope not for a blessing or an inheritance that is far off. But we live in the hope of an inheritance that is just at hand, and that is imperishable as well as undefiled and unfading. This blessing is ours henceforth and forever, although we do not now behold it. These are powerful and excellent words; into whosesoever mind they enter, he will, I imagine, not be greatly anxious after worldly good and pleasure. How can it be possible that one who assuredly believes this, should yet cleave to perishable possessions and lusts?

If worldly good is presented in contrast with this, it is at once seen how it all passes away and endures but for a time; but this alone lasts forever and will never consume away. Besides, *that* is all impure, and defiles us, for there is no man so devoted that worldly prosperity will not soil his purity. But *this* inheritance alone is pure; whoever has it is ever undefiled; it will not fade; it endures and does not corrupt. All that is on earth, however hard it be, is yet changeable and has no permanence. Man, as soon as he grows old, becomes deformed: but this does not change, but abides forever, fresh and green. On earth there is no pleasure that will not at length become irksome, as we see that men grow weary of all things; but with this blessing such is not the case. This do we possess only in Christ, through the mercy of God, if we believe, and it is freely bestowed upon us. For how is it possible that we poor wretches should be able to deserve such good through our own works as no human reason or sense can conceive?

That is reserved in heaven. Certain it is that our inheritance is imperishable, undefiled and unfading. It is only for a little while concealed from us, until we close our eyes and are buried, when, if we believe, we shall surely find and behold it.

V. 5. *Who are kept by the power of God through faith unto salvation.* We wait for this priceless inheritance, he says, in the hope to which we have attained through faith; for this is their order of succession: From the word follows faith, from faith is the new birth, from the new birth we pass to hope, so that we certainly expect and are assured of the blessing. So that Peter has here asserted, in a truly christian manner, that it must take place by faith, not by our own works.

But St. Peter says here, more particularly, *ye are kept by the power of God—to salvation.* But there are many people who, if they hear the Gospel,—namely, that faith alone, irrespective of works, justifies,—break in at once and say, "Yes! I believe too!" To think their thoughts which they themselves conceive, is faith. Yet we have also been taught from Scripture that we cannot do the least work without God's Spirit; how then by our own power should we be able to do the highest work,—namely, believe? Wherefore such thoughts are nothing else but a dream and a fiction. God's power must be present and work within us, in order that we may believe; as Paul also says, Eph. i., "God grant you the spirit of wisdom that ye may know what is the exceeding greatness of His power toward us who have believed, according to the working of His mighty power," &c. Not only is it God's will, but a power of God that is far from unimportant. For if God produces faith in men, it is certainly as great a work as though He recreated heaven and earth.

Therefore those fools know not what they say, who ask, How can faith alone answer, while many an one believes who yet performs no good work? For they imagine their own vain dream is faith, and that faith may exist without good works. But we say, just as Peter says, that faith is a divine power; when God produces faith, man must be born again and become a new creature; good works, flowing from a purified nature, must follow faith. So that we must not say to a Christian who has faith, Do this or that work,—for he performs of himself and unbidden, mere good works.

But this must be said to him, that he is not to deceive himself with a false, imaginary faith. Wherefore let those rude babblers go, who can say a great deal on the subject that is nothing after all but mere scum and vain prating. Of whom Paul also speaks, 1 Cor. iv., "I will come to you and will seek out not the speech of those that are puffed up, but the power; for the kingdom of God does not stand in word, but in power." Wherever this power of God is wanting, there is neither genuine faith nor good works. So that they are mere liars, who pride themselves on their Christian name and faith and yet lead a wicked life. For if it were of God's power, they would certainly be otherwise.

But what does St. Peter mean when he says, *ye are kept by the power of God to salvation?* This is his meaning: So tender and precious a matter is that which pertains to the faith which the power of God (that is with us and with which we are filled) produces in us, that He gives us a correct, clear understanding of all things that respect salvation, so that we may judge all that is on earth, and say, this doctrine is true, that is false; this conduct is right, that is not; this work is good and acceptable, that is evil. And whatever such a man determines is just and true, for he cannot be deceived; but he will be kept, and preserved, and remains, a judge of all doctrines.

On the other hand, wherever faith and this power of God are wanting, there is nothing but error and blindness; there reason suffers itself to be led hither and thither, from one work to another, for it would gladly reach heaven by its own works, and is ever imagining after this sort, "Yes! this work will bring you to heaven: do it and you shall be saved." Hence there are so many chapters, cloisters, altars, popes, monks and nuns in the world. Into such blindness does God permit the unbelieving to fall. But he keeps us, who believe, in a just apprehension, so that we may not fall into condemnation, but attain to salvation.

Which is ready to be revealed in the last time. That is, the inheritance that is appointed for them was long ago acquired, and prepared from the foundation of the world, but now is hidden, as yet covered up, reserved and sealed. But this is only for a little while, when in a moment it shall be opened and revealed, so that we shall behold it.

V. 6. *In which ye rejoice greatly, though now for a season (if need be), ye are in heaviness through manifold temptation.* Are you a Christian, and do you look for this inheritance or this salvation? then must you cleave to this alone, and despise all that is upon earth, and confess that all worldly reason, wisdom and glory are nothing—a thing the world will not be able to bear; wherefore you are to expect that men shall condemn you and persecute you. Thus St. Peter joins faith, hope, and the holy cross together, for one follows upon the other.

And here he gives us a source of consolation if we suffer and are persecuted. This sadness shall last a little while; afterward ye shall be exceeding glad, for this salvation is already prepared for you; wherefore be patient under your sufferings.

This is moreover a truly christian consolation,—not such comfort as human doctrines give, which attempt nothing more than to find relief from outward ill. I speak not of bodily comfort (he seems to say); it is no real injury that ye have to endure outward ill, only go onward vigorously and be steadfast;

inquire not how you may be free from the trouble, but think with yourself, My inheritance is prepared and held out to me; it is only a short time before my suffering must cease. Thus we should lay aside temporal consolations, and over against them place that eternal consolation which we have in God.

Besides, it is here to be observed that the Apostle continues and tells us in what circumstances all this will be, as he will hereafter say in the third chapter, *if it be God's will.*

There are many people who would storm heaven and enter it at once, wherefore they impose a cross upon themselves for their own fancied good; for reason will do nothing but propose for ever its own works, that God will reject. They should not be our own works which we select, but we should wait for whatever God imposes upon us and ordains for us, that we may go on and follow wherever He leads us; so that you are not to run after your own pleasure, in case it should be (that is, by God's appointment) that you are to suffer, but accept it and comfort yourself with the salvation which is not temporal but eternal.

V. 7, 8. *That the trial of your faith (or that your tried faith) be found much more precious than the perishable gold, (that is tried in the fire), to praise, honor, and glory, when Jesus Christ shall be revealed, whom ye have not seen, yet love, in whom ye also believe though ye see him not.* This should be the end of the cross and all kinds of reverses,—to enable us to distinguish between false and real faith. God lays his hand upon us, therefore, to try our faith and reveal it to the world, so that others may be induced to believe, and we also be praised and honored. For just as we exalt God, so will He in return exalt, esteem and honor us, insomuch that the false hypocrites, who do not walk in the right way, shall be put to shame.

Scripture throughout likens temptation to fire. Thus St. Peter here compares the gold that is tried by fire to the trial of faith by temptation and suffering. The fire does not take away from the gold, but it makes it pure and bright, so that all dross is removed. So God has imposed the cross upon all Christians, that they might thereby be purified. And it has been well said, let faith remain pure as the word is pure, so that we shall depend on the word alone, and trust to nothing else: for we need such fire and cross as this daily, because of the old corrupt Adam.

Thus, it is characteristic of a christian life that it should continually grow and become more holy; for if we are led to faith through the preaching of the Gospel, then shall we be justified and grow in holiness; but while we remain in the flesh we can never be fully purified. Therefore God throws us into the midst of the fire,—that is, into suffering, shame and calamity,—so that we may become more and more purified, until we die—a point we can attain by no works of our own. For how can an outward work make the heart inwardly clean? Moreover, if faith is to be tried (purified), all that is additional and false must be separated and removed. Thence will result a noble reward,—praise and glory when Christ shall be revealed. On this it follows:

V. 8, 9. *But because of your faith, rejoice with joy unspeakable and glorious, and attain also the end of your faith, even the salvation of your souls.* An unspeakably glorious joy shall that be, says St. Peter, whereof we have honor and praise. The world has such a joy that we receive nothing from it but shame, and of which we are compelled to be ashamed. Here St. Peter has evidently spoken of future joy,—and there is scarcely so clear a passage on the subject of the future joy as the one in this place,—and still he finds himself unable to express it.

This is one point of the introduction, in which the Apostle has shown what faith in Christ is, and how we must be tried and purified by reverse and suffering when God appoints it for us.—Now follows further how this faith is in Scripture constituted and denominated.

V. 10, 11, 12. *Of which salvation the prophets have inquired and searched diligently, who have prophesied of the grace that should come unto you; searching what or as to what time, the spirit of Christ which was in them, designated and testified beforehand the sufferings of Christ and the glory that should follow; to whom it was revealed, that not for their own sake, but for ours, did they minister that which is now preached to you, by those who have preached the Gospel, through the Holy Ghost sent down from heaven; into which also the angels desired to look.*

Here St. Peter directs us back to the Holy Scriptures, that we may therein see that God keeps whomsoever He has called of us, for no merit of ours, but of mere grace; for the whole of Scripture is directed to this end, that it may draw us away from our own works and bring us to faith. And it is necessary that we should study the Scriptures carefully that we may be well assured of our faith. Paul also teaches us the same thing in the Epistle to the Romans, chap. i., where he says that God promised the Gospel before by His prophets in the Holy Scriptures. So Rom. iii.: that the faith whereby we are justified, is testified of through the law and the prophets.

So we read also in Acts xvii. how Paul preached faith to the Thessalonians, leading them to the Scripture and explaining it to them, and how day by day they had recourse to the Scripture, and examined whether those things which Paul had taught them were so. So likewise ought we to do, going back, and from the Old Testament learning on what to base the New. Besides, we shall there discover the promise of Christ, as Christ himself also says, John v.: "Search the Scriptures, for it is they that testify of me." And "if ye believe Moses, ye must also believe me, for he wrote of me." Therefore we should let vain babblers go who despise the Old Testament, and say it is of no further use,—since from thence alone must we derive the ground of our faith; for God sent the Prophets to the Jews to this end, that they should bear witness of the Christ that was to come. Therefore it is that the Apostles throughout convicted and convinced the Jews out of their own Scriptures that this was the Christ.

Thus the books of Moses and the prophets are the Gospel, since they have first preached and written of Christ that which the Apostles afterward preached and wrote. Yet there is a distinction between them. For although both, as to the letter, have been written out on paper, yet the Gospel, or the New Testament, cannot be said so properly to be written, but to have consisted in the living voice which published it, and was heard generally throughout the world. But that it should also have been written, is an extraneous matter. But the Old Testament was composed only in writing, and is therefore called the letter; and the Apostles give Scripture this same name also, as it only pointed to the Christ that was to come. But the Gospel is a living proclamation of Christ who has already come.

Besides, there is also a distinction among the books of the Old Testament. In the first place, there are the five books of Moses, the foundation of the Scriptures, and which are especially called the Old Testament. Then come both histories and books of narration, wherein examples of all kinds are recorded, whether of those who held or rejected the law of Moses. In the third place, there are the prophets that are based on Moses, and what he has written they have in clear language more fully explained and elucidated. But the bearing of all the prophets and of Moses is one and the same.

But you ought to understand also about that which men say, that the Old Testament is given up and laid by. In the first place, there is that distinction between the Old and New Testament, as we have said above, that the Old prefigured Christ, but that the New gives us that which was promised first in the Old, and pointed out to us by types. But these types have now ceased, because the end which they were to subserve has been answered and attained, and that which was prefigured by them has been fulfilled. So that now there should be no further distinctions of food, clothing, place and time. All are alike in Christ, in whom all has been fulfilled. The Jews have not been saved by this, for it was not given them to this end that it should make them holy, but to foreshadow to them the Christ who was to come.

Besides, in the Old Testament God introduced a twofold government,—an external and an internal. There He undertook to rule His people, both inwardly in the heart, and outwardly in person and in property. Therefore He gave them such a variety of laws, commingled one kind with the other. So it was under the government that pertained to the person, that a man might give his wife a bill of divorce and put her away.

But to the spiritual government pertained the command, Thou shalt love thy neighbor as thyself. But now He rules in us only spiritually, by Christ; while the government that pertains to the body and the outward state, he exercises through the instrumentality of civil magistracy. So that when Christ came the external ceased, and God gives us direction no more as to the *outward* person, time and place. But He rules us only spiritually through the word, so that we may direct as to all that is outward, and be bound in nothing that pertains to the body.

But what pertains to His spiritual government has not been abandoned, but stands forever, now as then,—the law of love to God and our neighbor, contained in the books of Moses, which God will still have sustained, and by which He will condemn all the unbelieving.

Besides, the figures, as to their *spiritual* import, remain; that is, whatever is signified by the outward figures, although the outward part has been done away. Thus that a man should separate from his wife and send her away, because of adultery, is a figure and type which even now is spiritually fulfilled; for thus also has God rejected the Jews when they would not believe on Christ, and has chosen out the Gentiles. So, also, He does still; if any one will not walk in the faith, He suffers him to be excluded from the Christian Church, that he may be led to reform.

Of a similar import also is this, that a woman after her husband's death must take her husband's brother, and bear him children, and he must suffer himself to be called by his name, and must enter on his possessions. This, although it has now ceased, or rather become invalid, so that it may be done or neglected without sin, is a figure which even now has a significance in respect to Christ. For He is our brother, for us has died and ascended to heaven, and has commanded us that we, through the Gospel, should plant the seed in our souls and make them fruitful, be named after him, and enter on his possessions. Therefore I must not boast that I convert men, but it must all be ascribed to the Lord Christ. It is the same also with all the other figures of the Old Testament, which it would be too tedious to specify.

But all in the Old Testament which is not external, is still in force, as all those passages in the prophets concerning faith and love. Wherefore Christ also confirms it in Mat. vii.: "All things whatsoever ye would that men should do unto you, do ye even so to them; for this is the law and the prophets." Besides, Moses and the prophets testify of the Christ that was to come. As, when I preach of Christ that He is the only Saviour by whom all must be saved, I may quote to sustain me the passage in Gen. xxii.: "In thy seed shall all nations be blessed." Thence I draw a living voice and language. Through Christ, who is Abraham's seed, must all men be blessed. From that it follows, that we were all cursed and condemned in Adam; wherefore it is necessary that we should believe on the Seed, if we would escape condemnation. Out of such passages may we lay down the ground of our faith, and let it remain, that we may therein see how they bear witness of Christ, so that our faith may be strengthened thereby. That is what St. Peter intends now by these words, in which he says:

V. 10. *Of which Salvation the Prophets have searched and inquired diligently, who have prophesied of the grace that should come to you.* In this same manner Paul also speaks, toward the close of the Epistle to the Romans, of the revelation of the mystery which was hidden from all ages of the world, but is now revealed and made known through the writings of the prophets. And so you find in the New Testament many passages quoted from the prophets, by which the Apostles show that all has been fulfilled just as the prophets foretold.

This Christ Himself proves from the prophet Isaiah, Mat. xi.: "The blind see, the lame walk," &c. As though He had said, just as it was written there it is taking place now; so also we read in Acts ix., of Paul, and in the xviii., of Apollos, how they confounded the Jews, and convinced them out of Scripture that this was the Christ. For whatever the prophets had foretold, all had now come to pass in Christ. So (Acts xv.) the Apostles show how the Gospel must be preached to the heathen that they might believe. This has also come to pass, and been put in train, so that the Jews might be convinced and compelled to confess, that all had taken place just as Scripture had foretold.

V. 11. *And have investigated what or at what time the Spirit of Christ which was in them;* St. Peter would say, although the prophets have not particularly known of a set and definite time, yet have they in general testified to all the circumstances of time and place;—as, that Christ should suffer, and what death he should die, and that the Gentiles should believe on him: so that one might certainly know by these signs when the time had come. The prophet Daniel has approached still nearer, but yet speaks somewhat darkly thereof, as to when Christ should suffer and die—when that or this should take place. So, also, they had a sure prophecy that the kingdom of the Jews should cease before Christ came. But the day and exact time when this should come to pass was not fixed. For it was enough when this time came, that they should thereby know for a surety that Christ was not far off. The prophet Joel also prophesied of the time when the Holy Spirit should come, where he says, "I will in the last days pour out my spirit upon all flesh," &c., which passage St. Peter quotes in Acts ii., and shows that he speaks of that very time and of the particular persons.

From all which you perceive how, with great diligence, the Apostles exhibit throughout the ground and confirmation of their preaching and doctrine. The Councils and the Popes now reverse this course, and would deal with us apart from Scripture, commanding us, by obedience to the church and the terrors of excommunication, that we should believe on them. The Apostles were filled with the Holy Spirit, and were certain that they were sent by Christ, and preached the true Gospel; yet they did not exalt themselves, and did not ask men to believe them, unless they conclusively proved from Scripture that it was just as they said, so that the mouth of the unbelieving was stopped, insomuch that they could object nothing further. And shall we believe those grossly unlearned heads who do not preach God's word at all, and can do nothing else but cry out continually, "Surely the fathers cannot have been in error, and this has been decided now for a long time, so that it must no more be a question?" But this we can clearly prove from the Scriptures, that no one can be saved but he who believes on Christ, so that against this they can say nothing. But on their side they will never be able to prove to us from Scripture that he is to be condemned who does not fast on this or that day. Therefore we ought not and shall not believe them.

Now St. Peter says further:

V. 11. *Which spirit testified beforehand the sufferings of Christ, and the glory that should thereafter be revealed.* This may be understood of both kinds of suffering,—that which Christ, and we also, suffer. St. Paul calls the sufferings of all Christians the suffering of Christ. For just as the faith, the name, the word and work of Christ are mine, inasmuch as I believe on Him, so His suffering is also mine, since I suffer also for His sake. Thus will the sufferings of Christ be daily fulfilled in Christians, until the end of the world.

This is then our consolation in all the sufferings that we experience, that all that we suffer Christ shares with us, that He accounts it all as His own suffering. And of this we are assured, that speedily after suffering glory shall follow. But this we must also understand, that Christ was not glorified before He suffered, so that we are to bear our cross with Him first, that afterward we may share His joy.

All that we now preach, he says, the prophets previously foretold and described in the most explicit manner, just as the Holy Spirit revealed it to them. That we so imperfectly understand the prophets is, because we do not understand their language, since they have spoken clearly enough. Therefore they that are acquainted with the language, and have the Spirit of God, which all believers have, to them it is not difficult of apprehension since they know the scope of all Scripture. But if any one does not understand their language, and has not the spirit, or a christian apprehension, it might seem to him as though the prophets were drunken and full of new wine; although where we must want one, the spirit without the language is better than the language without the spirit. The prophets have a peculiar phraseology, but the sentiment is the same which the Apostles preach, for both have spoken largely of the suffering and of the glory of Christ, as well as of those things that relate to faith. As when David speaks of Christ (Ps. xxi.), "I am a worm and no man," whereby he shows how deeply he is cast down and despondent in his suffering. Likewise, also, he writes of his people and of the affliction of Christians, in Psalm xlv.: "We are despised, and accounted as sheep for the slaughter."

V. 12. *That not for their own sakes but for ours did they minister that which is now preached unto you, by those who have preached the Gospel to you, through the Holy Ghost sent down from heaven;* that is, the prophets possessed enough thereof to know the fact. But that they should have left it behind them (on record) calls for our gratitude; they have become our servants, and have so ministered to us, that we, through them, might go to school and learn the same lesson. There we have an argument to show that our faith should grow stronger, and we be enabled to arm and sustain ourselves against all false doctrine.

Into which also the angels desired to look. So great things have the Apostles declared to us, through the Holy Spirit, which descended upon them from heaven, as even the angels would gladly look into. When this Spirit opens our eyes and makes us see what the Gospel is, we shall have an appetite for it and a joy in it, although we cannot behold it with bodily eyes, but must believe that we are partakers and fellow-heirs of the righteousness, truth, salvation and all the blessings which God has to bestow. For since He has given us His only Son, that highest good, He will also, through Him, give us all good things, riches and treasures, whereof the angels in heaven have all their joy, and of which they are most desirous. All this is offered to us through the Gospel, and if we believe we shall also have a like desire for them. But our desire for them cannot be as perfect as that of the angels, so long as we live on earth; but it is a good beginning in us, if we experience, through faith, something of it. But in heaven it is so great that no human heart can conceive it; but if we reach that place we shall ourselves feel it.

Thus you see how St. Peter teaches us to arm and equip ourselves with Scripture. For hitherto he has described what it is to preach the Gospel, and shown that as it heretofore has been preached by the prophets, so it should still be, and should be preached in like manner. Now he proceeds farther, and admonishes us in this chapter that we should cleave to the same preaching of the Gospel by faith, and follow after it by love, and therefore says,—

V. 13-16. Gird up therefore the loins of your mind; be sober, and fix your hope firmly on the grace which is offered you through the revelation of Jesus Christ, as obedient children, not conformable to the previous lusts of your ignorance; but as He who has called you is Holy, be ye also holy in all your conduct, as it is written, Be ye holy for I am Holy.

This is an admonition to faith, and the sense is this: while such things are preached to you and bestowed upon you through the Gospel as the angels would rejoice and be desirous to behold, rely on them, and fix your confidence thereon with all firmness, so that it shall be a real faith, and not a painted or fictitious fancy or dream.

Gird up the loins of your mind. Here Peter speaks of a spiritual girding of the mind, just as one girds his sword to the loins of his body. This girding has Christ also enforced, Luke xii., where he says, "Let your loins be girt about." In some places the Scriptures speak of the loins with reference to bodily lust; but here St. Peter speaks of the loins of the spirit. As to the body, Scripture speaks of the loins with reference to natural generation from the father; as we read, Genesis xlix., that from the loins of Judah Christ should come. Likewise the bodily girding of the loins is the same with chastity, as Isaiah says, chapter xi., "Righteousness shall be the girdle of his loins, and faith the girdle of his reins." That is, only by faith is wicked lust subdued and restrained.

But this spiritual girding, whereof the Apostle speaks, means more. As a virgin is pure and inviolate in body, so is the soul spiritually inviolate through faith, by which it becomes Christ's bride. But if it falls from faith into false doctrine, it must be brought to shame. Hence Scripture uniformly calls impiety and unbelief, adultery and whoredom,—that is, when the soul relies on human doctrines, and thus lets go its hold on faith and Christ. This St. Peter here forbids, when he calls on us to gird up the loins of our mind; as though he would say, ye have now heard the Gospel and have come to believe, therefore see to it that ye abide therein, and do not suffer yourselves to be drawn away with false doctrine, so that ye shall not waver and run hither and thither with works.

And here he adopts a peculiar mode of speech, not after the manner of St. Paul, where he speaks of "the loins of your mind." He calls *that* mind here which we speak of as disposition; as when I say, "This seems to me right and as Paul speaks, so we understand it, so we are *disposed.*" In this he refers especially to faith, and would say: ye have attained a correct apprehension that we must be justified through faith; abide in that mind; gird it up well, hold fast thereon, and suffer not yourselves to be torn from it; then shall ye stand well. For many false teachers shall come in and set up human doctrines that they may pervert your understanding and loose the girdle of your faith; wherefore be admonished, and bind it well to your mind.

The hypocrites who rest on their own works, and hence pass a carefully abstemious life, are thus minded, that God must bring them to heaven for their works' sake; they are puffed up, become proud, abiding in their own opinion and blindness, like the Pharisees, Luke xviii. Of whom also Mary speaks, in the *Magnificat,* where she uses the same word that stands here in Peter, He hath scattered the proud in the disposition of their hearts,—that is, in their own minds.

Be sober. To be sober is of service outwardly to the body, and is the chief work of faith. For though a man has been justified, he still is not secured from evil lusts; faith has indeed begun to subdue the flesh, but this is ever bestirring itself, and likewise running riot in all sorts of lusts, which would gladly break forth again and act after their own will. Therefore the spirit must daily work to restrain and subdue it, and must charge itself therewith, without intermission, and have a care of the flesh that it do not destroy faith. Therefore those persons deceive themselves, who indeed say they have faith, and imagining that this is enough, live thenceforth according to their own caprice. Where the faith is genuine it must control the body and hold it in check, so that it shall not do what it lusts after. Therefore St. Peter says that we should be sober.

Yet he would not have us destroy the body or weaken it too much, as we find many do who have fasted and tortured themselves to death. St. Bernard, even, continued for a long time in this folly, although he was truly a holy man, for he mortified his body to such an extent that his breath was offensive and could not be endured. Yet he afterwards forsook it, and charged his brethren that they should not inflict injury upon the body; for he saw very well that he had rendered himself unfit to be of service to his brethren. Therefore St. Peter requires nothing more than that we should be sober,— that is, mortify the body to such an extent as to prevent its being in our apprehension too wanton; for he fixes no definite time how long we should fast, as the Pope has done, but leaves it to each, individually, to fast so that he remain sober and do not burden the body with gluttony, to the end that he remain in possession of reason and reflection, and consider how far it is necessary for him to hold the body in check. For it is utterly idle to impose one and the same command upon a whole congregation and church, since we are so unlike one to the other; one strong, another weak in body,—so that one must mortify it more, another less, provided the body is to remain sound and in the best state for exertion.

But another multitude mistake here, determined that they will not fast, and that they may eat flesh, and herein are wrong. For these persons reject the Gospel also, and are unprofitable as well as the others; doing no more than contemn the Pope's command, unwilling to gird up their mind and spirit, as Peter says, leaving the body to its own caprice, that it may become corrupt and wanton. It is well to fast; but that only can be called true fasting, when we give the body no more food than is needful for it that it may retain its health and endure labor and watchfulness—that the old ass do not become too obstinate, and going on the ice to dance, break a bone; but go on subject to control, and following the spirit; not after the manner of those who, whenever they fast, fill themselves so full of fish and the best wine, that their bellies are puffed out. Thus St. Peter directs us to be sober, and now says further:

And fix your hope firmly (or with all deliberation) on the grace which is offered you. The christian faith is of such a nature that it plants itself freely on the word of God with entire confidence, ventures freely thereupon, and goes joyfully onward. Therefore Peter would say: The loins of your mind are girt about, and your faith is genuine, when you venture it thus on that Word, let it cost what it will,—property, honor, limb, or life.

Thus has he with these words in truth well described a genuine and unfeigned faith. It must not be a corrupt and sleepy faith, becoming thus only a dream, but a living and active reality, that we may with all deliberation devote ourselves to it and cleave to the Word, so that, let God permit it to go with us as it will, we will yet press onward through good and ill. Thus when I come to die I must venture promptly on Christ, lift my head boldly, and rely upon the word of God which cannot deceive me. Thus must faith go straight forward, in nothing permit itself to be led astray, and subject to scrutiny all that it sees, hears and feels. Such faith St. Peter requires as consists, not in thought or word, but in such power as this.

Again, St. Peter says: Set your hope on the grace which is offered you. That is, ye have not deserved this great grace, but yet it is freely offered you; for the Gospel, which reveals this grace, is no invention or discovery of our own, but the Holy Spirit has sent it down from heaven into the world. But what is it that is offered to us? This, that we have already heard, that whosoever believes on Christ and cleaves to the Word possesses *Him*, with all the blessings He has to give, so that He is Lord over sin, death, the devil and hell, and is assured of eternal life. This treasure is brought to our doors and laid in our bosom without our help or desert, yes, beyond our expectation and without our knowledge or thought. Therefore the Apostle would have us venture thereon cheerfully, for God, who offers us such grace, will surely not deceive us.

Through the revelation of Jesus Christ. God permits none to make the offer of His grace except through Christ. Therefore no man should attempt to approach Him apart from this Mediator, as we have already above heard sufficiently. For He will hear no one but him who brings His dear Son with him, whom He alone regards, and for His sake those that depend upon Him. Therefore He would have us confess the Son, that we are reconciled through His blood to the Father, so that we may approach before Him. For to this end did Christ come into the world, assume flesh and blood, and joined Himself to us, that He might obtain such grace for us with the Father. So, too, all the prophets and patriarchs have been kept and saved, through such faith on Christ. For they all have exercised faith in the promise which God made to Abraham, "Through thy seed shall all nations be blest." Therefore, as we have said, to the Jews and to the Turks, faith is of no avail, neither to any that rest upon their own works and would thereby reach heaven. So Peter says, this grace is offered you, but it is through the revelation of Jesus Christ (or to render it more clearly into our language), because that Jesus Christ has been revealed to you.

Through the Gospel it is made known to us what Christ is, that we may learn of Him, moreover, that He is our Saviour. He rescues us from sin and death, and helps us out of every evil, reconciles us to the Father, and, apart from our own works, justifies and saves us. Whoever then does not thus confess Christ must be lost; for although you may know that He is the Son of God, that He died and has risen, and sits at the right hand of the Father,—still you have not yet truly known Christ, it is all of no avail to you; but you must know and believe that He has done it all for your sake, if your faith is to help you. Therefore that is a vain, senseless doctrine that has been hitherto preached and taught in the great schools, which have had no experience of this knowledge, and have only attained to imagine how the curse afflicted Christ our Lord, and how He sits above in heaven unemployed, and possesses a joy with Himself; and thus their hearts remain barren, so that faith cannot live in them. But Christ does not stand there for Himself, but He is to be preached that He is ours. For what necessity could there then have been that He should have come down to earth and have shed His blood? But since He has been sent into the world, as He says, John iii., "that the world through Him might be saved." He certainly must have fulfilled this mission, because He was sent from the Father. For this sending forth and proceeding from the Father is to be understood not only of the divine nature, but also of the human nature and of His ministry. As soon as He was baptized this began, and He has fulfilled it, for which end He was sent and came into the world, to wit, that He might preach the truth and obtain it for us, that all who believe on Him shall be saved. Thus has He revealed Himself, and presented Himself to our knowledge, and offered us grace.

V. 14. *As obedient children.* That is, conduct yourselves as obedient children. Obedience in Scripture means faith. But the Pope, with his high schools and cloisters, has even wrested the word from us, and falsely rendered what is recorded in Scripture concerning this obedience, as the passage in I. Kings xv.: "Obedience is better than sacrifice." For while they perceive that obedience is highly praised in Scripture, they have usurped the claim of it to themselves, so that they might blind the people, and that men should think it was obedience to their stuff of which the Scripture speaks. Thus they would bring us away from God's word to their lies, and to the obedience of the devil. Whoever hears the word of God and believes thereon, is an obedient child of God. Therefore, whatever is not the word of God, tread it under your feet and pay no attention to it.

Not conformed to the former lusts of your ignorance. That is, that you should not exhibit such ostentation and lead such a course of life as before, and that you be not found in the same condition in which you formerly were. Once you were godless, and lived in lewdness, gluttony, drunkenness, avarice, pride, anger, envy and hate, which was an evil, heathen-like state, and one of unbelief, and when you had gone into such a state like the blind, you have not known what you have done. Avoid now those same evil lusts. Here you perceive how he makes the charge against ignorance, that all evil proceeds therefrom. For where faith and the knowledge of Christ are wanting, there remains mere error and blindness, so that men are ignorant of what is right and wrong, insomuch that the people fall into every kind of vice.

Thus has it been hitherto: where Christ has been kept out of sight and eclipsed, there error has begun to prevail; and throughout the world the question has torn its way, how man may be saved. This is at once a sign of blindness or ignorance, that the true apprehension of faith is lost, and no one knows anything more about it. Hence the world is so full of such various sects, and all are divided, for every one will devise for himself a way to heaven of his own. In our misfortune we must be continually falling deeper in our blindness, since we cannot help ourselves. Therefore St. Peter would say: Ye have already befooled yourselves enough; now desist therefrom, since ye have been instructed and have attained to a correct understanding.

V. 15, 16. *But according as He that hath called you is holy, so be ye also holy in all your conduct, as it is written, Be ye holy for I am holy.* Here St. Peter quotes a passage from the Old Testament, Lev. xix., where God says: "Be ye holy for I am holy;" that is, since I am your Lord and God, and ye are my people, ye too must be as I am. For a faithful master secures that his people shall be like him, and walk in obedience, and be conformed to the master's will. As then God our Master is holy, so are His people holy also, and we are all holy if we walk in faith. Scripture says not much of the saints that have died, but of those who live on the earth. So David puts forth his claim in Ps. lxxxv.: "Lord, preserve my soul, for I am holy."

But here our learned men have for once perverted the passage, and they say: the prophet had a particular revelation, in that he called himself holy; whereby they themselves confess that they do violence to faith, and have not the revelation of Jesus Christ, otherwise they would surely be sensible of it. For whoever is a Christian experiences within himself such a revelation; but they who do not experience it are not Christians. For whoever is a Christian enters into a participation with Christ our Lord, of all his good things. Since, then, Christ is holy, he must also be holy, or deny that Christ is holy. Hast thou been baptized? then thou hast put on the holy garment, which is Christ, as Paul says.

The word Holy means that which is God's own, and which belongs to Him alone, or as we render it in Dutch (*geweiht*), consecrated. Thus, Peter here says: you are merely required to give God His own; therefore beware that ye do not suffer yourselves to be led back again to worldly lusts, but let God alone rule, live and work within you; then shall ye be holy, even as He is holy.

Thus he has hitherto described the grace which is extended to us through the Gospel and the preaching of Jesus Christ, and has taught us how we should therefore conduct ourselves, namely: that we abide in a pure, inviolate mind of faith, since we know that no work that we can do or imagine, can at all help us: when such doctrine as this is preached, reason objects, and says, Ah! if that is true, I need not do any good work. And then the great heads fall foul of it, and from a christian condition, educe a freedom of the flesh, imagining they may do what they will. These St. Peter here meets, and anticipates them, and teaches how we are to use our christian freedom only towards God. For nothing more is needed but faith, to the end that I should give God the honor due Him, and embrace Him as my God, confessing that He is just, true and merciful; such faith sets us free from sin and all evil. If now I have made such a return to God, whatever time I yet live I am to live for my neighbor, so as to serve and help him. The greatest work that follows from faith is this: that with my mouth I should confess Christ, sealing that confession with my blood, and laying down my life for it, if so it be. Yet God does not need this work; only I am to perform it, that my faith may thereby be tried and known, so that others also may be brought to believe. Thereafter follow also other works, which must all be directed to this end, that I may thereby serve my neighbor,—all of which God must work in us; for it profits not that we should lead a carnal life and do whatever we please. Therefore St. Peter now says:

V. 17-21. *And since ye call on the Father, who judgeth without respect of persons, according to every man's work, pass the time of your sojourning here in fear; and be aware that ye are not redeemed with corruptible silver or gold, from your vain conduct in the traditions of your fathers, but with the precious blood of Christ, as of an innocent and unspotted Lamb, who indeed was provided previously before the world began, but is revealed in these last times for you, who through Him believe on God, who raised Him from the dead, and hath given Him dominion, that your faith and hope might be in God.*

So says St. Peter: Ye have through faith hereunto attained, that ye are the children of God, and He is your Father. And ye have obtained an incorruptible inheritance in heaven, (as has been already said.) Thus nothing more now remains, except that the veil be taken away, and that be uncovered which is now concealed, for which ye are still to wait until ye shall behold it. Though ye are now arrived at that state in which ye may joyfully call God your Father, yet is He so righteous that he will reward every man according to his works, and respect not persons. Wherefore thou art not to imagine, although thou hast that great name so that thou art called a Christian or a child of God, that He will therefore continue thine if thou livest without fear, and thinkest that it is enough that thou dost glory in such a name. The world indeed judges by the person, since it does not punish all alike, and respects those who are friendly, rich, reputable, learned, wise, and powerful. But God regards nothing of this kind; it is all alike to him, be the person as great as he may. Thus in Egypt he struck the son of King Pharaoh dead, as well as the son of the poor miller.

Therefore the Apostle would have us expect such judgment from God, and stand in fear, so that we do not glory in our title that we are Christian, and thereupon become negligent, as though he would for this reason pass us over more readily than others. For in this the Jews were formerly deceived, who boasted that they were Abraham's seed and God's people. Scripture makes no difference in respect to the flesh, but in respect to the spirit. It is true that

Christ was to be born of Abraham's seed and that a holy people should spring from him, but it does not therefore follow that all who are born of Abraham are the children of God. He also promised that the Gentiles should be saved, but he has not said that he would save *all* the Gentiles.

But here now a question arises: When we say that God saves us alone by faith, without regard to works, why does St. Peter say that He judges not according to the person, but according to works? Answer. What we have taught as to faith alone justifying before God, is true beyond doubt, since it is so clear from Scripture that it cannot be denied. That which the Apostle here says, that God judges according to the works, is also true; but we must certainly hold, therefore, that where there is no faith, there can be no good work; and on the other hand, that there is no faith where there are no good works. Therefore join together faith and good works, since it is in both that the sum of the whole christian life consists. As you now live, so will it be with you, for thereafter God will judge you. Therefore, although God judges us according to our works, still it remains true that works are only the fruits of faith, by which we perceive when there is faith or unbelief; therefore God will sentence you from your works and convict you, either that you have or have not believed. So it is that no one can convict and judge a liar, except from his words. Yet it is evident that he is not made a liar by the word, but became a liar before he spoke the lie, for the lie must come from the heart into the mouth. Therefore, understand this passage thus, in the plainest way: that works are fruits and signs of faith, and that God judges men according to such fruits which must certainly follow it, so that it shall be openly seen whether there is faith or unbelief in the heart. God will not judge by this whether you are *called* a Christian, or have been baptized, but will ask you, "*Art* thou a Christian? then tell me where are the fruits by which you can evidence your faith."

Therefore St. Peter goes on to say: Since ye have such a Father, who judges not after the person, pass the time of your pilgrimage in fear; that is, stand in fear before the Father, not of pain and punishment,—as the Christless, and even the devil, is afraid,—but lest He forsake you and withdraw His hand; just as a dutiful child is afraid lest he provoke his father, and do something that might not please him. Such a fear would God have within us, that we guard ourselves against sin, and serve our neighbor, while we live here upon the earth.

A Christian, if he truly believes, possesses all the good things of God, and is God's child, as we have heard. But the time which he yet lives is only a pilgrimage: for the spirit is already in heaven by faith, through which he becomes Lord over all things. But to this end God permits him yet to live in the flesh, and his body to remain on earth, that he may help others and bring them also to heaven. Therefore we are to use all things on earth as a guest, who goes on wearily and arrives at an inn where he must tarry over night, and can receive nothing from it but food and lodging; yet does not say that the property of the inn is his. So must we also proceed in regard to our temporal possessions, as though they were not ours, and we enjoyed only so much of them as is needful to sustain the body, and with the rest we are to help our neighbor. Thus the christian life is only a night's sojourning; for we have here no abiding city, but must find it, where our Father is, in heaven. Therefore we should not here live in wantonness, but stand in fear, says St. Peter.

V. 18. *And be aware that ye are not redeemed with corruptible silver or gold, from your vain conduct in the traditions of your Fathers, but with the precious blood of Christ.* This should draw you, he would say, to the fear of God, wherein ye should stand, that ye should remember how much it has cost that ye might be redeemed. Before, ye were citizens of the world, and were held in subjection to the devil, but now, God has rescued you from such a state, and set you firm in another, so that your citizenship is in heaven; but ye are strangers and guests upon earth. And see at how great a cost God has reclaimed you, and how great the treasure is, wherewith ye are purchased, and brought into this state, to become the children of God. Wherefore pass your sojourning in fear, and see to it that ye do not despise such redemption, and lose the noble, precious treasure.

What now is the treasure wherewith ye are ransomed? Not corruptible gold or silver, but the precious blood of Christ the Son of God: the treasure is so costly and noble, that no human sense or reason can conceive it, insomuch that only one drop of this innocent blood were more than enough for the sin of all the world: yet has the Father been willing to dispense his grace so richly upon us, and denied Himself so much as to suffer Christ His Son to shed all His blood for us, and has bestowed upon us the whole treasure. Therefore He would not have us disregard such great grace, and count it as a small matter, but continue on our guard, so as to live in fear, that this treasure be not taken away from us.

And here it is well to remark, that St. Peter says, ye are ransomed from your vain conversation in the traditions of your fathers; for he thereby strikes to the ground all the supports whereon we lean when we imagine our view must be right because it has thus been preserved from of old, and our forefathers all of them have so held it, among whom there were certainly wise and pious people. It is as much as to say, all which our fathers have ordained and done, was evil; what from them has been taught you of the worship of God, is also evil; for it has cost the Son of God His blood to redeem the people therefrom; whatever, therefore, has not been washed in this blood, is all poisoned and cursed by reason of the flesh. Thence it follows, the more a man undertakes to make himself righteous and has not Christ, the more only he confounds himself, and sinks deeper in blindness and wickedness, and condemns himself in respect to this precious blood.

External matters, important in themselves, are even trifling in comparison with this, that a man should teach how we may be justified by works, and devise a worship of God according to our reason; for thereby the innocent blood is most deeply dishonored and reviled.

The heathen have committed many great sins, in that they have prayed to the sun and moon, which they held for the true worship of God, though this was joined with other sins. But human justification (justification by human works) is mere reviling of God, and the greatest of all sins that a man commits. So, also, that mode of life wherewith the world is now busied and which it holds as the worship of God, and piety, is in God's sight more provoking than any other sin, as is the priestly and monkish order, and which while it appears fair before the world, is yet without faith. Therefore whoever will not obtain favor before God through this blood, it were better for him that he should never come into God's presence, for he thereby only the more and more dishonors His Majesty.

V. 19. *As of an innocent and unspotted lamb.* But here St. Peter explains the Scripture,—for this though so short is an exceedingly rich Epistle,—since as soon as he had spoken of their vain course in the traditions of the fathers, he finds much instruction for us in the prophets—as in the prophet Jer. xvi.: "The heathen shall come to you from the end of the world, and say, our fathers have gone astray with lies," as though St. Peter had said, there the prophets foretold that ye should be redeemed from the tradition of your fathers.

So when he says here, ye are redeemed by the blood of Christ, as of an innocent and unspotted lamb, he would again refer to the Scripture, and explain that which is contained in the prophets and Moses—as Is. liii.: "Like a lamb he is led to the slaughter." So as to the type, Ex. xii., of the Paschal Lamb, all this he here explains, and says, this lamb is Christ; and as the one of old was to be unspotted, so must this, also, whose blood is shed for us, be unspotted and innocent.

V. 20. *Which indeed was provided previously, before the world began, but is revealed in these last times for you.* That is, we have not deserved nor even prayed this of God, that the precious blood of Christ should be shed for us, therefore we can glory in no respect; the glory belongs to none but God alone. God has promised and revealed or made known to us, not for any merit of ours, that which He from all eternity had provided and foreordained, before the world was made. In the prophets it is indeed promised, yet dimly and not openly; but now, since Christ's resurrection and the sending of the Holy Spirit, it is publicly preached and disseminated throughout the whole world.

This is now the latter age (the last time), as St. Peter says, wherein we live—now—from the ascension of Christ until the last day. So the Apostles and prophets, and Christ Himself, also, call it the last hour; not that the last day was to come immediately after Christ's ascension, but because after this preaching of the Gospel of Christ no other should ever come; and there will be no further revelation or manifestation, except as this is explained and revealed. One revelation after another has indeed gone forth. Therefore God says, Ex. vi., "By my name Jehovah was I not known to them." For the patriarchs, although they knew God, yet at that time had not so clear a manifestation of Him as was afterwards put forth through Moses and the prophets; but now there has no more glorious or clear manifestation of Him come into the world than the Gospel. Therefore it is the last; all dispensations have run their course, but the present,—the last,—which is revealed to us.

Besides, the time hereafter is not long to the end of the world, as St. Peter shows, II. Pet. iii., where he says: "One day is with the Lord as a thousand years, and a thousand years as one day." And so he would lead us by this reckoning of time, to conclude, after God's method, that it is the last time, and that the end approaches, but the time which still remains is nothing in the sight of God. The salvation is already revealed and completed: God permits the world to stand yet longer, merely that His name may be more widely honored and praised, although He for Himself is now fully revealed.

V. 21. *For you, who through Him believe on God, who raised Him from the dead, and hath given Him dominion that your faith and hope might be in God.* For our sakes, he says, is the Gospel revealed. For God and the Lord Christ have not needed it, but have done it for our profit, that we might believe on them; and that, not through ourselves, but through Christ, who intercedes for us with the Father, whom He has raised from the dead, that He might be Lord over all things; so that whoever believes on Him possesses all His good things, and through Him has access to the Father. Thus we have faith in God, and a hope through the same faith. Faith alone must save us, but it must be a faith in God; for if God does not help us, then we are not holpen; so that it is not enough, although you had all men's friendship, but you must have the friendship of God, that you may boast that He is YOUR Father, and that you are His child, and confide in Him even more than in your beloved father and mother, that He will help you in all your troubles, and this only through the one Mediator and Saviour, the Lord Christ. Such faith comes not (he says) from human power, but God creates it in us, because Christ has merited it by His blood; to whom He has given glory, and whom He has seated at His right hand, that He, by God's power, should produce faith in us.

Hitherto we have heard St. Peter admonishing us that we should gird up the loins of our mind, that we may remain undefiled and live in faith; then, also, that which meanwhile is so important, that we should walk in fear and never forget that we are called Christians, since God is a judge who respects none, but judges one like the other, without distinction of persons.

V. 22-25. *And purify your souls, through obedience of the truth in the Spirit, to unfeigned love of the brethren, and have fervent love toward one another, out of pure hearts, as those who have been born again, not of corruptible seed but of incorruptible, namely, of the living word of God, which endures forever. For all flesh is as grass, and all the glory of man like the flower of grass. The grass withereth and the flower thereof falleth away, but the word of the Lord endureth forever; and this is the word which is preached unto you.*

Paul, in Gal. v., points out the fruits which follow faith. The fruits of the Spirit, he says, are joy, peace, long-suffering, kindness, goodness, faith, meekness, temperance. So St. Peter speaks here of the fruit of faith,—to wit, that we should purify our souls, through obedience to the truth in the Spirit. For where there is real faith it brings the body in subjection to itself, and controls the fleshly lust; and although it does not entirely destroy it, yet it makes it subject and obedient to the Spirit, and holds it in check. St. Paul implies the same thing when he speaks of the fruits of the Spirit. It is a great achievement that the Spirit should attain control over the flesh, and restrain the evil lust which descends to us from our parents: for it is not possible that we should succeed without grace in leading a chaste life in the married state, to say nothing of the unmarried.

But why does he say then, purify your souls? He is well aware that the desires of the flesh remain with us after baptism, even to the grave. Therefore it is not enough that a person should refrain from works and remain pure outwardly, while he permits evil lusts to cleave to his heart, but must thereafter beware that the soul be pure, as well as whatever proceeds out of the heart, and that the soul be opposed to these wicked lusts and desires, and continually contend therewith, until it is free from their power.

And here he adjoins an excellent provision: that we should purify our souls,* *through obedience to the truth in the Spirit.* Much has been preached on chastity, and many books have been composed on the subject. They have said, we should fast for so long a time, we should not eat flesh, we should not drink wine, etc., that we may be free from temptation. These things may perhaps have aided somewhat to that end, but it has not been enough, it has not subdued lust.

 * Make them chaste.

So St. Jerome writes of himself, that he had mortified his body to such an extent that he had become like a Moor; still it had been of no avail, and he had dreamed of being at Rome at a revelry among harlots.

St. Bernard also subjected himself to such austerities, and so mortified his body that it became offensive, as I said above. They endured severe temptation, and purposed thus to subdue it by external methods. But since it is external, it is only an outward plaster, with no inward application. So that it does not suffice to subdue lust.

But here St. Peter has prescribed an appropriate remedy,—namely, obedience to truth in the Spirit, as Scripture also has done in other places,—as Isaiah xi.: "Faith shall be the girdle of his reins." This is the true plaster that girds the reins, for it must proceed from within outward, not from without inward. For it has penetrated into the flesh and blood, the marrow and other parts of the living system; it is not outward in the dress or clothing. Therefore it is not to be expected that we should subdue lust with outward things; we may weaken the body and destroy it with fastings and labors, but the evil lusts are not thereby banished; yet faith can subdue them, and guard them, that they shall be compelled to give the Spirit place.

So likewise speaks the prophet Zachariah, ix., of the wine which Christ has, whereby the pure grow, and of which he gives them to drink. Other wine usually invites to wicked lust, but this wine,—that is, the Gospel,—subdues it, and makes the heart chaste. This is what St. Peter speaks of when any one heartily embraces the truth, and is obedient to it in spirit. This is the true help and the most powerful remedy for it, since you will find none which can still all evil thoughts like it; for if this enters our hearts, evil inclinations quickly leave; let whoever will try it, he shall find it true, and whoever has tried it, knows it well; but the devil lets no one easily attain it, and comprehend the word of God so as to delight in it; for he well knows how powerful it is to subdue evil lusts and thoughts.

St. Peter, therefore, would here say, if you would remain chaste, then must you render obedience to the truth in the Spirit, that is,—we must not only read and hear the word of God, but apprehend it in our hearts. Therefore it is not enough that a man should preach or hear the Gospel once, but he must ever press after it and persevere; for such grace does the word possess, that the more we taste it the more delightful it is; although there is, throughout, one and the same doctrine of faith, yet it cannot be listened to too much where the heart is not wanton and untamed.

To unfeigned love of the brethren. To what end, then, are we to live a chastely holy life? In order that we may be saved thereby? No! but in order that we may be useful to our neighbor. What am I to do that I may restrain my sin? I am to have obedience to the truth in the Spirit. But why am I to restrain it? In order that I may be of service to others, for I must first control my body and the flesh by the Spirit, and thus I can afterward be of service to others.—It follows further:

And have fervent love toward one another out of pure hearts. The Apostles Peter and Paul distinguish brotherly love, and love in general, from one another. Brotherhood is, that Christians should dwell altogether as brethren, and make no distinctions between themselves. For since we all have a common Christ, one baptism, one faith, one treasure, I am no better than thou; that which thou hast, I have also, and I am just as rich as thou. The treasure is the same, except that I may have it in a better shape than thou, since I may have it lying in gold, but thou in a poor garment. Therefore as we have the grace of Christ and all spiritual blessings in common, so should we also hold body and life, property and honor, in common, that one should be of service to another in all things.

Here he speaks plainly: *in unfeigned brotherly love.* The Apostles love to make use of the word, but have clearly perceived that were we called Christians and brethren universally one with another, it would be false, a feigned or imagined thing, and would be only hypocrisy. We have many brotherhoods set up in the world, but they are vain deceptions and corruptions, which the devil has devised and brought into the world, which are only antagonist to the true faith and to genuine brotherly love. Christ is mine as well as St. Bernard's; thine as well as St. Francis'; if one therefore should come to you and say, I shall go to heaven if I belong to this or that brotherhood, then tell him that he is deceived; for Christ cannot suffer, and will not allow any other than the common brotherhood, which we all have one with another; yet you come here, you fool, and will set up one of your own. This I will readily permit, that they be set up, not to help the soul, but as some one's endowment, and thus serve as a fund from which they who need shall be helped.

Thus we all of us, as Christians, have attained a brotherhood in baptism, whereof no saint possesses more than I or you. For just as costly as that one was purchased, at the same price was I also purchased. God has devoted as much toward me as to the greatest saint, except that *he* may have employed the treasure better, and may have a stronger faith than I.

But love is greater than brotherhood, for it extends even to our enemies, and especially to those who are not worthy of love. For as faith performs its work where it sees nothing, so also should love see nothing, and there especially exercise its office where there appears nothing lovely, but only disaffection and hostility. Where there is nothing that pleases me I should the more seek to be pleased. And this spirit should go forth fervently, says St. Peter, from the whole heart, just as God loved us when we were not worthy of love.— Now follows further:

As those who have been born again. Again we should do this, because we are not what we were before (he says), but have become new creatures. This has not come to pass through works, but is a consequence of the new birth. For thou canst not make the new man, but he must grow, or be born; as a husbandman cannot make a tree, but it must grow, itself, out of the earth, and as we certainly do not become the children of Adam, except as we are born and derive sin from our parents. So here it cannot come to pass through works that we should become the children of God, but we must also experience the new birth. This, therefore, is what the Apostle would say: since ye then have become new creatures, ye should conduct yourselves otherwise than ye did, and lead a new life. As ye before lived in hate, ye are now to walk in love— in all respects the reverse. But how has the new birth taken place? This, also, follows:

V. 23. *Not of corruptible, but of incorruptible seed, even of the living word of God which endures for ever.* Through a seed are we born again, for nothing grows as we see otherwise than through seed. Did the old birth spring from a seed? then must the new birth also spring from a seed. But what is this seed? Not flesh and blood! What then? It is not corruptible, but an eternal word. It is, moreover, that whereon we live,—food and nourishment. But especially is it the seed whereby we are born again, as he here says.

But how does this take place? After this manner: God lets the word—the Gospel—go forth, and the seed falls in the hearts of men, and wherever it fastens on the heart the Holy Spirit is present, and makes a new man; then the man becomes another, of other thoughts, of other words and works. Thus you are entirely changed. All that you before avoided you now seek out, and what you before sought after that you fly from. In respect to the birth of the body, it is the case that when conception takes place the seed is changed, so that it is seed no longer. But this is a seed which cannot be changed; it remains for ever; it changes me, so that I am transformed in it, and whatever is evil in me passes away from my nature. Therefore it is indeed a wonderful birth, and of extraordinary seed.—Now St. Peter says, further:

V. 24, 25. *For all flesh is grass, and all the glory of man like the flower of grass; the grass withereth, and the flower thereof falleth away, but the word of the Lord endureth for ever.* This passage is taken from the prophet Isaiah, xl., where the prophet speaks in this manner: "Cry! what shall I cry? Cry thus: all flesh is grass, and all its glory like a flower of the field; the grass withereth and the flower falleth away, but the word of God endureth for ever." These words St. Peter introduces here; for this is, as I have said, a rich epistle, and well spiced with Scripture.

Thus speaks the Scripture, then: *The word of God endures for ever.* What is flesh and blood is corruptible, like the grass which is yet green, so that it blooms; so whatever is rich, strong, wise and fair, and thus is flourishing (which all belongs to the bloom), yet you observe its bloom wither; what was young and vigorous will become old and ugly; what is rich will become poor, and the like. And all must fall by the word of God. But this seed cannot perish.—Now Peter concludes:

This is the word which is preached unto you. As though he would say, ye are not to look far in order to reach the word of God; ye have it before your eyes; the word is that which we preach; therewith may you subdue all evil lusts. You are not to seek it from afar; you have nothing more to do than fully to apprehend it when it is preached. For it is so near us that we may hear it, as Moses also says, in Deut. xxx.: "The word that I command you is not far from thee, that thou must go therefor far away; ascend into heaven or go beyond the sea, but it is near thee, even in thy mouth and in thy heart." It is indeed soon spoken and heard. But if it enters our hearts it cannot die or perish, and will not suffer you to perish; as long as you cleave to it, it will cleave to you.

As when I hear that Jesus Christ died to take away my sins, and has purchased heaven for me, and bestows upon me all that He has, then I hear the Gospel; the word quickly is gone if some one preaches it, but if it falls into the heart and is apprehended by faith, it can never pass away. This truth no creature can overthrow; the clearest reasoning avails nothing against it; and if I too would strike the devil while I am in his jaws, and am able to lay hold on this, I must oppose him from this and abide fast by the word. Therefore he well says, ye must look for no other Gospel than that which we have preached to you.

So St. Paul also says, in the first part of the Epistle to the Romans: "I am not ashamed of the Gospel, for it is the power of God which saves all that believe in it." The word is a divine and eternal power; for although the voice or speech is soon gone, yet the substance remains,—that is, the sense, the truth, which is conveyed by the voice. As when I put a cup to my mouth in which wine is contained, I swallow the wine, although I do not thrust the cup down my throat.

So likewise is the word which the voice conveys; it falls into our hearts and lives, while the voice remains without and passes away. Therefore it is indeed a divine power; yea, it is God Himself. For thus He speaks to Moses, Exodus iv.: "I will be in thy mouth;" and Ps. lxxx.: "Open thy mouth wide, proclaim glad tidings; say thou art hungry, I will satisfy thee, I will presently speak to thee comfortable things."

So, also, in John xiv., Christ says: "I am the way, the truth, and the life." Whoever confides in this is born of God; so that this seed of our Lord is itself divine. All this goes to teach us that we cannot be helped by works. Although the word is a small matter, and seems as nothing while it proceeds out of the mouth, yet is there such an immense power in it that it makes those who confide in it the children of God. John i. Thus does our salvation raise us to an exalted blessedness.

This is the first chapter of this Epistle, wherein you perceive in what a masterly manner St. Peter preaches and treats of faith, whence we easily see that this Epistle is true Gospel. Now comes the second chapter, that will instruct us in matter of works, how we should conduct ourselves toward our neighbor.

CHAPTER II.

V. 1-5. Wherefore lay aside all malice, and all guile, and hypocrisies, and hatred, and all evil speakings, and desire the sincere milk of the word, as new-born babes, that ye may grow thereby, if ye have besides tasted that the Lord is gracious, to whom ye are come as to a living stone, which indeed is rejected by men, but before God is elect and precious. And be ye also as living stones built up into a spiritual house, and a holy priesthood, to offer up spiritual sacrifices acceptable to God by Jesus Christ.

Here he begins to show what the characteristic and fruit of a christian life should be. For we have said often enough that a christian life consists in two things,—faith toward God and love toward our neighbor. Besides, although christian faith has been given us, yet as long as we live many evil lusts remain in the flesh, since every saint must be in the flesh, but what is in the flesh cannot be entirely pure. Therefore St. Peter says, be ye armed, that ye may guard yourselves against the sins which still cleave to you, and strive continually against them. For the worst enemies that we have hide themselves in our bosoms, and in our very flesh and blood, wake, sleep, and live with us, like a wicked spirit which we have brought home with us and cannot send off. Wherefore, since through faith Jesus Christ is entirely yours, and ye have obtained salvation and all His blessings, let it be your aim henceforth to lay aside all wickedness, or all that is evil, and all guile, so that no one act toward another deceitfully or falsely; as with the world it has become a common expression to say, the world is full of falsehood, which is indeed so. But we Christians should not act with such deceit, but uprightly and with pure hearts, toward men as toward God, fairly and justly, so that none take the advantage of another in sale, purchase or promise, and the like.

Likewise also St. Paul says to the Ephesians, ch. iv., "Lay aside lying, and speak truth every one with his neighbor." Truth is, that yea be yea, and nay, nay,—but hypocrisy, when any one represents himself by his outward mien as being what he is not in his thoughts. For solemn is the obligation that we should show ourselves to be what we are at heart. A Christian should so act that he could permit all men to see and know what he thinks in his heart. Let him, then, in all his walk and conduct, be anxious only to praise God, and serve his neighbor, and be afraid of no one; and let every one be in heart what he is in appearance, and not act a feigned part, whereby he shall make others gape with wonder.

Furthermore, St. Peter says that we should lay aside hatred and evil speaking. Here he fitly takes up the common vices among men, in their intercourse with one another. This evil speaking is exceedingly common and injurious,—is soon done, insomuch that none of us is aware of it. Therefore he says, be on your guard, if ye already have a christian spirit, that ye may know what are the fruits of this spirit.

V. 2. *And desire the sincere milk of the word, as new-born babes.* Here he institutes a comparison, and would say,—ye are like those new-born babes who seek nothing but the milk: like them, striving for the breasts and milk, so be ye also eager for the word; endeavor for it, have an appetite for it, that ye may suck in the intelligible, sincere milk.

These words are, indeed, figurative; for he did not mean literal milk, or literal sucking, as he does not speak of a literal birth. But he speaks of another milk which belongs to the mind, which is spiritual, which is procured by the soul, which the heart must draw in. It must be, moreover, sincere (or unfalsified), not as the custom is, to sell false wares; since there is truly strong obligation, and great necessity, that to the new-born and young Christian, the milk should be given pure, and not corrupted. But this milk is nothing but the Gospel, which is also the same with seed, whereby we are conceived and born, as we have heard above. Yet it is also the food which nourishes us when we arrive at maturity; it is also the harness wherewith we equip and clothe ourselves,—yea, it is all these in common. But whatever is appended to it is human doctrine, whereby the word of God is falsified; therefore the Holy Spirit would have it so that every Christian shall see to it, what he sucks for milk, and shall himself learn to decide in regard to all doctrines.

But the breasts which yield this milk, and which the babes suck, are the preachers in the christian Church. As the bridegroom says to the bride, in Cant. iii., "Thou hast two breasts like two young roes; they are as though they were hung with a bundle of myrrh;" as the bride says, Cant. i., "My beloved is like a bundle of myrrh that lies continually between my breasts." That is, we should ever *preach* Christ. The bridegroom must resort to the breasts; so that it is unjust, and the milk will be corrupt, if we do not preach Christ alone.

There is this, besides: when it is preached that Christ died for us, and rescued us from sin, death, and hell,—this is delightful and sweet, like milk; but after this, the cross also must be preached, that we are to suffer, as we have done; and this is a strong draught, it is strong wine. Therefore, Christians should have at first given them the weakest drink,—that is, milk. For it cannot be preached in its simplicity, except Christ be preached first of all; which is not bitter, but is mere sweet, rich grace, from which you receive yet no smart. This is the sincere milk of the word.

But here St. Peter has supported himself by Scripture, as he is throughout rich from the Scriptures. In the Old Testament it is written, both in Exodus xxiii., and Deuteronomy xiv., "Thou shalt not seethe the kid in its mother's milk." For what reason did God permit that to be written? Of what concern to Him was it that no suckling should be killed while as yet it sucks milk? Because He would thereby give us to understand that which St. Peter here teaches; and it is as much as if he had said, preach gently to the young and weak Christians; let them be carefully fed, and thrive in the knowledge of Christ; burden them not with strong doctrine, for they are as yet too young, but after they have become strong, let them then be slaughtered and sacrificed on the cross.

So, also, we read in Deut. xxiv., "If any one have recently taken a wife, then he need not go out to war for the first year, lest he should be slain,—but abide at home cheerfully with his wife." All goes to this point, that we should bear for a time with them that are young Christians, and proceed tenderly with them. But when they have grown, God brings them to the holy cross, lets them even die like other Christians, so that then the kid is slain.—Now follows further:

V. 2, 3. *That ye may grow thereby, if ye have besides tasted that the Lord is gracious.* It is not enough that we should hear the Gospel once; we must ever be anxious for it, that we may grow. After faith has become strong, we may provide and eat each kind of food. But to those who have not heard the Gospel, this is not said; they know neither what is milk or what is wine. Therefore he adds, if ye have besides tasted that the Lord is gracious; as though he had said, whoever has not tasted it, to him it is not a thing of the heart, to him it is not sweet; but they who have tried it, who grow by the food and by the word, to them it tastes pleasant and is sweet.

But it is said to be *tasted*, when I believe with my heart that Christ has given Himself for me, and has become my own, and my sin and misery are His, and His life also is mine. When this reaches my heart, then it *tastes;* for how can I but receive joy and gladness therefrom? I am heartily glad, as though some good friend should bestow on me a hundred florins. But as to him whose heart it does not reach, he cannot rejoice himself therewith. But they taste it best who lie in the straits of death, or whom an evil conscience oppresses; for in that case hunger is a good cook, as we say, that makes the food have a good relish. For the heart and conscience can hear nothing more soothing, when they feel their misery; after *this* they are anxious, they smell the provision afar off and cannot be satisfied. So also speaks Mary, in the *Magnificat:* "The hungry also has he filled with good things." But that hardened class who live in their own holiness, build on their own works, and feel not their sin and misery, they taste this not. Whoever sits at table and is hungry, he relishes all, readily; but to him who is previously full, nothing relishes, but he can only murmur at the most excellent food. Therefore the Apostle says, if ye have besides tasted that the Lord is gracious. But it is as though he had said, If ye have not tasted it, then I preach to you in vain.— He further says:

V. 4. *To whom ye art come as to a living stone.* Here he falls back again upon the Scripture, and quotes the prophet Isaiah, chap. xxviii., where he also says: "Hear now what God says to you, scorners: ye say, we have made a league with death and with hell, and have made lies our trust. Therefore thus saith the Lord, I lay in the foundation of Zion an elect, precious corner stone, a sure foundation," etc.

This passage Paul has also quoted, and it is an important passage of Scripture, for Christ is the precious head-stone which God has laid, on which we must be built.

And observe how St. Peter quotes the expression, and shows the stone to signify Christ. Just as Isaiah had spoken of setting confidence upon Him, St. Peter likewise says, it is as much as trusting in Him; thus is Scripture truly explained. The builders lay the foundation stone where it may stand sure and firm, that it may bear up the whole building. So Christ, the living stone, bears up the whole building; and it is called the building, in order that we, bound one to another, may set our confidence and security on Him.

V. 4. *Which indeed is rejected of men, but before God is elect and precious.* Here he brings forward a passage of the prophet David, in Ps. cxvii.: "The stone which the builders rejected has become the corner stone, and it is wonderful in our eyes." Which passage Christ also refers to in Mat. xxi. So Peter, in Acts iv., where he says: "This is the stone which ye builders rejected." Ye are builders, he says: for they taught the people, went about with great speeches, laid down many laws, but made mere work-saints and hypocrites. Then Christ comes and tells them, ye are hypocrites and broods of vipers; pronounces upon them many terrible judgments; judges them as sinners, and not as great saints, so that they could not endure it; they even reject Him— say to Him, "You are a heretic; do you caution that a man should not do good works? Ay! you must die." Therefore Peter says, here, this is the corner stone which indeed was rejected of men, whereon ye must be built by faith. This is now wonderful in our eyes, as the prophet says; it seems strange to us, and where the Spirit does not teach it, it is utterly incomprehensible. Therefore he says, in God's eyes the stone is elect, and an extremely precious stone; it is of great importance also that it takes away death, satisfies for sin, and rescues from hell, besides that it freely bestows heaven.

V. 5. *And be ye also as living stones, built up into a spiritual house.* How can we build ourselves up? By the Gospel and that which is preached. The builders are the preachers; the Christians who hear the Gospel are they who are built, and the stones which are to be fitted on this corner stone; so that we are to repose our confidence on Him, and let our hearts stand and rest upon Him. I must therefore take heed to myself that I have the form which this stone has, for if I am laid upon Him by faith, then I must also bear such marks and fashioning as He had, and every one else with me. It is the fruit of faith and a mark of love, that we all be fitted one to another, and all thus become one building. To the same end, also, St. Paul speaks on this subject, although in a different manner, I. Cor. iii.: "Ye are the temple of God." The house of stone or wood is not His house: He will have a spiritual house,—that is, the christian congregation, wherein we are all alike, in one faith, one like the other, and all laid and fitted one to the other, and locked into one another by love, without any wickedness, deceit, hypocrisy, hatred and slanders, as He has said.

And a holy priesthood. There he casts down the outward and bodily priesthood, which had existed before under the old dispensation, as also the outward Church, which he takes entirely away, as though he had said, "That outward institution with the priesthood has all ceased, wherefore another priesthood now begins, and another sacrifice is offered, even one that is entirely spiritual." We have had much disputing on this point, maintaining that those who are now called the clergy are not priests in the sight of God; and this is confirmed out of this passage of St. Peter. Therefore apprehend it well, and if one should meet you with the objection, and attempt to show, as some have done, that He speaks of a twofold priesthood,—of outward and spiritual priests,—then bid him lay aside his vain speeches that he may see clearly, and take nieswort* that he may clear his brains. St. Peter says, also, Ye are to build yourselves up into a spiritual or holy priesthood. Ask now those priests whether they are holy: their life clearly shows, as we see, that this wretched set is plunged into avarice, fornication, and all manner of vice. Whoever has this priesthood must certainly be holy. Whoever is not holy, he does not possess it. Therefore St. Peter speaks here only of one kind of priesthood.

* Aromatic snuff.

We ask further, whether he makes a distinction between spiritual and worldly, since the clergy are now called spiritual, and other Christians worldly?

Yet they must confess, no thanks to them, that St. Peter here speaks to all those that are Christians, even to those who lay aside all wickedness, deceit, hypocrisy and malice, etc., and are like new-born children, and drink the pure milk: so that their lie must bite itself in their mouth, since it stands forth a thing not to be gainsaid, that St. Peter speaks to all that are Christians; whence it is clear that they lie, and that St. Peter says nothing of their priesthood, which they have fancied and arrogate to themselves alone; wherefore our bishops are nothing but Nicholas-bishops, and as is their priesthood so are also their laws, sacrifices and works. It might be an excellent play to act out in the deep night, except that under the mask the divine name is reviled.

Therefore those alone are the holy and spiritual priesthood, who are true Christians and built upon this stone.

For since Christ is the bridegroom, and we all of us are the bride, so then the bride has all which the bridegroom has, even His own body; for if He gives Himself to the bride, He gives Himself for what He is, and on the other hand the bride gives herself to Him. Now Christ has been anointed the high and most exalted priest by God Himself; has also sacrificed His own body for us, which is the office of the high priest; besides, He prayed on the cross for us. Again, He has also preached the Gospel, and taught all men to know God and Himself.

These three offices has He also given to all of us: therefore, since He is a priest and we are his brethren, so all Christians have it in their power and charge, and an obligation rests upon them, to preach and to come before God, and that one should entreat for another and offer himself up to God; and provided that any one begin to preach the word of God or address it to others, he is then a priest.

To offer up spiritual sacrifices acceptable to God through Jesus Christ. As to spiritual offerings, it is not necessary that we should present them to the Pope; neither is sacrifice such as it was in the Old Testament, when men were required to sacrifice the tenth of all they had. Such outward sacrifices and priesthood have all now ceased, and all has become new and spiritual. The priest is Christ; and we all, since He has sacrificed His own body, must offer up ourselves. Here is now fulfilled all that was typified by outward sacrifices in the Old Testament, since they have all passed away, and all of them may be said compendiously to preach the Gospel. Whoever preaches this exercises and carries out all that former—strikes the calf dead,—that is, kills the carnal mind and the old Adam. For this stubborn nature in flesh and blood must be slain by the Gospel; thus do we permit ourselves to be offered upon the cross and to die. Herein is exercised the true priest's office, in that we sacrifice to God that wicked rogue, the corrupt old dolt (of our nature); if the world does it not, we must do it ourselves; but it must in the end be all removed, whatever we have of the old Adam, as we heard above in the first chapter. This is the only sacrifice that pleases and is acceptable to God. From this you may perceive whereto our foolish and blind leaders have brought us, and how this text has been kept under the bench. Now you may say, If that is true, that we are all priests and ought to preach, what sort of an institution is there? must there then be no distinction among the people, and are the women, also, to be priests? Answer. In the Old Testament it is permitted to no priest to wear the tonsure. Not that it is wrong in itself; a person might very well suffer himself to be shorn if he chose, but it is reason that none make a distinction between himself and common Christians,—a thing which faith will not permit. So that they who are now called priests are all laymen like the others, and only some, for the office' sake, are selected out of the Church to preach. Thus there is only an outward distinction for the office' sake, inasmuch as one is called of the Church; but before God there is no difference, and some individuals are selected from the multitude, in order that they may bear and exercise the office which they all have; not that one is more elect than another. Therefore, no one should rise up of himself and preach in the Church, but one is to be selected and instituted out of the congregation, who may be removed when it is desirable.

Yet have these men assumed a position of their own; as though directed by God, they have arrogated to themselves such license, that almost in the heart of christendom there is a greater distinction than that which exists between us and the Turks. When you look upon Christians you must observe no distinction, and you are not to say, this is a man or a woman, a servant or a master, old or young; as Paul tells us, Gal. iii.: They are all one and a purely spiritual people. So that all alike are priests, all alike may proclaim God's word, except that a woman is not to speak in the Church; but let the men preach, because of the command that they are to be subject to their husbands—as St. Paul teaches us, I. Cor. xiv.: Such order God permits to remain, but makes no distinction of the election. But where there are no men, but women only, as in the Nun's Cloisters, there a woman may be selected to preach.

This is now the true priesthood, which consists in those three points as we have heard,—namely, that we sacrifice spiritually; that we pray for the Church; that we preach. Whoever will do this, he is a priest, as all are bound to be, inasmuch as they should preach the word, pray for the Church, and offer themselves up before God. Let those fools then go who call the institution of the priests spiritual, who yet bear no other office but just to wear the tonsure and to be anointed. If the being shorn and anointed makes a priest, then might I easily shear an ass and anoint him, so that he should be a priest also.

Finally, St. Peter says, that we are to offer up spiritual sacrifices, acceptable to God through Jesus Christ. Since Christ is the corner stone whereon we are laid, it must be only through him that we are to treat with God, as we have heard sufficiently above; for God does not look upon my cross even though I torture myself to death, but he looks upon Christ through whom my works are acceptable before God, which otherwise would not be worth an alms of a straw's value. Therefore Scripture calls Christ properly a precious corner stone which imparts its virtue to all who through faith are built upon it. So, also, St. Peter teaches us in this passage how Christ is the living stone—what Christ is; and the figure is a fine one, since it is easy to understand by it how we are to believe on Christ.—It follows, now, further:

V. 6-10. Therefore it is contained in Scripture, Behold I lay in Zion an elect precious corner stone, and whoever believeth on Him shall not be put to shame. To you therefore who believe, He is precious, but to the unbelieving, the stone which the builders rejected is made a corner stone, and a stone of stumbling and a rock of offence, even to those that stumble at the word and believe not thereon, whereunto they were appointed. But ye are the chosen generation, the royal priesthood, the holy nation, the peculiar people, that ye should show forth the praise of him who has called you out of darkness into his wonderful light: who once were not a people, but are now the people of God, to whom God did not show mercy, but (now have obtained mercy) to whom He is now merciful.

I have before said, that St. Peter has enriched and fortified his Epistle well with Scripture, just as all preachers should do, in order that their foundation may rest entirely on the word of God. Here also he introduces four or five texts, one upon another. The first he has taken from the prophet Isaiah, word for word, that Christ is a precious corner stone or foundation, and is the very passage which we have just treated of and somewhat explained. It is truly an eminent proof text of the doctrine of faith, which is to be laid down as a foundation when we are to preach in a place where Christ has not been preached before. For it must be confessed that Christ is the stone on which faith should be built and should stand.

But that the prophet does not speak in this place of a material stone is evident from this, that it afterward follows, "whoever believes on Him shall not be made ashamed." If I am to *believe* on Him, it must be a stone in a spiritual sense. For how am I to believe on stone and wood? Besides, He must be truly God, since, in the first commandment, God has forbidden that we should believe on anything else, but on Him only. Since then this stone is laid as a foundation on which we are to trust, it must be God Himself. On the other hand, He cannot be God alone, but must also therewith be like man, because He must be a part of the building, and not merely a part, but the head. If a man then erects a building, one stone must be like the other, that each have the complexion, nature, and form of the other: therefore, since we are built on Christ, he also must be like us, and of the same nature with the other stones that rest upon Him, even a real humanity as we all have. Thus does the Scripture, by simple and few words, express so great a matter, even the entire *summa* of our faith, and in such brief words comprises more than any man can express.

Now what this that builds us up is, I have already said—namely, faith, whereby we are laid on Christ, and repose our trust upon this stone, and thus become like Him; and then this also must follow, that the building must be fitted one part to the other, for the other stones must all be laid and placed upon this stone. That is, of course, that love is a fruit of faith.

But why does the prophet call Him a foundation stone? For this reason: that no man can build a house except he lay one stone first as a foundation, for the other stones in the building cannot stand except on the foundation stone.

So we must all of us rest on Christ, and confess Him for a foundation stone. Therefore we are not to pride ourselves that the stone must receive something from us, but we must receive blessing from it alone; for we do not bear it up, but it bears us up, and upon Him lies sin, death, hell, and all that we have to bear. So that all this—and whatever jars against us—cannot injure us if we have been placed on this foundation.

For if we remain resting on him, and leave ourselves upon Him, we must then remain where He is; just as natural stones must be left on their foundation stone.

Besides, the prophet calls Him a corner stone. The Holy Spirit has a way of His own of saying much in few words. Christ is a corner stone because he has brought Gentiles and Jews together who were at dead enmity one with another, and thus the Christian Church has been gathered of both classes, whereof the Apostle Paul writes largely. The Jews gloried in the law of God, and that they were God's people, and so despised the heathen. But now Christ has come, has taken away their boasting from the Jews, and called us who were Gentiles; and thus he has made us both one, by one faith, and He has so dealt with us that we both must confess that we have nothing of ourselves, but are all sinners, and only must expect righteousness and heaven from Him, and that we Gentiles may as justly claim that Christ has come to help us, as the Jews; wherefore He is the corner stone that joins both together in one, so that it becomes one building and one house.

This, now, is the conclusion to which the prophet comes: Whoever believes on Him shall not be put to shame. When the Holy Spirit says, that they shall not be ashamed who believe on Christ, he gives us to understand what he has in view,—to wit, that he has already published and confirmed the sentence, that the whole world must be confounded and put to shame. Yet he would draw forth some out of the multitude, so that no one may escape the shame but he who believes on Christ. So Christ explains Himself in the last of Mark: "Whoever believes and is baptised shall be saved; but he who believes not shall be damned;" in which words, moreover, He accords with the prophets. So that Peter said well in the first chapter, that the prophets sought out the time, and diligently inquired after the salvation and concerning the future grace that was previously promised. So now Christ is to be preached, that He it is who has rescued us from this shame into which we were all plunged.

Now let any one come forward who chooses, and exalt free-will, and defend human ability. Though you should commingle together all human works and doctrines, and whatever springs from man, you have enough in this single passage to overthrow it all, so that it must all fall like dry leaves from the tree.

For it is doomed that whatever does not rest upon this stone, *that* is already lost. He does not suffer that you should attain anything by works. With such simplicity speaks forth the Spirit and the Divine Majesty, that it despises no one, yet with such authority that it overcomes all things. Who, then, will set himself against it, or who will not be terrified by it? Therefore God would have us entirely despair as it regards ourselves, and appropriate to ourselves only the blessings which *He* has, and build on that foundation which no creature can overthrow; so that no one should trust in his own righteousness, but on Christ's righteousness, and on all that Christ has. But what is it to rest upon His righteousness? Nothing else but that I should despond in regard to myself, and think with myself,—my righteousness, my truth, must go to pieces, and what is built thereon; while His righteousness, His truth, His life, and all the blessings which He has, are eternal. There lies the foundation on which I stand; whatever stands not on this foundation, will all necessarily fall. But he who lets himself fall back on this, he alone shall not be put to shame, and shall rest safe, so that no violence shall ever injure him at all. Therefore Christ must be not only a stone, but God will lay Him also as a foundation on which we should confide. God has said this, who cannot lie.

Now this stone is not subservient to itself, but suffers itself to be trodden on, and buried in the earth so that it cannot be seen, and the other stones lie upon it and can be seen. Wherefore, it is given to us that we should partake of Him, and rest upon Him, and believe that what He has shall all be ours, as what He has procured; that He has done it for us; so that I may say,—this is my own property and treasure, over which my conscience can exult.—But St. Peter says further:

V. 7, 8. *To you, therefore, who believe, He is precious; but to the unbelieving, the stone which the builders rejected has become a corner stone, and a stone of stumbling and a rock of offence.* This exceedingly precious stone, says Peter, is indeed, to some, precious and honorable. But on the other hand, it is also to many not precious, but despised, and a stone of stumbling. How is this? The Scripture ascribes to it a twofold aspect, inasmuch as there are some that believe thereon, and, on the other hand, many who do not believe thereon. To them who believe, is He precious; so that my heart must be glad if I repose my confidence and trust upon Him. Therefore he says,—to you that believe, He is precious; that is, ye are greatly dependent on Him; for although He in Himself is precious and excellent, yet this may be of no service or help to me. Therefore He must be precious to us for this reason, because He gives us so many precious blessings; as an excellently precious stone, which does not retain its virtue in itself, but breaks forth and imparts all its powers, so that I have all that *it* is.

But the unbelieving hold Him not as such a precious stone, but reject Him, and stumble upon Him, because He is not pleasing to them, but obnoxious and hateful; although He is yet delightful in Himself. These are not only the great, openly avowed sinners, but much more those great saints who rest on their free-will, on their own works and righteousness, who must stumble on this stone and run upon it. Now God pronounces the sentence, that they who rest thereon, without works, come to be justified through faith alone; but these do not attain thereto, for they would be justified by their own righteousness, as St. Paul says, Rom. x.

Therefore this has become the stone, says St. Peter, which the builders rejected. And here he dovetails the Scriptures into one another, but explains the passage which he quoted above from the cxvii. Psalm, "The stone which the builders rejected, has become the corner stone." Who the builders are, I have sufficiently shown: even those who taught, preached the law, and would justify men by works; who agree with Christians, as summer and winter with each other; therefore those preachers who preach of works, reject this stone.

Besides this, he quotes another passage still, from the prophet Isaiah, chap. viii. The prophet has there described that which was to take place, as St. Peter here does, and speaks thus: "The Lord shall be your fear, who shall be to you for holiness; but for a stone of stumbling and a rock of offence shall He be, to both houses of Israel." This is the sense of the prophet: The Lord shall be to you for holiness,—that is, He shall be hallowed in your hearts; ye are to have no other sanctification, neither this nor that, except as ye believe. To the others, He shall be a stone whereon they shall stumble and be offended.

But what, now, is this offence and perplexity, or stumbling? This is it: when we preach Christ, and say, See why this stone is laid for a foundation, that you, wholly desponding and despairing in yourself, might hold your works and your own righteousness as a merely condemned thing, and might place your confidence upon Him alone, and believe, that Christ's righteousness may become your righteousness; when those men hear this, they revolt at it, stumble and vex themselves, and say, "How? do you mean to say that virginity, and masses, and the like good works, amount to nothing? It is the devil that bids you say that!" For they cannot understand, in this matter, that their claims are not good; they think they have done well in the sight of God; quote passages to prove it from the Scriptures, and say, God has commanded that we should perform good works. If we dispute this, they begin and cry out, "Heretic! Heretic!" "Fire! Fire!" So that they cannot endure this stone, and they stumble against it. So inconsistent are they one with another, that upon this stone they must stumble; as Christ says, Matt. xxi., "Have ye not read in Scripture,—the stone which the builders rejected is become the corner stone? (and it follows) and whosoever shall fall upon this stone shall be dashed in pieces, and on whom it shall fall, it shall grind him to powder." Therefore, do as ye will, ye cannot dishonor the stone; it is laid, and it will continue to lie. Whoever, then, will run upon it and dash himself thereon, must necessarily be broken.

That is the stumbling and the vexation whereof Scripture has much to say. Thus the Jews stumble to this day against this stone,—and this will not cease until the last day shall come; then shall this stone fall upon all the unbelieving and grind them to powder. Wherefore, although Christ is such an elect, precious stone, He must yet be called a stone of offence and stumbling, by no fault of His. And just as the Jews did, we continue to do at the present day; for as they gloried in the name of God, that they were God's people, so it is the case now, that men, under the name of Christ and the christian church, deny Christ, and reject the precious stone. He has come that they might reject their works; but this is a thing they cannot suffer, and they reject Him. Therefore it follows:

Who stumble at the word and believe not thereon, whereunto they were appointed. If they are told that their works are not good and are of no avail before God, they cannot and will not hear it. Now God has laid down Christ as a foundation, whereon they should have been placed, and through Him have obtained complete salvation; and He has caused Him to be preached throughout the whole world, that they, through the proclamation of the Gospel, might be grounded on Him. Yet would they not receive Him, but rejected Him, and remain in their own nature and works; for if they suffered themselves to rest upon Him, then would their own honor, riches, and power fall, insomuch that they would never rise again.—St. Peter says further:

V. 9. *But ye are the chosen generation, the royal priesthood, the holy nation, the peculiar people.* There he gives Christians a true title, and has quoted this passage from Moses, Deut. vii., where he says to the Jews, "Ye are a holy people to the Lord your God, and the Lord your God has chosen you as his peculiar people out of all the nations that are on the earth." So, Ex. xix., he says: "Ye shall be my possession before all peoples, and shall be to me a kingdom of priests and a holy people." There you see where Peter's words are from. As I have said before, so I say again, that it should be understood how Scripture is wont to speak of priests. Let no one be troubled as to those whom the people *call* priests; let every one call them as he pleases, but abide thou by the pure word of God, and what *this* calls priests do thou call priests also. We could well endure it that those should call themselves priests whom the bishops and the Pope consecrate, and let them call themselves as they will, only see to it that they do not call themselves priests of God, for they cannot quote a word from Scripture in proof of it.

But should they claim that in this passage he speaks of them, answer them as I have instructed you above, and ask them to whom St. Peter is here speaking,—so shall they of necessity be made ashamed; for it is certainly clear and plain enough that he speaks to the whole congregation, to all Christians, in that he says, ye are the chosen generation and the holy people, since he has hitherto spoken of none but of those who are built upon this stone and believe. Therefore it must follow, that whoever does not believe is no priest. If they say, then, "Ah! we must explain the passage just as the holy fathers have interpreted it;" then do you say, Let the fathers and teachers, whoever they may be, explain as they will, yet St. Peter, who has received greater testimony from God than they, besides being more ancient, tells me so and so, therefore I will hold with him. The passage, moreover, needs no gloss, for he speaks in express words of those that believe. Now those are not the only believers who are anointed and wear the tonsure; therefore we will readily grant them that they call themselves by this name, for the question is not what they permit themselves to do; but the dispute is here,—whether they are styled priests in Scripture, and whether God calls them by this name. There may be some selected out of the Church, who are its officers and ministers, and appointed to this end, that they should preach in the Church and administer the sacraments; but we are all priests before God if we are Christians. For since we are built upon this stone, which is our high priest before God, we must also possess all that He has.

Therefore I would be glad to find this word priests becoming as common as it is for us to be called Christians. For it is all the same,—priest, baptized, Christian. As little as I would suffer that those who are anointed and shorn should call Christians un-baptized, so little would I endure that they only should be regarded as priests. Yet have they arrogated it entirely to themselves. So too they have named *that* the church which the Pope and his cardinals rule over, but Scripture refutes this. Therefore mark this well, that you may know how to establish the distinction as to how God names us priests, and how men call themselves such.

For we must yet again state that this word *priest* should become as common as the word Christian. For to be a priest belongs not to an office that is external, it is only such a service as has to do with God's presence.

So we conclude that we are all kings. Priests and kings are all spiritual names, as Christians, saints, the Church. And just as you are not called a Christian because you have much gold or wealth, but because you are built upon this stone and believe on Christ, so you are not called a priest because you wear a tonsure or long robe, but for this reason, that you come into God's presence. Likewise you are not a king because you wear a gold crown, and have many lands and people subject to you, but because you are lord over all things, death, sin, and hell. For you are as really a king as Christ is a king, if you believe on Him. Still He is not a king as the kings of this world are, wears no crown of gold, rides forth with no great splendor and large equipage. But He is a king over all kings,—one who has authority over all things, and at whose feet all must lie. As He is a lord, so also am I a lord; for what He possesses that have I also.

But perhaps some one may object. St. Peter says here, also, that Christians are kings, while we have it before our eyes that they are not all kings, so that this passage is not to be understood as though He spoke of all in the Church. For whoever may be a Christian, he certainly is not a king in France or a priest at Rome. But when I ask whether the King of France is also a king in the sight of God, this he passes over, for God will not judge by the crown. On earth, indeed, and before the world, he is indeed a king, but when death comes then his kingdom is gone, for then he must lie at the feet of those that believe. We are speaking of an eternal kingdom and priesthood, inasmuch as every one who believes is in truth a king before God; but who does not know that we are not all shorn and anointed priests? But because those men have been anointed, they are not therefore priests in the sight of God, just as they are not kings before God because they have been crowned. Crowned kings and anointed priests are of the world, and are made by men; the Pope may make as many such priests as he chooses, but far be it that he should make one a priest before God, for these God himself will make.

Therefore, when St. Peter says here, "ye are the royal priesthood," it is as much as though he had said, "ye are Christians." Would you now know what sort of a title, and authority, and glory, Christians have: you learn it here, that they are kings and priests, and a chosen people.—But what this priest's office is, follows after:

That ye should show forth the praises* of Him that hath called you out of darkness into His wonderful light. This belongs to the office of a priest, that he be a messenger of God, and receive from God himself the command to preach His word. The praises, (says St. Peter,) that is, the wonderful work that God has performed in you, in that he brought you out of darkness into light, you are to proclaim,—which is the office of the High Priest. And this is the way in which your preaching is to be discharged, that one brother proclaim to another the powerful work of God: how ye have been ransomed from sin, death, hell, and all evil, by Him, and have been called to eternal life. Thus shall you also instruct others how they may come also to the same light. For your whole duty is discharged in this, that you confess what God has done for you; and then let this be your chief aim, that you may make this known openly, and call every one to the light, whereto ye have been called. Where you see people who are ignorant, you are to direct and teach them as you have learned, namely, how a man may be saved through the virtue and power of God, and pass from darkness to light.

* In the German, *tugend* or virtue.

And here you observe that St. Peter plainly says, that there is only one single light, and concludes that all our reason, however sharp-sighted it is, is mere darkness; for although reason may count one, two, three, and also discern what is black or white, great or small, and judge outwardly of other matters, still it cannot understand what faith is. Herein it is stark blind, and if all men should put their shrewdness together, they could not understand a letter of this divine wisdom. Therefore St. Peter speaks here of another light, that is truly wonderful; and tells us earnestly, all alike, that we are all in darkness and blindness if God hath not called us to his true light.

Experience teaches us this, also. For when it is preached that we cannot come before God by our works, but must have a mediator, who may come into God's presence and may reconcile us to him, reason must confess that she never could have known such a thing; so that if she would understand it she must have another light and knowledge. Therefore all that is not of God's word and faith is darkness. For here reason gropes like a blind man,—is ever changing from this to that, and knows not what it does. But if we speak in this manner to the worldly, learned, or wise, they begin to cry out and bluster against it. Therefore St. Peter is a bold Apostle indeed, in that he dares make that darkness that all the world calls light.

So we see that the first and most eminent office which we as Christians are to discharge is, that we should make known the praise of God. What then are the praiseworthy things and the noble deeds which God has put forth? They are, as we have often said, that Christ, through the power of God, has wounded death, chained hell, subdued sin and brought us to eternal life: these are praises so great that by no man are they possibly to be conceived; we can only be silent. Therefore it is of no avail that to us Christians human doctrines should be preached, but we should be taught of such a power as subdues the devil, sin and death. And here St. Peter has once more brought together many proof-texts, and it is throughout common with him thus to heap passage on passage, for all the prophets speak of this, that God's name and honor, and his arm or power should be honored and extolled, and that he would perform such a work that the whole world would sing and speak of it. Of this are the prophets in all places full. On this same St. Peter here expatiates. Besides, they have spoken much of light and darkness, that we must be enlightened with God's light, thereby showing that all human reason is darkness.—St. Peter says, further:

V. 10. *Ye who once were not a people, but are now a people of God, to whom God did not show mercy, but to whom he is now merciful.* This passage is found written in the prophet Hosea, chap. ii., and St. Paul has also quoted it in Rom. ix.: "I will make those to be called my people, who were not my people." The import of all is this: Almighty God chose his people Israel as a peculiar people, and manifested his great power in their behalf, and gave them many prophets, and performed many wonderful works toward them, that He from that people might permit Christ to become man; and for the children's sake has it all taken place. Therefore they are called in Scripture the people of God. But the prophets have extended this further, and said that this election should be more comprehensive, and should even include the Gentiles. Therefore St. Peter says here, ye are now the people of God, who once were not the people of God. Hence it is evident that he wrote the epistle to the Gentiles and not to the Jews. Thereby he shows that the passage out of the prophet has been now fulfilled—that they are now a holy people—they have the property, priesthood, kingdom, and all which Christ has, if they believe.—It follows further, in Peter:

V. 11-12. *Dearly beloved, I admonish you as strangers and pilgrims, abstain from fleshly lusts which war against the soul, and lead an honest life among the Gentiles, so that they, if they slander you as evildoers, may see your good works, and praise God when it shall come to that day.*

St. Peter here uses a somewhat different mode of speech from St. Paul, who would not speak in the same manner, as we shall hear: for every Apostle has his own way of speaking, just as each prophet has also. He has hitherto been firmly laying down his foundation of the christian faith, which may serve as his text. Now he proceeds and teaches how we should conduct ourselves toward all men. This is the true method of preaching, that faith should be first set forth,—what it does, and what its power and nature are, even that it gives fully to us everything that is necessary to holiness and salvation,—that we can do nothing except by faith, and through this we have all which God has. God has thus proceeded with us and given to us all that is His, and has Himself become our own, so that we have, through faith, all things that are good and needful for us. What then are we to do? Are we to live in indolence? It were far better that we should die, though we had all. But while we live here we should act in our neighbor's behalf, and give ourselves to him for his own, as God hath given Himself to us. Thus faith saves us, but love leads us to give to our neighbor whenever we have enough to give. That is, faith receives from God; love gives to our neighbor. This matter is spoken of in few words, yet much may easily be preached thereon, and it may be further extended than it has here been by St. Peter.

This is now the sense of the Apostle, when he says, Dear brethren, I admonish you as strangers and as pilgrims. Since, then, you are one with Christ, form one household, and His goods are yours, your injury is His injury, and He takes as His own all that you possess; therefore you are to follow after Him, and conduct yourselves as those who are no more citizens of the world. For your possessions lie not upon the earth, but in heaven; and though you have already lost all temporal good, you still have Christ, who is more than all else. The devil is the prince of this world and rules it; his citizens are the people of this world; therefore, since you are not of the world, act as a stranger in an inn, who has not his possessions with him, but procures food, and gives his gold for it. For here it is only a sojourning, where we cannot tarry, but must travel further. Therefore we should use worldly blessings no more than is needful for health and appetite, and therewith leave and go to another land. We are citizens in heaven; on earth we are pilgrims and guests.

Abstain from fleshly lusts that war against the soul. I will not determine, here, whether St. Peter speaks of outward impurity,—or as St. Paul's language is, all that is called carnal,—whatever man does without faith, while he is in the body and a carnal life. I hold, indeed, that St. Peter had a somewhat different mode of speech, yet do not think that he uses the word soul, as St. Paul does, for spirit; but St. Peter has given in more to the common Greek word, than St. Paul. Yet much stress is not to be laid upon this: let it be understood of all kinds of lusts, or all kinds of carnal desire or impurity. But this at least he would teach us, that no saint on earth can be fully perfect and holy. Yet the high schools have even trodden the passage under their feet, nor do they understand it; they think it is said only of sinners, as though the saints had no more wicked lusts remaining. But whoever will study carefully into the Scriptures, must note a distinction, because the prophets sometimes speak of the saints in an obvious way, as though they were perfectly holy in every respect; while on the other hand they speak also of them as having evil lusts and being troubled with sins.

In regard to those two positions, those persons cannot see their way. Understand, then, that Christians are divided into two parts,—into an inward nature which is faith, and an outward which is the flesh. If we look upon a Christian as it respects faith, then he is pure and entirely holy; for the word of God has nothing impure in it, and wherever it enters the heart that depends upon it, it will make that also pure. Because, in respect to faith all things are perfect: according to that, we are kings and priests and the people of God, as was said above. But since faith exists in the flesh, and while we yet live on earth we feel at times evil dispositions, as impatience and fear of death, &c.

These are all the fault of the old man, for faith is not yet mature, has not attained full control over the flesh.

This you may understand from the parable in the Gospel, Luke x., of the man who went down from Jerusalem to Jericho and fell among thieves, who beat him and left him lying half dead, whom the Samaritan afterward took up, and bound up his wounds, and took care of him, and saw to it that he should be nursed. There you perceive that this man, since he is to be attended upon, is not sick unto death,—his life is safe; all that is wanting is, that he should be restored to health. Life is there, but he is not completely restored, for he lies yet in the hands of the physicians and must yet give himself up to be healed. So it is with us as respects the Lord Jesus Christ; we are assured of Eternal life, yet we have not complete health; something of the old Adam still remains in the flesh.

Similar also is the parable in the xiii. of Matthew, where Christ says, the kingdom of heaven is like leaven which a woman takes and mingles in the meal until it is leavened throughout. When the meal is made into dough, the leaven is all in it, but it has not penetrated and worked through it, but the meal lies working, until it is leavened throughout, and no more leaven need be added. Thus though you have what you should have, through faith, whereby you apprehend the word of God, yet it has not penetrated throughout, wherefore it must continue to work till you are entirely renewed. In this way you are to discriminate in regard to the Scriptures, and not mangle them as the Papists do.

Therefore I say, when you read in Scripture of the Saints, that they were perfect, understand it thus: that they as to faith were entirely pure and without sin, but the flesh still remained, that could not have been entirely holy. Therefore Christians desire and pray that the body or the flesh be mortified, that it may be entirely pure. This those who teach otherwise have neither experienced nor relished, which leads them to speak just as they imagine and conceive by reason; wherefore they must err. In regard to this, those great saints who have written and taught much, have greatly stumbled. Origen has not a word of it in his books. Jerome never understood it. Augustine, had he not been driven to contend with the Pelagians, would have understood it as little. When they speak of the saints, they extol them as highly as if they were something different from, and better than, other Christians: certainly as though they had not felt the power of the flesh and complained thereof as well as we.

Therefore St. Peter says here, as ye would be pure and have complete sanctification, continue to contend with your evil lusts. So also Christ says in the Gospel of John xiii.: "Whoever is washed, must also wash his feet;" it is not enough that his head and hands be clean, therefore he would yet have them wash their feet.

But what does St. Peter mean, in that he says, refrain from the lusts that war against the soul? This is what he would say: You are not to imagine that you can succeed by sports and sleep. Sin is indeed taken away by faith, but you have still the flesh which is impulsive and inconsiderate; therefore take good care, that ye overcome it. By strong effort must it be; you are to constrain and subdue lust, and the greater your faith is, the greater will the conflict be. Therefore you should be prepared and armed, and should contend therewith without intermission. For they will assault you in multitudes, and would take you captive.

Hence St. Paul says, also, Rom. vii.: "I have a desire toward the law of God after the inward man; but I find another law in my members, which opposes itself to the law in my spirit, and takes me captive, that I cannot do as I would,"—as though he had said, I fight indeed against it, but it will not finally yield. Therefore I would gladly be free, but in spite of my wishing it, it may not come to pass. What then am I to do? "Wretched man that I am, (says he,) who shall deliver me from the body of this death." In this same manner, also, all the saints cry out. But those people who are without faith, the devil leads in such a way that he permits them only to enter on sinful courses, to follow him and make no opposition. But as to the others, he thinks, I have already taken them captive by unbelief. I will permit them then to go so far only, as to do no great sin and have no great assault and be kept from swearing and knavery.

But believers have always opposition enough,—they must ever stand in the (attitude of) struggle. Those who are without faith and have not the Spirit, do not feel this, nor do they have such an experience; they break away and follow their wicked lusts; but as soon as the Spirit and faith enter our hearts, we become so weak that we think we cannot beat down the least imaginations and sparks (of temptation), and see nothing but sin in ourselves, from the crown of the head, even to the foot. For before we believed, we walked according to our own lusts, but now the Spirit has come and would purify us, and there arises a conflict. Here the devil, the flesh, and the world, oppose themselves to faith; whereof the prophets complain, here and there, in the Scriptures.

Wherefore St. Peter here means, that the strife does not take place in sinners, but in believers, and gives us an encouragement, inasmuch as when we are on our guard against wicked lusts, we are repelling them. If thou, then, hast wicked thoughts, thou shouldest not on this account despair; only be on thy guard, that thou be not taken prisoner of them. Our teachers have proposed to relieve the matter in this way (by directing,) that men should torture themselves until they had no more evil thoughts, that they might be at last bold and free. But you are to understand, if you are a Christian, that you must experience all kinds of opposition and wicked dispositions in the flesh. For wherever there is faith, there come a hundred evil thoughts, a hundred strugglings more than before; only see to it that you act the man, and not suffer yourself to be taken captive; and continue to resist, and say, I will not, I will not. For we must here confess, that the case is much like that of an ill-matched couple, who are continually complaining of one another, and what one will do the other will not.

That may yet be called a truly christian life that is never at perfect rest, and has not so far attained as to feel no sin, provided that sin be felt, indeed, but not favored. Thus we are to fast, pray, labor, to subdue and suppress lust. So that you are not to imagine that you are to become such a saint as these fools speak of. While flesh and blood continue, so long sin remains; wherefore it is ever to be struggled against. Whoever has not learned this by his own experience, must not boast that he is a Christian.

Hitherto we have been taught, that when we made confession, or joined ourselves to some spiritual institution, we were at once pure and needed no longer to contend with sin. They have said, moreover, that baptism purifies and makes holy, so that nothing evil remains in the person. Then they have thought, "now will I have a pleasing rest," but the devil has come and assaulted them worse than before. Therefore understand the thing well, though you confess and permit yourselves to receive absolution, you must do even as the soldier, who in battle runs upon the points (of the javelins); whenever the critical moment approaches, and the conflict rages, compelling him to strike right bravely, as if to repel outrage, then he must draw out his sword and lay about him; but while the strife threatens only, so long must there be untiring vigilance. So, although you have been baptized, be on your guard, inasmuch as you are not safe for an hour from the devil and from sin, even though you think you will have no more assaults.

Therefore a christian life is nothing else but a conflict and encampment, as the Scripture says; and therefore the Lord our God is called the Lord of Sabaoth,—that is, a Lord over the hosts. So also, *Dominus potens in prælio*— the Lord mighty in battle.

And thereby He shows how powerful He is, that He permits His people to be exposed in the conflict and rush upon the points (of the javelins). Yet so that while the trumpets are ever sounding He is ever observant, (saying) beware here, beware there; thrust here, strike there. Besides, it is a lasting conflict, in which you are to do all that you can, so that you may strike down the devil by the word of God. We must therefore ever make resistance, and call on God for help, and despond of all human powers.—Now follows further:

V. 12. *And lead an honest life, that those who have slandered you, as evil-doers, may see your good works and praise God.* Mark now what an excellent order St. Peter has observed. He has already taught us what we should do in order to subdue the flesh with all its lusts. Now he teaches us again why this should be. Why should I subdue my flesh? that I may be saved? No, but that I may lead an honest life before the world. For this honest life does not justify us, but we must first be justified and believe before we attempt to lead an honest (pious) life. But as to outward conduct, this I am not to direct to my own profit, but that the unbelieving may thereby be reformed and attracted, that they through us may come to Christ; which is a true mark of love, though they slander and asperse us, and hold us as the worst wretches. Therefore we should exhibit such an excellent course of action, that men shall be compelled to say, Certainly they cannot be blamed.

We read that when the emperors reigned, and persecuted the Christians, no fault could be found with the latter, except that they called on Christ and considered Him as God. So Pliny writes in his letter to Trajan, the Emperor, that he knew of no wrong that the Christians did, except that they came together every morning, early, and sang songs of praise in order that they might honor their Christ and receive the sacrament; besides this, none could bring any charge against them. Therefore St. Peter says: Ye must endure to have men asperse you as evil-doers, and for this reason you are to lead such a life that you shall do no man injury, and in this manner you shall bring about their reformation. *Till that day arrive;* that is, ye must endure it as long as men reproach you, till all shall be set forth and revealed, so that it shall be seen how unjust they have been toward you, and that they must glorify God on your account. So St. Peter continues:

V. 13-17. *Submit yourself to every ordinance of man for the Lord's sake, whether to the king as supreme, or to governors, as those that are sent by Him for the punishment of evil-doers and to the praise of those that do well. For this is the will of God, that by well-doing ye may silence the ignorance of foolish men. As free, and not as though ye had your freedom as a cover of wickedness, but as the servants of God. Be respectful toward every man. Love the brotherhood; fear God; honor the king.*

In such a beautiful order does St. Peter proceed, and teaches us how we should conduct ourselves in all things. Hitherto he has spoken in a general manner of the conduct that belongs to every condition. Now he begins to teach how we should act toward civil magistracy. For since he had said enough as to the first matter, of our duty to God and ourselves, he now adds how we are to conduct toward all men.

And now he would say, in the first place, and before all else, since ye have done all that was necessary that ye might attain to a true faith and hold your body in subjection, let this now be your first business, to obey the magistracy.

This, which I have here rendered in the Dutch, every *ordinance* of man, is in the Greek [Greek: ktiois], and in Latin *creatura*. This thing has not been understood by our learned men. The Dutch language well expresses what the word means, where it is said, we are to obey what the ruler enacts (creates). So he uses the word here as though he said, what the magistracy enacts (creates) yield obedience to. For to enact (create) is to lay down a command and ordinance; it is a human creation. But they have hence inferred that *creatura* means an ox or an ass, as the Pope also speaks of it. If this were Peter's meaning, then we should need to become subject even to a slave. But he here means a human ordinance, law or command,—and what they enact we are to do.

What God makes, authorizes, and requires,—that is His ordinance, as that we should believe. So, also, that is a human and secular creation which is constituted by commands, as external government must be. To this we are to be subject. Therefore understand the expression as meaning, *creatura humana, quod creat et condit homo* (what man makes and constructs).

For the Lord's sake. We are not bound to obedience to the sovereign power for its own sake, he says, but for God's sake, whose children we are; and we should be drawn to this, not that we may thereby acquire a merit,—for what I do for God's sake, I must freely do as an act of service: moreover, I would do from mere cheerfulness, what His heart desires. But why should we be obedient to the magistracy for God's sake? Because it is God's will that evil-doers should be punished, and those that do well should be protected, that there may be concord in the world. So we should demand that there be civil peace, which God requires; but the majority are unbelieving, so that He has enacted and ordained, in order that the world might not go to anarchy, that the magistracy should bear the sword and restrain the wicked, in order that if they are not disposed to be at peace, they may be compelled to it. This He executes through the magistracy, so that the world may be ruled to the good of all. Whence you see that if there were none wicked, there would be no need of magistracy; wherefore he says, *to the punishment of evil-doers, and to the praise of those that do well.* The just should have the honor of it when they do right, since they exalt and crown worldly magistracy, insomuch that others may take example from them,—not that any one may thereby merit any thing before God. Such is Paul's language, also, in Rom. xiii.: "The power is not established to the fear of those that do well, but for the evil; therefore, if thou wouldst not be afraid of the power, do well."

V. 15. *For this is the will of God, that by well-doing ye should silence the ignorance of foolish men.* In these words St. Peter silences those vain babblers who glory in their christian name, and prevents them from coming forward and saying, Since faith is sufficient for a Christian, and works do not justify, what is then the necessity of being subject to the civil power, and paying tribute and taxes? And he tells them thus, that although we have no need of it, we ought readily to do it to please God, so that the mouth of those enemies of God who asperse us may be stopped, and they be able to bring up nothing against us, and be compelled to say that we are honest, obedient people. So we read of many saints, that they were summoned to war, under heathen rulers, and slew the enemy, yet were subject and obedient (to those that summoned them), as we Christians are bound to be to the magistracies, although it is now maintained that we could not be Christians if we lived among the Turks.

Now you may perhaps say here, But still Christ has commanded that we should not resist evil, but if any one strike us on one cheek we are to turn the other also; how, then, can we strike and execute others? Answer: the heathen formerly objected in like manner to the Christians, and said, if such and such should come to pass, your government must be suppressed. But we reply, it is true that Christians for themselves should not resist the evil, neither should they revenge themselves when they are injured, but endure injustice and violence, so that they cannot be severe even toward those who do not believe. But the magistracy of the sword is not thereby forbidden; for although honest Christians have no need of the sword and law (since they live so that none can complain of them, do no man wrong, but treat every one kindly and cheerfully, endure all that is done to them), yet the sword must be borne on account of the unchristian, that these, when they injure others, may be punished, so that the general peace shall be preserved and the just be protected. Thus God has provided another rule, that they who would not of themselves be restrained from evil, might be so compelled by the power that they should do no injury. Therefore God has established magistracy for the sake of the unbelieving, insomuch that even christian men might exercise the power of the sword, and come under obligation thereby to serve their neighbor and restrain the bad, so that the good might remain in peace among them. And still the command of Christ abides in force, that we are not to resist evil. So that a Christian, although he bears the sword, does not use it for his own sake nor to revenge himself, but only for others; and, moreover, this is a mark of christian love, that with the sword we support and defend the whole Church, and not suffer it to be injured. Christ teaches those only who, while they believe and love, obey also. But the greater multitude in the world, as it does not believe, obeys not the command. Therefore they must be ruled as unchristian, and their caprice be put under restraint; for if their power was suffered to obtain the upper hand, no one could stand before them.

Thus there are two kinds of government in the world, as there are also two kinds of people,—namely, believers and unbelievers. Christians yield themselves to the control of God's word; they have no need of civil government for their own sake. But the unchristian portion require another government, even the civil sword, since they will not be controlled by the word of God. Yet if all were Christians and followed the Gospel, there would be no more necessity or use for the civil sword and the exercising of authority; for if there were no evil-doers there certainly could be no punishment. But since it is not to be expected that all of us should be righteous, Christ has ordained magistracy for the wicked, that they may rule as they must be ruled. But the righteous He keeps for Himself, and rules them by His mere word.

Therefore christian government is not opposed to the civil, nor is civil magistracy opposed to Christ. Civil government does not cease by Christ's ministry; but it is an outward thing, like all other offices and institutions. And as these exist distinct from Christ's office, so that an unbeliever may exercise them just as well as a Christian, so it is also with the exercise of the civil sword, since it neither makes men Christian or unchristian. But of this I have spoken often enough elsewhere.—It follows, further:

V. 16. *As free, and not as though ye had your freedom as a cover for wickedness, but as the servants of God.* This is said especially for us, who have heard of christian freedom, that we may not go on and abuse this freedom; that is to say, under the name and show of christian freedom do all that we lust after, so that from this freedom shall spring up a shamelessness and carnal recklessness, as we see even now takes place, and had begun even in the Apostle's times, as is easily discovered from the epistles of St. Peter and St. Paul, when men did what the great multitude do now. We have now, again, through the grace of God, come to the knowledge of the truth, and we know that that is mere deception which popes, bishops, priests and monks have hitherto taught, laid down and enforced; and our conscience is enlightened and has become free from human ordinances and from all the control which they have had over us, so that we are no longer obliged to do what they have commanded under peril of our salvation. To this freedom we must now hold fast, and never suffer ourselves to be robbed of it; but for this very reason we should be carefully on our guard not to make this freedom a cloak of our shame.

The Pope has here proceeded unrighteously in aiming to force and oppress men by his laws. For among a christian people there should and can be no compulsion, and if the attempt is made to bind the conscience by outward laws, faith and the christian life are soon suppressed; for Christ's are only to be led and ruled in the spirit, since they know that they, through faith, already have all whereby they are to be saved, and stand in need of nothing more to this end, and henceforth are under obligation to do nothing more than good to their neighbor, helping him with all they have, as Christ has helped them, and moreover that all the works which they do should be done freely and without constraint, and flow forth from willing and happy hearts; this is grateful to God, exalts and praises Him for the blessings that have been received. So St. Paul writes (I. Tim. i.), That for the righteous no law is made, for they do freely of themselves, and unsummoned, all that God requires.

Since now such enforcement of human doctrines is rejected and christian freedom is preached, the reckless spirits that are without faith coïncide with it, and thereby would become good Christians, inasmuch as they keep not the law of the Pope, claiming this freedom which relieves them from obligation to it; and yet they observe not that which true christian freedom requires,—namely, to do good to their neighbor with cheerfulness, and irrespective of its being commanded, as real Christians do. Thus they make christian freedom just a cloak, under which they work only their shame, and disgrace the noble name and title of that freedom which Christians have.

This St. Peter here forbids, for this is what he would say: although ye are free in all external matters (if ye are Christians), and should not be forced by laws to subject yourselves to the control of worldly rule, since for the righteous no law is given (as we have said), yet ye should do it of yourselves, voluntarily and without compulsion,—not that ye must be held in obedience by necessity, but in order to please God, and for the advantage of your neighbor. This also Christ did Himself, as we read in Matt. xvii., that he paid tribute when he need not have done it, but was free, and Lord over all things. So likewise he subjected Himself to Pilate and permitted Himself to be judged, while as yet He said to him, "You could have had no power or authority over me except it had been given you from above," in which words He gave confirmation to the authority to which He meanwhile subjected Himself, that He might please His Father.

Whence you see that that multitude has no claim to christian freedom who will do nothing, neither what the world nor what God requires, but abide in their insubordinate disposition, although they make their boast of the Gospel.

Though we be free from all laws, we must yet have respect to weak and ignorant Christians, since this is a work of love. Hence Paul says, Rom. xiii.: "Owe no man anything, but to love one another." Therefore let him who would glory in his freedom, do first what a Christian should do: let him first do good to his neighbor, and thereafter make use of his freedom in such a way as this. When the Pope, or even any one, imposes his authority upon him, and would force him to obey it, let him say, "My good fellow, Pope, I will not do it, for this reason, because you choose to make a command of it, and invade my freedom."* For we are to live in freedom as the servants of God, (so St. Peter here says,) not as servants of man. Yet in case any one desires that of me in which I can be of service to him, I will cheerfully do it out of good will, not scrupulous whether it have been commanded or not, but for the sake of brotherly love, and because God also requires that I should do good to my neighbor. Thus I will not be forced to become subject to worldly princes and lords, but what I do I will do of my own self,—not because they command me, but for service to my neighbor. Of this kind should all our works be, springing forth from affection and love, and all having respect to our neighbor, since we have no need on our own account to do good works. It further follows:

> * In the views presented by Luther, in this connection, we have a distinct enunciation of the noble principles of the Non-conformists of England—principles which were

familiar to the great Reformers and to the early Puritans. They could not admit any human authority to invade the domain of divine legislation. To a conformity in externals which did not require them to admit the right of the civil magistracy to enact laws for the church, they were willing to yield as far as was necessary to edification. But when the command issued from the ruling power, in usurpation of the prerogative of the great and only head of the church, and obedience was to be construed as acquiescence in such usurpation, their reply was kindred in tone and spirit to that which Luther here puts into the lips of a christian man in answer to Papal arrogance.

V. 17. *Be respectful toward every man.* This is not a command, but a faithful admonition. We are each of us assuredly under obligation, although we are free; for this freedom does not extend to evil-doing, but merely to well-doing. Now we have repeatedly said, that every Christian, through faith, attains to all that Christ has Himself, and is, moreover, His brother. Therefore, as I give all honor to the Lord Christ, so also should I do toward my neighbor. This consists, not merely in outward behavior, that I should bow to him, and things of that sort, but much more: that inwardly in my heart I should highly regard him, as I also highly regard Christ. We are the temple of God; as St. Paul says, I. Cor. iii., for the spirit of God dwelleth in us. If now we bend the knee before a place of worship, or a picture of the holy cross, should we not do it far more before a living temple of God?*

> * One is reminded here of the noble reply of that English martyr, John Bradford, when he was required to bow down to a wooden cross. Stretching out his arms, as he stood before his tyrannical judges, he exclaimed, "Why, here is a living cross, and God made it; yet would I not worship even that."

So St. Paul teaches us, also, in Romans xii., that each should esteem the other better than himself, so that each should place himself below the other, and give him the preference. The gifts of God are manifold and various, so that one is in a more exalted position than another; but no one knows who is most exalted in the sight of God, for he may easily raise hereafter to the highest place one who here occupies the meanest position. Therefore should every one, however high he be exalted, humble himself and honor his neighbor.

V. 17. *Love the brotherhood.* I have spoken above of the distinction which the Apostles make between love in general, and brotherly love. We are required even to love our enemies: this is common christian love. But brotherly love is, that we Christians should love one another as brethren, and communicate one to another, since we all alike have our blessings from God. This is the love which St. Peter here particularly requires.

Fear God; honor the King. He says not that we are to have great regard of lords and kings, but still that we are to honor them, although they are heathen, as Christ also did, and those prophets who fell at the feet of the King of Babylon. But here perhaps you will say, "hence, you perceive, that we are to be obedient to the Pope and are to fall at his feet." Answer: Certainly, if the Pope attains to temporal power and conducts himself like another sovereign, we are to be obedient even to him, as when he speaks after this manner: "I forbid you wearing the cowl or tonsure; besides, on this day you are to fast, not that it is of any avail before God, nor is necessary to salvation, but because I, as a temporal ruler, require it." But in case he goes further, and says, "This, in God's place, I forbid your doing—this you are also to receive as though it came from God Himself, and are to observe it under pain of excommunication and deadly sin," then you are to say, "Pardon, my master, I will not do it."

To the power we are to be subject, and are to do what it bids, while it does not bind the conscience and only forbids in respect to outward things, even though it should proceed tyrannically towards us; for "if any one will take away thy coat, let him take thy cloak also." But if it invade the spiritual domain and constrain the conscience, over which God only must preside and rule, we certainly should not obey it, but rather even slip our neck out from under it.

Temporal authority and government extend no further than to matters which are external and respect the body. But the Pope not only arrogates this to himself, but would seize upon the spiritual also; and yet he has nothing of it, for his commands have respect to nothing but clothing, food, canonries and prebends—a matter which belongs neither to civil nor spiritual control. For how is the world benefitted by these things? Besides, it is impious to make sins and good works to consist in such matters, where they do not belong; wherefore Christ cannot suffer it. But civil government he can well tolerate, since it does not encumber itself with the matters of sins and good works, and spiritual concerns, but has to do with other things,—as protecting and fortifying cities, building bridges, imposing taxes, gathering tribute, extending protection, guarding the land and the people, and punishing the evil-doers. Therefore, to such a prince, while he imposes no ordinance upon the conscience, a Christian may readily render obedience, and he does it unconstrainedly, since he is free of all things.

Therefore, whenever an emperor or a prince asks me what my faith is, I shall tell him, not because he commands it, but because I am under obligation to confess my faith publicly before every man. But in case he should go further, and command me that I should believe thus or so, then I shall tell him: "My good sir, do you attend to your civil government; you have no authority to intrude on God's domain, wherefore I certainly shall not obey you. You cannot yourself tolerate invasion into your sovereignty: if any one against your will passes the limits, you shoot him down with musketry. Do you imagine then that God will tolerate it, that you should thrust Him from His throne and seat yourself in His place?" St. Peter calls civil magistracy only a human ordinance. So that they (the magistracy) have no power to step into God's ordinances and to make laws against faith. But of this we have said enough. It follows now, further, in the Epistle:

V. 18-20. *Servants, be subject to your masters with all fear, not only to the good and gentle, but also to the froward. For this is thankworthy, when any one, for conscience toward God, endures grief, suffering wrongfully. For what praise is it, if ye endure buffeting for your faults? But if ye for well-doing suffer and endure, this is well-pleasing with God.*

St. Peter has thus far taught us how we should be subject to the civil power, and give it honor. Wherefore we have stated how far its authority extends, that it may not arrogate to itself in matters which pertain to faith. This is said of magistracy in general, and is a doctrine for every one (to receive). But now he proceeds, and speaks of such power as does not extend itself over a community, but only over individuals. Here he first teaches how domestic servants should conduct themselves toward their masters, and this is the substance of it:

Household servants are just as really Christians as any other class, if, like others, they have the word, faith, baptism, and all such blessings; so that, before God, they are just as great and high as others. But, as to their outward state and before the world, there is a difference, since they occupy a lower station, and must serve others. Wherefore, since they are called into this state by God, they should let it be their business to be subject to their masters, and have respect and esteem for them. Of this the prophet David gives a fine illustration, and shows how they are to serve, Ps. cxxiii.: "As the eyes of the servant to the hand of his master, and as the maiden looks to the hand of her mistress, so are our eyes directed to Thee."—That is, servants and maidens should perform with humility and care what the master or the mistress requires. This is the will of God, and therefore it should cheerfully be done. Of this you may be certain and assured, that it pleases God and is acceptable to Him, when you do this in faith. Wherefore, since these are the best works which you can do, you are not to run far after others. What your master or mistress commands you, that God Himself has commanded you. It is not a human command, although it is made by man. So that you are not to scruple as to the master you have, be he good or bad, kind, or irritable and froward; but think thus, let the master be as he will, I will serve him, and do it to honor God, since He requires it of me, and since my Master, Christ, became a servant for my sake.

This is the true doctrine which is ever to be urged, which now, alas! is buried in silence and is lost. But no one regards it except those who are Christians, for the Gospel preaches only to those who receive it. Wherefore, if you will be a child of God, purpose in your heart to render such service as Christ Himself bids you. As also St. Paul teaches, in Eph. vi., "Ye servants, be obedient to your masters that are upon earth, as to the Lord Christ; not with eye-service only, as men-pleasers, but as servants of Christ; that ye obey from the heart, for God's sake, with cheerfulness." Consider that ye serve the Lord, and not man. So, also, he says, in Col. iii., "For ye serve the Lord Christ." Ah! if the popes, monks and nuns were in such a state as this, how would they thank God and rejoice! For none of them can say, God has commanded me to celebrate mass, sing matins, pray the seven times, and the like,—for Scripture does not contain a word on the subject; so that if they are asked whether they are confident and assured that their state pleases God, then they say, No! But if you ask a little maid-servant why she scours the key or milks the cow, she can say, I know that the thing I do pleases God, for I have God's word and commandment. This is a great blessing, and a precious treasure of which no one is worthy. A prince should thank God for it, if he might do the same. It is true, he can do in his state what God requires,— namely, punish the wicked. But when, and how rarely, does it happen that he can discharge such a duty aright! But in this state it is all so ordered, that you may know that when you do what you are bidden, it pleases God.

God does not look to the work, how small it is; but to the heart that serves him in such little things. But in this it happens as in other matters: what God has commanded, no one performs; what men enact and God does not ordain, every one complies with.

But, say you, "Ah! how is this? What if I have such a strange and irritable master as no one can thankfully serve, for many such may be found?" To this St. Peter answers, "Are you a Christian and desirous to please God, you are not to inquire as to that matter how strange and froward your master is, but ever direct your eyes to this, and observe what God bids you." So that you are to reason after this manner: "I will in this way serve my Master, Christ, who requires it of me that I be subject to this froward master." If God should command you to wash the devil's feet, or those of the merest wretch, you are to do it; and this work would be just as much a good work as the highest of all, when God calls you to it. Therefore you are to have no regard to the person, but only to what God requires; and in this case the least work is more to be preferred in God's sight, when rightly performed, than all the popes' and monks' works in one heap. But whomsoever this does not incite, that it is God's will, and is acceptable to Him, the work will be of no avail to him. Better than it is you cannot make it, worse than it is you cannot leave it. And therefore this is to be done *with all fear*, (as St. Peter says,) that it may be rightly proceeded with, since it is not the command of men, but of God.

And here St. Peter speaks particularly of servants according to the circumstances of those times, when they were held as property, such as are to be found still in some places, and are exchanged like cattle, who are ill-treated and beaten of their masters; and the masters had such license that they were not punished although they put their servants to death. Wherefore it became necessary that the Apostles should carefully admonish and comfort such servants, that they might serve their hard masters, and endure it, though suffering and injustice were imposed upon them. Whoever is a Christian must also bear a cross; and the more you suffer wrongfully, the better it is for you; wherefore you should receive such a cross from God cheerfully, and thank Him for it. This is the right kind of suffering, that is well-pleasing to God. For what a thing would it be, that you should be cruelly beaten and had well deserved it, yet would glory in your cross? Therefore St. Peter says: When ye suffer and are patient for well-doing, this is well-pleasing with God,—that is to say, acceptable and exceedingly grateful in the sight of God, and a real service of God. Observe, here are those truly precious good works described, which we are to do; and we like fools have trodden this doctrine under foot, and have invented and devised other works; so that we should lift up our hands, thank God, and rejoice that we at length have such knowledge.—Now it follows, further:

V. 21-25. *For thereunto are ye called, since Christ also hath suffered for us, and left us an example, that ye should follow in His steps; who did no sin, and in His mouth was found no guile; who, when He was reviled reviled not again, when He suffered He threatened not, but committed it to Him that judgeth righteously; who Himself hath borne our sins in His own body on the tree, that we might be without sin and live to righteousness; by whose stripes ye are healed. For ye were as sheep going astray, but ye are now returned to the Shepherd and Bishop of your souls.*

Thus it is, as we have said, that the servant should resolve in his heart and be induced cheerfully to do and suffer what is required of him, since his Master, Christ, has done so much for him. Hence they are to reason thus: since my Master has thus become my servant,—a thing to which He was not obliged,—and has given up body and life for me, why should not I serve Him in return? He was perfectly holy and without sin, yet has He so greatly humbled Himself, and has shed His blood for me, and has died that He might take away my sin. How then shall not I also endure somewhat if it pleases Him? Whoever reflects on this must be a stone if it does not move him; for when the Master goes forward and steps in the mire, the servant should cheerfully follow Him.

Therefore St. Peter says, *Hereunto are ye called.* Whereto? That ye should suffer wrongfully like Christ. As though he would say, If you will follow after Christ you must not dispute and complain greatly, though you are unjustly treated, but endure the same and count it for the best, since Christ has suffered all without guilt of His own. He did not even defend His integrity when He stood before the judges. So that you are to neglect this right, and only say, *Deo gratias,* for this am I called that I should endure injustice; for what should I complain of when my master did not complain?

And here St. Peter has quoted some words from the prophet Isaiah,— namely, these, Chap. liii.: "Who did no sin, neither was deceit found in His mouth," also, "by whose stripes ye are healed." Christ was so pure that not an evil word was ever on His tongue. He deserved that all should fall at His feet, and bear Him in their hands. Although He had power and the right to avenge Himself, he yet permitted Himself to be derided, insulted, reviled, and besides all, put to death, and never opened His mouth. Why then should you not endure it also, when you are nothing but sin? You ought to praise and thank God that you are counted worthy of this,—that you should be like Christ; and not murmur nor be impatient though you be made to suffer, since the Master did not revile nor threaten in return, but even prayed for his enemies.

But perhaps you say, "How? Am I then to give that which is due to those who treat me unjustly, and say of them, they have done well?" Answer. No! but this is what you are to say: I will from my heart cheerfully suffer it, although I have not deserved it, and you do me injustice for my Master's sake, who also has endured injustice for me. You are to commit it to God, who is a righteous judge, and will richly reward it, just as Christ committed it to His Heavenly Father. *He who has borne our sins in His own body* (says St. Peter); that is, he has not suffered for himself, but for our welfare. We who have crucified him by our sins, are far from that condition ourselves. Wherefore, if you are a pious Christian, you are to follow after your Master, and mourn for those who make you suffer, and even pray for them, that God will not punish them; for they do far more injury to their own souls than to your body. If you lay this to heart, you shall easily forget your suffering, and suffer cheerfully. For we are to consider that we were once in such a Christless state as those, but have now, through Christ, been converted, as St. Peter concludes and says:

V. 25. *Ye were like sheep going astray, but ye are now returned to the Shepherd and Bishop of your Souls.* This, however, is a passage from the prophet Isaiah, who speaks after this manner: "We have all gone astray like sheep, and every one has gone in his own way." But now have we obtained a Shepherd, says St. Peter. The Son of God has come for our sake, that He might be our Shepherd and Bishop; He gives us His Spirit, feeds us, and leads us by His word, so that we now know how we are helped. Therefore, when you confess that through Him your sins have been taken away, then you become His sheep, and He becomes your herdsman. Just as He is thy Bishop, so art thou His Soul. This is, then, the comfort which all Christians have. Thus we have two chapters in this Epistle, wherein St. Peter has in the first place taught the true faith, then the true works of love, and has spoken of two kinds of works. First, what we all generally should practice toward civil government, then how domestics should conduct themselves toward their masters. And what St. Peter says here of servants, extends, also, to some other persons,—namely, artizans, day-laborers, and all kinds of hired servants. Now he goes on to teach us further, how husband and wife should conduct themselves toward one another in a christian manner.

CHAPTER III.

V. 1-6. Likewise ye wives be in subjection to your own husbands, so that they who do not obey the word may be won without the word, through the conduct of their wives, when they see your chaste conversation coupled with fear. Whose adorning is not outward, in the braiding of the hair, and the wearing of gold, or the putting on of apparel, but the hidden man of the heart, in that which is incorruptible, a meek and quiet spirit, which is, in the sight of God, of great price. For thus also did the holy women of old adorn themselves, who hoped in God and were subject to their husbands. As Sarah was obedient to Abraham and called him master, whose daughters ye are, if ye do well, and fear not of any terror.

Here St. Peter speaks especially of wives, who at that time had heathen and unbelieving husbands. And on the other hand, he speaks of believing husbands who had heathen wives; for it often occurred while the Apostles preached the Gospel among the heathen, that one was a Christian and the other not. If it *then* was commanded that the wife should be subject to the husband, how much more must it be so ordered now. Therefore it is the woman's duty, St. Peter would say, to be subject to her husband, although he is a heathen and unbeliever; and he gives the reason why this should be so.

V. 1, 2. So that even they who believe not on the word, may be won without the word, through their wives' conduct, when they see your chaste conversation coupled with fear. That is, when a man sees that his wife proceeds and conducts herself with such propriety, then he is drawn toward obedience, and holds the state of a Christian to be one that is truly blessed. And although it is not directed to women to preach, yet should they so conduct themselves in their demeanor and conversation that they may thereby attract their husbands toward obedience:—as we read of the mother of St. Augustine, who converted her husband, who had been a heathen, before his death, and so afterward her son Augustine. Still it is an external thing, which, as it is not to be performed in order to our justification for obedience, does not save you, for you may perhaps find an obedient wife who is yet unbelieving, but you should do it for this reason, that you may thereby benefit your husband. For thus has God ordained (Gen. iii.) when He says to the woman, "thou shalt submit thyself to thy husband, and he shall be thy master," which is also the punishment which he has imposed on the woman. But such is (I say) the outward conduct—that which belongs to the body, not to the spirit.

But this is a great thing, to know what works we should do to please God. By this rule are we to run, just as we see that the world runs, by the rule that it has falsely devised. It is a high, noble blessing which a wife may have when she so conducts herself as to be subject to her husband, inasmuch as she is saved, and her works please God; what can be a happier experience? Therefore whoever wishes to be a christian wife is to reason after this manner: I will not pay regard as to what sort of a husband I have, whether he be a heathen or a Jew, righteous or wicked; but to this I will pay regard, to the fact that God has placed me in the marriage state, and I will be subject and obedient to my husband. Then all her works are precious if she stands in such obedience.

But where the influence of attraction is not employed, nothing else will avail:—for you never will succeed by blows in making a wife pious and submissive. If you strike one devil out you will strike two devils in, as they say. Oh! if people who are in the marriage state knew this, how uprightly would they walk; but no one does cheerfully what God has commanded, but all run after that which men have invented. This command God has wished to be so carefully observed, that he authorized husbands to make void the vows which their wives made if they were displeasing to them, as we read in Num. xxx., so that all might go on peacefully and quietly at home. This is one point. Now the Apostle directs further how a woman should conduct herself toward other people.

V. 3, 4. *Whose adorning, let it not be outward, in braiding of the hair, and wearing of gold, and putting on of apparel, but of the hidden man of the heart, in that which is incorruptible, a meek and quiet spirit, which in God's sight is precious.* This treasure, which is internal, should be possessed not only by the wife, but by the husband. But here possibly some one might ask whether that which St. Peter here says of ornament is commanded or not. We read of Esther, that she wore a golden crown and precious ornaments, decking herself as a queen. So also of Judith. But near by it is recorded, that she despised the ornament and wore it from necessity. So that we say this much, that a woman should be so disposed as not to care for this adorning; yet, inasmuch as people convinced on the subject of ornament, cease not from the use of it, such is their habit and nature,—a christian wife should despise it. But if the husband requires it, or there is a reasonable cause for her adorning herself, it may well be done. But in such a way should she be adorned, as St. Peter here says, as to be inwardly attired in a meek and quiet spirit. You are vainly enough adorned when you are adorned for your husband; Christ will not suffer it that you should be adorned to please others, and that you should be called a vain harlot. Therefore you are to see to it, that you wear about in your heart the hidden treasure and precious adorning, in that which is incorruptible, as St. Peter says, and lead a pure, merciful, temperate life.*

> * "Here the Apostle pulls off from christian women their vain outside ornaments; but is not this a wrong to spoil all their dressing and fineness? No; he doth this only to send them to a better wardrobe: there is much profit in the change."—*Leighton on I. Peter.*

It is good evidence that there is not much of the spirit there, where so much is expended on ornaments, but this will be trodden under foot where faith and the spirit are present, and these will say, like Queen Esther, "Lord, thou knowest that I regard with aversion the crown which I wear on my head, and that I am compelled thus to adorn myself. If this was not required to be done of me out of love to my king, I would much rather trample it under foot." Where the wife is of such a disposition, she will so much the more please her husband. Therefore they are to take this into consideration (says St. Peter), that they adorn the inward man, where there is to be a quiet spirit, one that cannot be ruffled; not only that they do not run into excess, so that they may be kept from confusion and shame, but, his meaning is, that they should beware that the soul remain unruffled, and in the true faith, and that this be not forsaken. Thus is derived a heart such as does not break forth and busy itself as to how it shall appear before the world. Such a heart is a precious thing in the sight of God. If a woman were to adorn herself with pure gold, precious stones and pearls, even to her feet, it would be exceedingly splendid. But you cannot attach so much to a woman that it shall be preferable to that superior ornament of the soul which is precious in God's sight. Gold and fine stones are precious in the world's esteem, but before God they are an ill-savor. But she is truly and nobly adorned in the sight of God, who goes forth with a meek and quiet spirit; and since God himself accounts it precious, it must be a noble thing. A christian soul has all that Christ has, for faith, as we have said, brings us all the blessings of Christ in common. This is a great and precious treasure, and such an ornament as none can sufficiently prize. God himself makes much account of it. Thus the husband should withdraw and dissuade the wife from ornament, so long as she is inclined to it. When a christian wife gives ear and reflects, and determines thus, "I will not care for ornament, since God does not regard it,—but if I must wear it, I will do it to please my husband," then is she truly adorned and attired in spirit. Hereupon St. Peter now gives us an example of holy women, that he may draw wives to a christian conduct, and says:

V. 5. *For after this manner did holy women of old time adorn themselves, who set their hope on God and were subject to their husbands, as Sarah obeyed Abraham and called him lord.* As these women adorned themselves, he would say, so do ye also, as Sarah was obedient to her husband Abraham, and called him her lord. So Scripture speaks, Gen. xviii., where the Angel came to Abraham and said,

Within a year shall Sarah have a son; then she laughed and spoke thus: "Now that I am old, and my Lord is old also, shall I yet have pleasure?" This passage St. Peter has justly noticed and adduced in this place; for she would not have called Abraham thus her lord if she had not been subject to him and had him before her eyes. Therefore, he says, further:

V. 6. *Whose daughters ye are, if ye do well and stand in fear of no terror.* What does he mean by that? This is what he means. It is usually the nature of women to be troubled and frightened about everything, since they are so much occupied with charms and superstition, while one teaches the other, that it is not to be told what illusions they have. This should not be the case with a christian woman, but she should go forward securely, yet not be so superstitious, and run about here and there—pronounce here a blessing, there a blessing—inasmuch as it concerns her to let God direct; and she is to remember it cannot go ill with her, for as long as she knows her condition, that her state is pleasing to God, what will she then have to fear? Though your child die, though you are sick, it is well if it pleases God; if you are in a state which pleases God, what better can you desire? This, then, is what is preached to wives. Now follows the duty of husbands:

V. 7. *Likewise, ye husbands, dwell with them according to reason, giving honor to the wife as to the weaker vessel, and as being heirs together of the grace of life, that your prayers be not hindered.*

The woman is also God's instrument or vessel, he says, for God uses her to this end, that she may bear children, give them birth and nourishment, and watch over them, and rule the household. Such work is the wife to do. So that she is God's instrument and vessel, which He has created and instructed to this end. For this reason is the husband to respect his wife. Therefore, St. Peter says, Ye husbands, dwell with your wives according to reason, not that ye are to rule over them with a headstrong will. They are, indeed, to obey the law of the husband; what he bids and commands, that is to be done; but he is also to see to it that he walks soberly and according to reason with his wife, so as to give her that respect and honor which belongs to her as God's weaker vessel.

The husband is also God's instrument, but he is stronger, while the wife is weaker bodily, as well as timid and more easily dispirited; therefore, you are so to conduct and walk in respect to her, that she may be able to bear it. You must proceed in this case just as with other instruments wherewith you labor; just as when you would have a good sickle, you must not hack upon the stone with it. On this subject no rule can be laid down. God leaves the matter to each individually, that he shall treat his wife in accordance with reason, according to the circumstances of each woman: for you are not to use the authority which you have, according to your own will, for you are her husband for this very purpose, that you may help to guide and support her,— not that you should destroy her. Hence none can lay you down a rule with exact limitations; you must understand yourself how you are to proceed in accordance with reason.

Thus we have now heard in regard to husbands, also, what good works those who please God are to perform,—namely, that they dwell with their wives, endear themselves to them, and walk soberly with them. Things cannot always go on as you would be glad to have them. Therefore do you see to it that you act like a husband, and have so much the more discretion, when it is lacking in the wife, while you are to connive at some matters, tolerate and pardon some things,* and give to the wife, also, her honor.

> * "Not disclosing the weaknesses of the wife to others, nor observing them too narrowly himself, but hiding them both from others, and his own eyes, by love: not seeing them further than love itself requires."—*Leighton*.

This *honor* has been explained, I hardly know how. Some have interpreted it thus: that the husband should procure food, drink, and clothing for the wife, and should nourish her. Some have referred it to marriage duties. I hold this to be the meaning, as I have said, that the husband should treat the wife as consists with her being a Christian, and a vessel or instrument of God. And thus they are both to conduct: the wife is to hold the husband in honor, and on the other hand also the husband is to give to the wife her honor. If matters were thus directed, they would go on harmoniously, in peace and love. Yet where this course is wanting, there will be more disgust in the marriage state. Hence it comes to pass, when man and wife take one another from nothing but lust, and imagine they will have happiness and the gratification of appetite, that they experience mere heart-anguish. But if you have a regard to God's work and will, then may you live christianly in marriage,—not like the heathen, who know not what God requires.

As heirs together of the grace of life. The husband is not to dwell on this, that the wife is weak and fragile, but on this, that she also is baptized, and has the same that he has,—all blessings in Christ. For inwardly we are all alike, and there is no difference between man and woman, but as to the outward condition, it is God's pleasure that the husband rule, and the wife be subject to him.

That your prayers be not hindered. What does St. Peter mean by that? This is his meaning; if you do not act in accordance with reason, but will find fault, and murmur, and proceed arbitrarily, and in this give occasion for error, so that neither can overlook another's fault, and take all for the best, then will you be unable to pray, and say, "Father, forgive us our sins as we forgive." By prayer we are to strive against the devil, therefore we must be subject one to another. These are the truly precious good works which we are to do. If this is preached and understood, we shall all have our homes full of good deeds.—Thus we have heard how a Christian should conduct himself in all varieties of condition, but especially in his relations to others. It follows now, further, how we all, in common one with another, should lead, as to our outward condition, a christian life.

V. 8-12. *Finally, be ye all like-minded, have compassion one of another, be compassionate, affectionate as brethren, heartily kind, courteous. Render not evil for evil, or railing for railing, but on the contrary, blessing; and know, that ye are hereunto called, that ye should inherit the blessing. For whoso loveth life and would see prosperity, let him refrain his tongue, that it speak not evil, and his lips that they bear no guile. Turn thyself from evil and do good, seek out peace and pursue it. For the eyes of the Lord behold the righteous, and His ears are open to their prayer, but the face of the Lord is against them that do evil.*

All this is said only to this end, that we should have mutual love one to another. For here that which the Scripture sometimes expresses in few words, is much enlarged upon. St. Peter would say, the *summa summarum* as to how you are to treat one another in your outward conduct is, that ye be like-minded. This matter the Apostles Peter and Paul often bring forward, and this much is said, that we all should have one mind, one spirit, one thought; what seems to one right and good, let this also seem to another right and good. It is an important, note-worthy matter, that should be well understood; St. Paul has spoken much particularly upon it.

We cannot all of us do the same kind of work, but every one must labor each for himself,—a husband in a different sphere from the wife, a servant in a different sphere from the master, and so throughout. And it is a foolish thing to preach that we should all do one work, as those senseless preachers have done who preach the legends of the saints,—that *these* saints have done *that* work, *those*, another, and then insist and say we should do the same.

It is doubtless true that Abraham did a good work, highly to be esteemed, when he offered up his son, since this was particularly commanded him of God. When the heathen did the same and would sacrifice their children likewise, this was an act of cruelty in the sight of God. So, also, King Solomon did well in building the temple, and God justly rewarded him for it. And our blind fools, now, would also do the same,* and preach that we must build churches and temples for God, while God has given us no command on the subject. So it now comes to pass, that men busy themselves with a single kind of employment, and have many views in it directly in opposition to the Gospel.

> * Luther here doubtless refers to what he regarded as the foolish project of the Pope in attempting to build the church of St. Peter, at Rome,—the project which sent Tetzel into Germany, and made the sale of indulgences so common and obnoxious.—[*Trans.*]

But this is what should be taught, that there should be a single aim and many employments, one heart and many hands: all should not follow one business, but every one should attend to his own; otherwise there will not remain unity of aim and heart. As to what is external, it must be permitted to remain of a manifold character, so that every one abide in that which has been committed to him, and the work that he has in hand. This is a true doctrine, and it is exceedingly necessary that it should be well understood; for the devil expends his care particularly on this, and has brought things into such a state, that judgment is passed on the employment, and every one thinks that his own should be counted better than another's; hence it has come to pass, that men are so disunited one with another, monks against priests, one Order against another, for every one has wished to do the best work: thus they must satisfy themselves, and they have given themselves up to the Order, and think this Order is better than that. There is that of the Augustines against that of the Preaching Monks, that of the Carthusians against the Barefooted Friars, and nowhere is there greater want of unanimity than among the Orders.

But if it has been taught that, in the sight of God, no employment is better than another, but that through faith all are alike,—then will all hearts remain united, and we are all alike mutually disposed, and shall also say,—the Order, or the mode of life which the bishop leads, is in God's sight no more accounted of than that which a poor man leads; the mode of life which the nun leads is no better than that which a married woman leads; and the same in respect to all varieties of condition.

But this they will not hear to, but every one maintains his own for the best, and says, Ah! how much better and more important is my state, in the Order, than the state of a common man.

Thus to have one aim is, that every one should regard his own employment like the others, and that the condition of the married woman is just as good as that of the virgin, as all are indeed alike in the sight of God, who judges according to the heart and faith, not by the person or according to the works; so that we, also, are to judge as God judges, and then are we of one mind, and unanimity remains in the world, and hearts remain unestranged, so that there is no deriding on account of the external condition; all this I hold to be excellent, and am well satisfied with every man's employment, whatever it be, if it only be not sinful in itself.

Of this St. Paul also speaks, 2 Cor. xi., "I fear lest as the serpent beguiled Eve, so your minds should be corrupted from the simplicity that is in Christ Jesus,"—that is, lest the devil so beguile you, and pervert and divide that simplicity of aim which you have. So, Phil. iv., "The peace of God, which passeth all understanding, keep your hearts and minds through Jesus Christ." Why does the Apostle lay so much stress on the aim of the mind? Because it all consists in this, that when I am brought to cherish a false aim, everything is already lost; as in case I am a monk, and have adopted such a view as that my works are of more worth in the sight of God than others, and say, "God be thanked that I have become a monk; my state is now far preferable to the common one of marriage:" in which case, from such a view there must spring a proud spirit, and it cannot fail that I should count myself more righteous than another, and should despise other people while I deceive myself. For a married woman, if she abides in faith, is better in the sight of God than I am with the Order I belong to. So that when this is understood, that faith brings with it all that a Christian ought to have, we all of us have one aim and view, and there is no difference among works.

Wherefore we are thus to understand this passage of St. Peter, that he means the aim of the soul,—not that which refers to outward matters,—and an internal view or plan which aspires to those things that are esteemed with God; so that both the doctrine and the life be one, and I hold that for excellent which you hold as excellent,—and again, that is well-pleasing to you which is well-pleasing to me, as I have said. This sense of things is possessed by Christians, and to this view we should hold fast, that it may not be perverted, as St. Paul says; for when the devil has corrupted it, he has forced the castle of true purity, and all then is lost.

V. 8. *Be ye compassionate, affectionate as brethren, heartily kind, courteous.* To be compassionate is, that one should make himself a sharer with another, and have a heart to feel his neighbor's necessity. When misfortune overtakes him you are not to think,—Ah! it is right, it is no more than he should have, he has well deserved it. Where there is love, it identifies itself with its neighbor; and when it goes ill with him, the heart feels it as though it were its own experience. But to be brotherly (affectionate as brethren) is this much, that one should regard another as his own brother. This certainly may be easily understood, for nature itself teaches it; by which you see what those that are truly brothers are, that they are united more heartily together than any friends even. So ought we, as Christians, to act; for we are all brethren by baptism,—so that after baptism even father and mother are brother and sister, for I have the same blessing and inheritance that they have from Christ, through faith.

Heartily kind,—Viscerosi. This word I cannot explain except by giving an illustration. Observe how a mother or a father act toward their child,—as when a mother sees her child enduring anguish, her whole inward being is moved, and her heart within her body; whence is derived that mode of speech that occurs in many places in Scripture. Of this we have an example in I. Kings iii., where two women contended before King Solomon for a child, and each claimed the child. And when the king would discover which was the real mother of the child, he must appeal to nature, whereby he detects it; and he said to the two women, You say that the child is yours, while you say also that it is yours: well, then, bring hither a sword and divide the child into two parts, and give one part to this woman, and another to that. Thus he attained knowledge as to which was the real mother; and the text tells us that she was inwardly affected with anxiety for the child, and said, No! no! rather give the child whole to this woman, and let it live. Then the king pronounced his decision and said, That is the true mother; take the child and give it to her. Hence you may understand what this word *heartily* means.

This is what St. Peter would say: that we should conduct ourselves toward one another like those that are truly friends by blood, as with them the whole heart is moved, the life, the pulse, and all the powers; so here, also, the course should be heartily kind, and motherly, and the heart should be thoroughly penetrated. Such a disposition should one christian man bear towards another. But the standard is indeed set high; few will be found who bear such a hearty love to their neighbor,—as when it is seen that a necessity is imposed that they should have an affection like that which a mother has for a child,—such that it presses through the heart and through every vein. Hence you see what the monks' and nuns' state of life is; how far it is removed from such hearty love: if all they have were to be smelted together in one man, not one drop of such christian love as this would be found in it. Wherefore let us look to ourselves and be jealous over ourselves, whether we can find in ourselves such a kind of love. This is a short lesson and quick spoken, but it goes deep and spreads itself wide.

Courteous, is, that we lead outwardly a gentle, pleasing, lovely behaviour,—not merely that we should sympathize one with another, as a father and mother for their child, but also that we should walk in love and gentleness one with another.* There are some men rough and knotty, like a tree full of knots,—so uncivil, that no one will readily have anything to do with them. Hence it happens that they are usually full of suspicion, and become soon angry; with whom none of their own choice are familiar. But there are gentle people, who interpret all for the best, and are not suspicious; do not permit themselves to be soon irritated; can at least understand something as well meant; such persons as are called *Candidos*. This virtue St. Paul names [Greek: chrêstotês], as it is often praised by him.

> * "The least difficulties and scruples in a tender conscience should not be roughly encountered; they are as a knot in a silken thread, and require a gentle and wary hand to loose them."—*Leighton*.

Now consider the Gospel, which portrays the Lord Christ so distinctly, that we may trace this virtue especially in Him: now the Pharisees assault Him, and now again, others, that they might take Him,—yet He does not suffer Himself to become enraged. And although the Apostles often stumble, and act a foolish part here and there, He nowhere assails them with angry words, but is ever courteous, and attracts them toward Himself, so that they remained with Him cheerfully and heartily, and walked with Him. This likewise we see among kind friends and societies on earth, wherever there are two or three good friends, who have a good understanding one with another: though one acts a foolish part, the other can readily pardon him. There is represented in some measure that which St. Peter here intends, although it is not perfectly set forth, for this courteousness is to be considered obligatory upon every one individually. Hence you see the true nature of love, and how excellent a people Christians should be. The angels in heaven live with one another thus, and so should it also, in justice, be on earth; but rarely does it take place.

As St. Peter has already said, that the man servant and the maid servant, the husband and wife, should so conduct themselves that each should attend to that business of his own which he is to discharge, so would He have us all do generally, one with another. Therefore, if you would be certain and assured that you are doing an excellent deed, that is pleasing to God, set yourself in God's name in opposition to whatever has been preached in the devil's name, whereby the world walks and seeks to merit heaven. For how can you be better assured that you are acceptable with God, than when you observe, as he here says, the works which a man should do, the conduct which every one should lead, that he be compassionate, brotherly affectionate, heartily kind, courteous? In this he says nothing of those fool-works whereof we have been taught; says not, "build churches, found masses, be a priest, wear a cowl, vow chastity, &c.;" but this is his language: See to it that you be courteous. These are truly precious, golden deeds, precious stones and pearls, which are well pleasing to God.

But with this the devil cannot rest content, for he knows that thereby his interests are thrown to the ground; therefore he devises what he can to suppress such doctrine, incites monks and priests to cry out, "Do you say that our matters are nothing at all? that is for you to talk like the devil." But reply to them then, Do you not know that there must be good works, whereof St. Peter here speaks,—to wit, that we be brotherly affectionate, heartily kind, and courteous? if these are the best, as must be confessed, you must be false in regard to your works, if you think they are better. I am really astonished that such blindness could come upon us; for Thomas, the preaching monk, has written, and says, shamelessly, that monks and priests are in a better state than ordinary Christians. This the high schools have confirmed, and men have been Doctorated for it. After them the Pope and his multitude have gone, and have exalted those to be saints, who teach such doctrine.

Therefore understand this, as I have said,—for Christ Himself and all His Apostles have so taught,—if you would do the most excellent good works, and be in the best condition of life, you will find them nowhere else but in faith and love; that is the highest state of all. So that it must be an error, when they choose to say, their state is better than faith and love; for if it be better than faith, it is better than God's word, but if it be better than God's word, it is better than God Himself. Therefore Paul has truly said, that Anti-Christ should exalt himself before God. Be informed in this way so as to judge of these things; where love and friendship are wanting, there, certainly, all works are condemned and trodden under foot. Thus we see why St. Peter has so confidently expatiated on the external character of a truly christian life, as he taught us above, in a masterly manner, how the inward (spiritual) life should be ordered toward God. Wherefore this epistle is to be regarded as a truly golden epistle. Whereupon it follows, further:

V. 9. *Render not evil for evil, nor railing for railing, but on the other hand blessing, and know that ye are called thereunto, that ye should inherit the blessing.* But this is a still further illustration of love, showing how we should act toward those that injure and persecute us. If any one does you evil—this is his meaning—do him good; if any one rails at and curses you, then you are to bless and wish him well; for this is an important part of love. O Lord God! what a rarity such Christians are! But why should we return good for evil? Because, says he, ye are called thereunto that ye should inherit the blessing, so that ye should suffer yourselves to be attracted towards it.

In the Scriptures we Christians are called a people of blessing, or a blessed people. For thus said God to Abraham, Gen. xii.: "In thy seed shall all nations of the earth be blessed." Since God has so richly shed down this blessing upon us, in that He takes away from us all the malediction and the curse which we have derived to ourselves from our first parents, as well as that which Moses suffered to go forth upon the disobedient, so that we are now filled with blessing, we ought so to conduct ourselves that it shall be said of us, That is a blessed people. So that this is what the Apostle here means: See, God has shown you His favor, and has taken away from you the curse, and the reviling wherewith you have dishonored Him; He neither imputes nor punishes, but has bestowed upon you such rich grace and blessing, while ye were only worthy of all malediction, inasmuch as ye reviled God without intermission (for where there is unbelief the heart must ever curse God): do ye also as has been done toward you; curse not, rail not, do well, speak well, even though you are treated ill, and endure it where you are unrighteously used. Hereupon he quotes a passage out of the xxxiii. Ps., where the prophet David speaks thus:

V. 10. *Whoso will love life and see good days, let him keep his tongue from evil, and his lips that they do not deceive.* That is, whoever would have a pleasure and a joy in life, and would not die the death, but see good days, so that it shall go well with him, let him keep his tongue that it speak not evil, not only in respect to his friends, for that is a small virtue and a thing which even the wickedest of all may do, even snakes and vipers,—but also, he says, maintain a kind spirit, and keep your tongue silent even against your enemies, though you are even incited thereto—though you have cause to rail and speak evil.

Besides, keep your lips, he says, that they do not deceive. There are probably many who give good words, and say *good morning* to their neighbor, but they think in their heart, The devil take you. These are people who have not inherited the blessing; they are the evil fruit of an evil tree. Therefore St. Peter has introduced a passage which refers to works, even to their root,—that is, what springs from within out of the heart.* Furthermore, the passage in the prophet says:

> * "A guileful heart makes guileful tongue and lips. It is the workhouse where is the forge of deceits and slanders, and other evil speakings; and the tongue is only the outer shop where they are vended, and the lips the door of it. So then such ware as is made within, such and no other can be set out. That which the heart is full of, runs over by the tongue."—*Leighton*.

V. 11. *Let him turn away from evil and do good, let him seek peace and pursue after it, for the eyes of the Lord behold the righteous.* The world considers this as satisfaction when one man does injustice to another, that his head should be cut off. But this brings one none the nearer to peace. For no king, even, ever attained to be in peace before his enemies. The Roman empire was so powerful that it struck down all that set itself against it; still for all this it could not be preserved. Therefore this method is of no avail toward reaching peace, for though a man should prostrate and silence his foe, ten and twenty rise up again after it, till at length he is compelled to yield. But he who seeks after the true peace, and moreover would find it, let him restrain his tongue; let him turn away from evil and do good: this is a course different from that which the world pursues. To turn from evil and to do good is, that when a man hears evil words, he be able to overlook the wickedness and injustice. Seek thus after peace, so shall you find it; when your enemy has wasted his breath and done all that he can, if you hear him, but rail and rant not back, he must subdue himself by his own violence. For thus Christ also on the cross subdued his enemies, not by the sword or by violence. Therefore is it a saying, which should be written with gold, where it says, "Striking back again makes hatred, and whoever strikes back again is unjust." Thence it must follow that not to strike back again makes peace. But how can this be? Is it then a thing not human? Certainly it does not accord with human nature; but if you in this manner suffer unjustly and do not strike back again, but let the matter go, it shall come to pass as hereafter follows:

V. 12. *The eyes of the Lord are over the righteous, and his ears are open to their cry, but the face of the Lord is against those that do evil.* If you do not revenge yourself and do not repay evil with evil, there is the Lord in heaven above who cannot tolerate wrong, wherefore he that does not strike back must have his right. These He beholds; their prayer reaches His ear; He is our protector and will not forget us, while if we cannot escape from His eyes, we should comfort ourselves with the thought:—that is, this should induce a christian man to endure all injustice with patience, and not return evil. If I properly reflect, I see that the soul which does me wrong must burn forever in hell-fire. Therefore a christian heart should speak on this wise: Dear Father, since this man falls so sadly under Thy wrath and so miserably throws himself into hell-fire, I pray that Thou wouldest forgive him, and do to him even as Thou hast done toward me since Thou hast rescued me from condemnation. But how comes this? Thus: while He graciously looks down upon the righteous, He also looks angrily at the wicked, wrinkles His brow and turns it in indignation upon them; when we know then that He looks upon us graciously and upon them with disfavor, we ought to suffer ourselves to pity and mourn for them, and pray for them. Furthermore, St. Peter says:

V. 13-16. And who is he that will harm you, if ye follow after that which is good. Blessed are ye if ye suffer for righteousness' sake, and be not afraid for their terror, neither be troubled, but sanctify the Lord God in your hearts. But be ready always to give an answer to every man who asks the reason of the hope that is in you, with meekness and fear, and have a good conscience, so that they who speak of you as evil-doers may be put to shame, that they have falsely accused your good conduct in Christ.

If we follow after that which is good,—that is, do not reward evil with evil, but are heartily kind and courteous, etc., then there is none that can injure us. For though our honor, life and property should be taken away, we are still uninjured. Hence we have a blessing that is incomparable,—one that none can take from us. Those who persecute us have nothing but prosperity on earth, but thereafter, eternal condemnation, while we have an eternal, incorruptible good, although we lose a small temporal blessing.

V. 14. Blessed are ye if ye suffer for righteousness' sake. Not only, he says, can no one injure you if ye suffer for God's sake, but blessed are ye also, and ye should rejoice that ye are to suffer, as Christ also says in the sixth of Matthew: "Happy are ye when men deride and persecute you for my sake, and speak every kind of evil against you, falsely; rejoice, and be exceeding glad." Whoever then apprehends this, that it is the Lord speaks such things, and so tenderly speaks comfort to his heart, he stands well; but to whom this does not bring strength, it makes him sad and complaining,—he may well remain unstrengthened.

But be not afraid of their terror, neither be troubled, but sanctify God in your hearts. Here St. Peter quotes a passage from Isaiah viii., where he says: "Be not afraid of their terror, nor be frightened, but sanctify the Lord in your hearts, and let Him be your fear and your dread." There we have a great support and reliance, whereon we may trust, assured that no one can injure us. Let the world terrify, defy and threaten as long as it will, it must have an end, but our confidence and joy shall have no end; thus we shall have no fear on account of the world, but shall be courageous, while before God we shall humble ourselves and be afraid.

But how does St. Peter mean that we should sanctify God; how can we sanctify Him; must He not sanctify us? Answer. So it is that we pray, even in the *Our Father, hallowed be Thy name,* that we may sanctify His name, as He Himself also sanctifies His name. Therefore it comes to this: *in your hearts,* says St. Peter, ye are to sanctify Him; that is, if the Lord our God appoints anything for us, be it good or evil, bring it weal or woe, be it shame or honor, prosperity or adversity, I am not only to consider it as good, but even as holy, and say, this is nothing but a precious blessing that I am unworthy of, that comes to me. So the prophet says, Ps. cxliv., "The Lord is righteous in all His ways, and holy in all His works." If I give God praise in regard to such matters, and consider such doings good, holy, and excellent, then I sanctify Him in my heart. But they who scruple accounts, and complain that they are treated unjustly, and say God sleeps, and will not help the just and restrain the unjust, these dishonor Him, and account Him neither just nor holy. But whoever is a Christian, should attribute righteousness to God and unrighteousness to himself—should account God holy and himself unholy, and say that He in all His deeds and works is holy and just; this is what he requires. So also speaks the prophet Daniel, iii.: "O Lord, in all that Thou hast done towards us, hast Thou done in accordance with right and true judgment. For we have sinned; therefore be the shame ours, but the honor and the praise Thine." If we sing, *Deo gratias*, and *Te Deum laudamus*, and say, God be praised and blessed, when misfortune overtakes us, that is called by Peter and Isaiah a true hallowing of the Lord. But He does not by this require that you should say that he has done right and well who has injured you, for it is an entirely different judgment between God and me, and between me and thee. I may have within me anger, hatred, and wicked lusts, whereby I intend your damage, while you are yet still uninjured, and have nothing against me; but in God's sight I am unjust,—therefore He does right if He punishes me; I have well deserved it. If he does not punish me in that case, He shows me favor, and thus is right in every way. But it does not therefore follow, that he does right who persecutes me, for I have not done injustice to him as I have done in the sight of God. If God sends the devil or wicked people upon you to punish you, He uses them to this end, that they may execute His righteousness; so wicked wretches and injustice itself become a blessing.

So we read in Ezekiel, xxix., of King Nebuchadnezzar, where God says by the prophet, "Knowest thou not that he is My servant, and has served Me?" Now, says he, "I must give him his hire, I have not paid him as yet; well, then, I will give him Egypt, and that shall be his hire." The king had no right to the land, but God had a right to it, so that He might punish it through him; for, in order that even wicked wretches might serve Him, and eat not their bread in vain, He gives them enough, lets them serve Him even to this end, that they persecute His saints. Here reason is at fault, and thinks He does well and right when He remunerates them only here; gives them much land, and does it simply for this, to make them His executioners, and persecutors of pious Christians.

But when you endure and sanctify God, and say, *Just Lord*, then you do well, while He casts them into hell and punishes them because they have done wickedly, but takes you into His favor and gives you—Eternal Salvation. Therefore let Him manage them; He will give a just reward.

Of this we have an example in holy Job, when all his cattle and all his sons were slain, and his property was taken away; when he said, "The Lord gave and the Lord hath taken away; as it was well pleasing to God, so has it been ordered, therefore praised be His name." And when his wife came, deriding him, and railed at him, and said: "See! what hast thou now, abiding in thine integrity? Curse God and die:" then he answered her—"Thou hast spoken like a foolish woman: are we to receive good at God's hands,—why should we not also receive evil from Him, for He hath done as it hath pleased Him? God hath given, and God hath taken away," he says; not God has given it, the devil hath taken it away, while yet it was the devil that did it. This man truly sanctified the Lord; therefore is he so highly praised and exalted of God. It follows, further:

V. 15. *But be always ready to give an answer to every man that asketh you, the reason of the hope that is in you.* We must here acknowledge that St. Peter addressed these words to all Christians, clergy and laity, male and female, young and old, of whatever state or condition they may be. From thence it will follow that every Christian should know the ground and reason of his faith, and be able to maintain and defend it where it is necessary. But up to this time, the idea that the laity should read the Scriptures has been treated with derision. For in this matter the devil has hit on a fine measure, in tearing the Bible out of the hands of the laity,—and this is what he has thought: "If I can keep the laity from reading the Scripture, I will then bring the priests over from the Bible to Aristotle, so that gossip they what they will, the laity must hear just what they set forth; while if the laity should read the Scripture, the priests must study it too, in order that they may not be detected and overcome." But look you now at what St. Peter tells us all, that we should give answer and show reason for our faith. When you come to die I shall not be with you, neither will the Pope; and if you know but this one reason of your hope, and say, "I will believe as the Councils, the Pope and the Fathers believed," then the devil will answer, "Yes! but how if they were in error?" Then will he have won, and will drag you down to hell. Therefore must we know what we believed,—namely, what God's word is, not what the Pope and holy Fathers believe or say. For you must not put your faith at all in persons—but on the word of God.

So when any one assaults you, and like a heretic asks why you believe that you shall be saved through faith—here is your answer: "Because I have God's word and the clear declarations of Scripture." As St. Paul says, "The just shall live by faith," and St. Peter, where he speaks of Christ, the living stone, quoting from the prophet Isaiah, "Whosoever believeth on him shall not be confounded; thereon do I build, and know that the word will not deceive me." But if you will speak like other fools, "Yes, we will hear how the council decides, and with that we will abide," then are you lost. Wherefore you should say, "Why do I then ask what this one or that believes or decides; if they speak not the word of God, I will hear nothing of it."

Do you say, then, it is so confusedly difficult a thing, that no one knows what he should believe, and so one must wait till it is determined what one shall hold? Answer. Then will you go to the devil the while; for if it comes to the pinch, and you should die and not know what you should believe, neither I nor any one else could help you. Therefore you must know for yourself, and turn to no one else, and cling fast to the word of God, if you would escape hell. And for such as cannot read, it is necessary that they should learn and retain some clear texts out of the Scriptures—one or two at least, and on this ground abide firmly. As for instance that of Gen. xii., where God says to Abraham, "In thy seed shall all the nations of the earth be blessed." If you have learned that, you may stand thereon and say, "Though Pope, bishop, and all the councils stood yonder and said otherwise, yet do I declare this is God's word, that I can rely on, and that does not deceive me." Whoever will be blessed, must be blessed through "the seed," and whoever is blessed is ransomed from the curse—that is, from sin, death and hell. Therefore it follows, from the text—whoever will not be blessed through "the seed," he must be lost. So that my works or good deeds can help nothing to my salvation.

To the same end also is the passage out of Peter,—"Whoever believeth on this stone shall not be ashamed." If any one now come upon you and demand a reason of your faith, reply—"There stands the foundation which cannot fail me, and so I ask nothing beside, what Pope or bishop teach or decide." Were they true bishops, then would they teach the ground of faith that they knew was common to all Christians. Yet they rush on and cry out, "The laity must not be suffered to read the Scriptures."

So if any one asks you whether you will have the Pope for a head, say at once, "I will hold him for a head—a head of wickedness and profligacy." And for this I have a passage of St. Paul, I. Tim. iv.: "There shall come the devil's teachers forbidding to marry, and commanding to abstain from meats which God has created." That too has the Pope forbidden, as is the case now. Therefore is he Antichrist. For what Christ commands and teaches, that *he* transgresses. What Christ makes free, that the Pope binds—Christ says, it is not sin, while the Pope rejoins, it is sin.

Thus should one now learn to give a reason and answer for his faith. For though not now, yet at death will it come to pass, that the devil will come forward and say, "Why have you charged the Pope as Antichrist?" If you are not prepared and ready to show reason, then has he won. It is as much as though St. Peter had said, If ye will now be faithful, ye must henceforth endure much persecution. But in this persecution must you have a hope, and must look for Eternal life. If one asks you why you hope for it, then you must have the word of God, on which you can build.

But the sophists also have perverted the text, as though one was to convince heretics with reason, and out of the natural light of Aristotle; therefore (say they) it is here rendered in the Latin, *Rationem reddere*, as if St. Peter had thought it should be done with human reason. Because, say they, the Scriptures are far too inconclusive that from them we should silence heretics. The method by which (according to them) it must be shown that the faith is a right one, must agree with reason, and come forth from the brain; whereas, our faith is above reason, and subject to God alone. Therefore, if the people will not believe, then should you be silent; for you are not responsible for compelling them to hold the Scriptures as the word or book of God. It is enough that you give your reason therefrom. But if they take exceptions, and say, "You preach that one should not hold to man's doctrine, while Peter and Paul, and Christ even, were men:" when you hear people of this stamp, who are so blind and obtuse that they deny that this is God's word, or doubt of it, then be silent—speak no more with them, and let them go—only say, "I will give you my reasons out of Scripture. If you will believe that, it is well; if not, I will give you no others." But do you say, "Must God's word be treated with such shame?" Leave that to God. So you see that this matter should be well apprehended, and we should know how to meet those who now rise up and present such objections.—It follows:

With meekness and fear. That is, if you are examined and questioned of your faith, you should not answer with haughty words, and proceed in the matter with contempt and violence, as if you would tear up a tree by the roots, but with such fear and humility as if you stood before God's tribunal, and were there to give answer; for if it were now to happen that you should be examined before king and princes, and had well prepared yourself a long time therefor with replies, and thus thinking with yourself, "Deliberate, I will answer him correctly," then shall it be a happy experience for you,—though the devil take the sword out of your hands, and give you a blow, so that you stand in shame, and have put on your armor in vain, and he can fairly take out of your hands the reply you have carefully composed, so that it fails you even though you have it fairly in your mind, because he has beforehand tracked out your thoughts. Even this God suffers to take place, that he may subdue your pride and make you humble.

So, if you would avoid such an experience, you must stand in fear, and not rely on your own strength, but on the word and promise of Christ, Matt. x. 19—"But when they deliver you up, take no thought how or what ye shall speak, for it shall be given you in that same hour what ye shall speak; for it is not ye that speak, but the Spirit of your Father which speaketh in you." It is right, when you are to answer, that you should prepare yourself well with passages out of Scripture; but beware that you do not insist thereon with a proud spirit, since God will even take the most forcible reply out of your mouth and memory, though you were previously prepared with all your replies. Therefore, fear is proper. And so, if you are summoned, then may you answer for yourself before princes and lords, and even the devil himself. Only beware that it be not the vanity of men, but the word of God.

V. 16. *Having a good conscience, that whereas they speak evil of you as of evil-doers, they may be ashamed that falsely accuse your good conversation in Christ.* Of this St. Paul has already spoken above. We cannot disregard it. If we will follow the Gospel, then must we be despised and condemned by the world, so that men shall hold us as contemptible rabble. But let the devil and all the world rave and rage—let them abuse as they will, yet they shall at last be made to understand, with shame, that they have injured and defamed us, when *that day* shall arrive,—as St. Peter has said above,—in which we shall be secure, and stand up with a good conscience. These are, in every respect, suitable and forcible replies, which can comfort us and make us courageous, and yet go on circumspectly, with fear.

V. 17, 18. *For it is better, if the will of God be so, that ye suffer for well-doing than for evil-doing. For Christ also hath once suffered for our sins, the just for the unjust, that he might bring us to God, being put to death in the flesh, but quickened by the Spirit.*

It will not, then, be the case that they who shall reach heaven shall have prosperity on earth, while even those who do not arrive at heaven may not have prosperity. For that which God said to Adam is imposed on all men—"In the sweat of thy brow shalt thou eat thy bread;" and to the woman: "In sorrow shalt thou bring forth children." Since, now, adversity is imposed in common upon us all, how much more must *we* bear the cross if we would attain to eternal life. Therefore, he says, since God will have it so, it is better that ye suffer for well-doing. They who suffer for evil-doing have an evil conscience, and have double punishment. But Christians have only the half of it. Outwardly, they have suffering; but inwardly, comfort.

Yet has he here set a limit,—as he also has said above,—if a case should occur of such severity as the Donatists experienced, of whom Augustine writes, who took such a resolution that, stung by their sufferings, they committed suicide, and threw themselves into the sea.

It is not the will of God that we seek out, and even invite, calamity. Go thou on in faith and love. If the cross comes, take it up; if it comes not, seek not for it.

Therefore these modern spirits commit sin, in that they lash and beat themselves, or subject themselves to torture, and so would storm heaven.

This has Paul also forbidden, in Col. iii., where he speaks of such saints as walk in a self-chosen spirituality and humility, and spare not their body. We should also restrain the body that it do not become too wanton, yet not so as to destroy it; and we should submit to suffer if another sends suffering upon us, but not of our own choice fall therein. That will be the question: if it is God's will—if he has appointed it—for then it is better; while you are also more happy and fortunate that you suffer for well-doing.

V. 18. *Since also Christ has once suffered for us—the just for the unjust.* There St. Peter presents us, once for all, the example of our Lord, and points us evermore to Christ's sufferings, that we all of us alike should follow his example, so that he need not present a particular exemplar for the estate of every individual. For just as Christ is held forth as an example to all in the whole Church, so it is the duty of every individual in the Church,—each for himself, of whatever state he is,—to copy thereafter, in his whole life, as it is set before him; and he will speak after this manner: "Christ was righteous; yet, for well-doing, has suffered on our account, who were unjust; yet he sought not the cross, but waited till it was God's will that he should drink the cup; and it is He that is our pattern, whom we are to imitate." Thus St. Peter here adduces this one example, to this end especially, that he may thus designate that by which every estate is to be instructed; and now he goes on to declare more fully the suffering of Christ.

But, more particularly, he says here, Christ has suffered *once* for us; that is, Christ has borne many sins upon himself, but he has not done it in such a way as to die for every individual sin; but at once, for all together, has done enough to remove the sins of all who come to Him and believe on Him—who are now freed from death, even as He is free.

The righteous for the unrighteous, he says. As though he had said, much rather should we suffer, since we die for the righteous who had no sin. But He has died for the unrighteous, and for the sake of our sins.

That He might present us to God. This is all said to teach the peculiar end of Christ's sufferings; namely, that He died,—not for His own sake,—but that He might present us to God. How is that consistent: has He not offered up Himself? Answer: It is true that He has offered up Himself upon the Cross for us all who believe on Him, but at the same time He offers up us with Himself, since all they who believe on Him must suffer also with Him, and be put to death after the flesh as He was. Yet God has taught us, that they are alive in the spirit and yet dead in the flesh, as He afterwards says. But are we a sacrifice with Him? Then, as He dies, so we are to die according to the flesh; as He lives spiritually, so do we also live in the spirit.

Being put to death in the flesh, but quickened by the spirit. The word *flesh* is common in Scripture, as is also the word spirit, and the Apostles usually present the two in contrast. The sense is this: that Christ, through His sufferings, is taken out of this life that consists in flesh and blood, as a man on earth who lives by flesh and blood,—walks and stands, eats, drinks, sleeps, wakes, sees, hears, grasps, and feels,—and, in brief, whatever the body does while it is sensible; to all this Christ has died. This is what St. Paul calls a natural body,—that is, the animal life. *In the flesh*, not *after* the flesh,—that is, in the natural functions which the body exercises, to such life is He dead: so that this life has now ceased with Him, and He is now removed to another life and quickened after the spirit, passed into a spiritual and supernatural life, that comprises in itself the whole life that Christ now has in soul and body. So that he has no more a fleshy body, but a spiritual body.

Thus shall it be with us at the last day, when spiritual life shall succeed to flesh and blood; for my body and yours will live without food and drink,—will not procreate, nor digest, nor grow wanton, and the like, but we shall inwardly live after the spirit,—and the body shall be purified even as the sun, and yet far brighter, while there probably will be no natural flesh and blood, no natural or corporeal labor.

This is the language of St. Paul thereon, I. Cor. xv.: "The first man Adam was made in natural life, and the last in spiritual life." And it follows, "As we have the image of the natural man, so shall we also bear the image of the spiritual man." From Adam we derive all our natural functions, so far as concerns our unreasoning animal nature as to the fine senses. But Christ is spiritual,—flesh and blood not according to the outward sense; He neither sleeps nor wakes, and yet knows all things, and is present in the ends of the earth. Like Him shall we be also, for He is the first fruits, the earnest and first born (as Paul says) of the spiritual life; that is, He is the first who has risen again and entered upon a spiritual life. Thus Christ lives now after the spirit; that is, He is really man, but has a spiritual body. Therefore we should not here question how we may distinguish flesh and spirit from one another, but understand that the body and flesh are spiritual, and the spirit is in the body and with the body. For St. Peter does not say here that the Holy Spirit has raised Christ up, but he speaks more generally; as when I say the spirit, the flesh, I do not mean the Holy Spirit, but that which is within us, that which the spirit impels, and that which proceeds from the spirit. It follows, now:

V. 19-21. *By which same He also went and preached to the spirits in prison, who aforetime were disobedient, when the long-suffering of God waited in the days of Noah, while the ark was preparing, in which a few, that is, eight souls, were saved by water. Which now also saves you through baptism, which is typical by it; not the putting away of the filth of the flesh, but the union of a good conscience with God, through the resurrection of Jesus Christ, who has ascended to heaven, and is seated at the right hand of God,—and angels, and principalities, and powers, are subject to Him.*

This is a strange text, and a more obscure passage, perhaps, than any other in the New Testament, for I do not certainly know what St. Peter means. At first sight, the words import as though Christ had preached to the spirits,—that is, the souls which were formerly unbelieving at the time Noah was building the ark; but that I cannot understand, I cannot even explain it. There has been no one hitherto who has explained it. Yet if any one is disposed to maintain that Christ, after that He had suffered on the Cross, descended to these souls and preached to them, I will not dispute it. It might bear such a rendering. But I am not confident that St. Peter would say this. Yet the words may well be understood in this sense,—that our Lord, after His ascension into heaven, came and preached in spirit, yet so that His preaching was not in the body. For He speaks not with bodily voice; He does no more what pertains to the natural functions of the body. Whence it must also follow, as it seems, that inasmuch as He preached to the spirits in that same spiritual body, such preaching must also be a spiritual preaching, so that He did not go there in body and with oral preaching. The text does not require us to understand that He went down to the spirits and preached to them at the time of His death. For this is his language, *by which same,*— namely, when He had been put to death in the flesh and made alive after the spirit,—that is, when He had unclothed Himself of His fleshly existence and had passed into a spiritual being and life, just as He now is in heaven,—*thus* He went and preached. Now He certainly could not have gone to hell, after He had taken to Himself such a new existence; wherefore we must understand that He has done it after His resurrection.

While the words only require that he be considered as speaking here of spiritual preaching, we may rest in this view, that St. Peter speaks of the office that Christ performs by means of external preaching. For He commanded the Apostles personally to preach the Gospel. But with the word preached He comes Himself, and is spiritually present there, and speaks and preaches to the people in their hearts; just as the Apostles speak the word orally and in body to the ears, so He preaches to the spirits that lie captive in the prison-house of the devil. So that this also should be understood spiritually, like the preaching.

But here the expression follows, *to the spirits which aforetime were unbelieving*, &c. We should observe, in accordance with the divine account, that in that state of existence in which Christ is at present, those who have lived aforetime and those that are living now, are alike to Him, for His control extends itself alike over dead and living: and in that life, the beginning, middle and end of the world are all in one. But here on earth it has properly a measure, so that one age passes on after another, the son succeeds the father, and so it continues. But to give an illustration: If a high wood lies before you, or you look upon it as it stretches along in length before you, you cannot well overlook it; but if it lies near before you, and you stand above it and can look down directly upon it, then you have it in full view. So it is, that here on earth we can form no conception of this life (I speak of), for it passes on (piecemeal as it were) foot by foot, to the last day. But as to God, it all stands in a moment. For with Him a thousand years are as one day, as St. Peter says, in the next Epistle. Thus the first man is just as near to Him as the last that shall be born, and He sees all at once, just as the human eye can bring together two things widely separated at a single glance. So the sense here is this, that Christ preaches no more in person, but is present with the word and preaches to spirits, spiritually, in the heart. Yet you are not to understand that He preaches in this manner to all spirits.

But to what spirits has he preached? To those who aforetime were unbelieving. This is the figure of speech which is called Synecdoche. That is, "from a part the whole" (*ex parte totum*),—that is to say, not to these very spirits, but to those who are like them, and are just as unbelieving as they. Thus must we look away from this outward, to that inward life.

That is the best rendering, as I think, of those words of St. Peter;* still I will not too strenuously insist upon it. This at least I can scarcely believe, that Christ descended to those souls and preached to them; while the Scripture is against it, and declares that every one, when he arrives there, must receive according as he has believed and lived. Besides, while it is uncertain what is the state of the dead, we cannot easily explain this passage as one that refers to it. But this is certain, that Christ is present and preaches in the heart, wherever a preacher of God's word speaks to the ear. Therefore may we safely draw to this conclusion: let him to whom a better understanding is manifest, follow the same.

> * The view generally taken by Protestant expositors of this passage is, that the preaching here referred to took place in the days of Noah, by means of himself or others who were inspired by God to teach and warn. Their interpretation would be in effect,—"For Christ also suffered for our sins, the just for the unjust (that he might bring us to God), being put to death in the flesh, but quickened by the Spirit (of God). By which Spirit also he went (formerly) and preached to the spirits (now) in prison; which were disobedient, when once the long-suffering of God waited, in the days of Noah, (120 years,) while the ark was preparing, wherein few,—that is, eight souls,—were saved *by* or *through* water."

This is the summary of the sense which I have exhibited: Christ has ascended to heaven and preached to the spirits,—that is, to human souls; among which human souls have been the unbelieving, as in the times of Noah.

V. 20. It continues,—*when once the long-suffering of God waited in the days of Noah, while the ark was preparing, wherein few, that is, eight souls, were saved by water.* Thus does St. Peter bring us into the Scriptures, that we may study therein; and gives us an illustration out of them, from the ark of Noah, and interprets this same figure. For it is pleasant to have one bring forward illustrations from such figures, as St. Paul also does when he is speaking, Gal. iv., of the two sons of Abraham, and the two women; and Christ, in John v., of the serpent which Moses had erected in the wilderness. Such comparisons, when well drawn, are delightful; wherefore St. Peter introduces this here, that we may be able to comprehend faith under a pleasing image.

But he would also tell us, that as it happened when Noah was preparing the ark, so it takes place now. As he took refuge in the ark which swam upon the waters, so, it is to be observed, must you also be saved in baptism. Just as that water swallowed up all that was then living, of man and beast,—so baptism also swallows up all that is of the flesh and corrupt nature, and makes spiritual men. But we rest in the ark, which means the Lord Christ, or the christian Church, or the Gospel that Christ preached, or the body of Christ, on which we rest by faith, and are saved as Noah in the ark. You also perceive how the image comprises in brief what belongs to faith and to the cross, to life and death. Where there are only those that follow Christ, there is surely a christian Church, where all that springs from Adam, and whatever is evil, is removed.

V. 21. *The like figure whereunto, even baptism, doth now save us; not the putting away of the filth of the flesh, but the answer of a good conscience toward God.* But you are not kept and saved by merely washing away the filth of the flesh, that the body be clean, as was the practice of the Jews; such purification has no further value. But the answer of a good conscience toward God,—that is, that you feel your conscience to be rightfully at peace within you, that it stands in harmony with God, and can say, "He has promised to me that which He will fulfil, for He cannot lie." If you shall rely upon and cleave to His word, then shall you be preserved. Faith, alone, is the band whereby we shall be held; no outward work which you can do will suffice.

Through the resurrection of Christ Jesus. This St. Peter adjoins, in order to explain that faith which rests on the fact that Christ died, descended to hell, and has risen again from the dead. Had He continued subject to death, it would not have advantaged us; but since He has risen and sits at the right hand of God, and suffers this to be proclaimed to us so that we may believe on Him, we have a union with God, and a sure promise, whereby we shall be saved as Noah in the ark. Thus has St. Peter given to the ark a spiritual significance throughout, within which is not flesh and blood, but a good conscience toward God,—and that is faith.

V. 22. *Who is gone into heaven, and is on the right hand of God; angels, and authorities, and powers, being made subject unto Him.* This he says for the enlightening and strengthening of our faith. For it was necessary that Christ should ascend to heaven and become Lord over all creatures and powers universally, that He may bring us thither, and make us conquerors. This is said for our consolation, that we may know that all powers, whether they be in heaven or earth, must serve and aid us, even death and the devil,—since all must become subservient, and lie at the feet of the Lord Christ. This closes the third chapter. The fourth follows.

CHAPTER IV.

V. 1. *Forasmuch, then, as Christ hath suffered for us in the flesh, arm yourselves likewise with the same mind; for he that hath suffered in the flesh hath ceased from sin.*

St. Peter continues still in the same strain. Just as he hitherto has admonished us generally that we should suffer, if it be the will of God, and has set Christ before us as an example,—so he now confirms it more broadly, and repeats it again, saying, While Christ, who is our captain and head, has suffered in the flesh and presented us an example, (besides that He has ransomed us from our sins,) we also should imitate Him, and prepare ourselves, and put on the same armor. For in the Scriptures the life of the Lord Christ, and especially his suffering, is presented before us in a twofold manner.

Sometimes as a gift, as St. Peter has already exhibited it in the third chapter; and to those first, who are built up and instructed in the faith that we are ransomed, and our sins taken away by the blood of Christ; and so he is a gift and bestowment upon us, which none can receive except by faith. Whereof he speaks where he says, "Christ has once suffered for our sins." That is certainly the grand doctrine, and the most precious one of the Gospel.

Again, Christ is set before us and offered to us as an example and pattern for us to follow. For if we only receive Christ, through faith, as a free gift, we shall go farther and do ourselves as He has done for us, and imitate Him in His whole life and sufferings. In this manner St. Peter presents it here. But he does not speak here particularly of those marks of the love which leads us to befriend our neighbor, and do good, which are called, specifically, good works (for he had said enough of this above), but of such evidences as concern our personal experience, and are of service in strengthening our faith, that sin may be put to death in the flesh, and we thereby become of so much better service to our neighbor. For if I control my body so that it be not lustful, then can I leave my neighbor, his wife or child, at peace; while if I subdue hate and envy, I shall become so much better prepared to be kind and friendly toward my neighbor.

We have repeated often enough already that we are justified through faith, and thus have the Lord Christ as ours; still we must also do good works and show kindness to our neighbor. For we are never entirely purified while we live on earth, and every one still finds in his body evil lusts. The believer indeed prays for the death of sin and the gift of heaven, but is not yet become entirely and completely strong; but as Christ described the Samaritan, who was not yet healed, but was laid under restrictions and directions that he might become sound, so it is also with us. If we believe, then is our sin restrained,—that is, the disease which we have derived from Adam, and we begin to recover. But it is the case, in one more, in another less, that in proportion as one mortifies and subdues the flesh, so much does his faith increase. So that if we have these two things, faith and love, our future experience will be, that we shall continue to drive sin before us till we die.

Therefore St. Peter says, *arm yourselves with the same mind;* that is, take up a firm purpose, and strengthen yourselves with the mind which you receive from Christ; for, if we are Christians, then must we also say, My Master has suffered and spilt His blood for me, and has died for my sake. Should I then be so base as not to love Him? While the Master runs upon the spears' points in the conflict, how much more should the servant advance with joy? Thus do we awaken a courage such that we press onward, and arm ourselves in our own minds so as joyfully to persevere.

The word *flesh* refers in Scripture not only outwardly to the body, but includes all that is derived from Adam. As when God says, in Gen. vi.: "My Spirit shall not always strive with men, for they also are flesh;" and Isaiah, chap. xl., "All flesh shall see the Salvation of God,"—that is, it shall be revealed for all men. So we also make confession in our own form of faith, "I believe in the resurrection of the flesh," that is, that men shall rise again. So man uniformly throughout is called flesh, as he lives here in this state of being.

The marks of the flesh are carefully recounted, one after another, in Paul's Epistle to the Galatians v., not only the gross carnal works, as lasciviousness, but also the highest and most reckless blasphemies, as idolatry and heresy, which belong not only to the flesh, but to the reason. We must understand, therefore, that man, with his intellectual nature,—and with respect both to that which is inward and that which is outward—that is, the body and spirit,—has the appellation of flesh; and this, because with all his faculties, internal and external, he seeks only that which is carnal, and can serve to gratify the flesh. St. Peter says here, too, that Christ suffered in the *flesh*, while it is certain that His suffering extended further than to the body merely, for His soul suffered the greatest anguish, as is said by the prophet Isaiah.

In the same way, also, you are to understand that which follows, in the passage before us: "*Whoever hath suffered in the flesh hath ceased from sin.*" For this implies not only such things as the death and the torture of the body, but whatever can work misery to man—whatever he endures through calamity and necessity. For there are many people who are sound in body, and yet inwardly experience much heart-sorrow and anguish. If it comes upon us for Christ's sake, it is serviceable and profitable. For whoever suffers in the flesh (says he) ceases from sin, and therefore the Holy Cross is profitable, that sin may thereby be subdued; since it requires you to mortify lust, envy and hate, and other wickedness. Therefore God has imposed the Holy Cross upon us that He might urge and constrain us to believe, and extend the hand of kindness one to the other. Hereupon it follows:

V. 2. *That he henceforth, in the time that still remains for him in the flesh, should live not according to the lusts of men, but the will of God.*

We should henceforth, as long as we live, hold the flesh captive through the Cross, and by mortifications, so as to do that which pleases God, and not with the idea that we should or can deserve anything by it. *Not according to the lusts of men* (says he),—that is, that we should not do that to which we might yet be tempted by others; for we are not to be conformed to this world, as Paul says, Rom. xii. What the world demands of us we must refuse.

V. 3. *For the time past of our life is enough to have wrought the will of the Gentiles, when we walked in lasciviousness, lusts, excess of wine, revellings, banquetings and abominable idolatries.*

We have already gone altogether too far, that before our believing we have so shamefully spent our life in accordance with the will of the Gentiles, which is the same with lusts of men. Therefore as long as life continues we should see to it that we do that which is well-pleasing to God; for we have our enemy in our flesh, the one that is the real knave—not gross matter merely, but more particularly blindness of mind, which Paul calls carnal wisdom,—that is, the policy of the flesh. If we have subdued this depravity, that other is carefully to be constrained, which does our neighbor injury in so secret a manner as not to be observed.

St. Peter calls that lasciviousness that is accompanied with outward gestures or words by which evil intentions are expressed, though the deed itself be not performed, and it is that which is unchaste to the sight and hearing, upon which afterward the lust and the act also follow. Thereupon there succeeds such idolatry as is abominable. And we may easily bring all this upon us, for when we have lost faith we have certainly lost God, also, and may fall into more abominable idolatries than the heathen, if we view the matter aright.

V. 4-5. *And it surprises them that ye run not with them to the same excess of disorderly life, and they calumniate you, who must give account to Him that is ready to judge the living and the dead.*

That is, ye have hitherto lived after the manner of the heathen, but since you have now forsaken it, it appears strange to men, and seems shameful and foolish, and they say, "What great fools they are to withdraw themselves from all worldly good and gratification." But let it seem strange to them; let them libel you; they shall yet be compelled to give in their account; wherefore leave it to Him that will judge righteously.

V. 6. *For to this end also was the Gospel preached to the dead, that they should be judged according to men in the flesh, but live to God in the spirit.*

Here we have, however, a strange and remarkable text. The words clearly declare that the Gospel is preached not only to the living, but also to the dead, and adds besides, "in order that they may be judged according to men in the flesh." Now they certainly have not flesh, which can be understood only of the living. It is a wonderful passage, however understood: whether it should be made to refer to us, or to concern something foreign, I do not know, yet this is my understanding of it. We are not to be anxious how God will condemn the heathen who died many centuries ago, but only how He will judge those that are now living; so that the passage should be considered as spoken of men on earth.

But as to the word *flesh*, you are to understand, as I said above, that the entire man is called flesh, according as he lives, just as he also is called in respect to his whole nature, spiritual, while he follows after that which is spiritual. Still there is also a commingling of the two things with one another, just as I say of a man who is wounded, that he is whole and yet is wounded; and so, too, though the sound part is greater than the wounded part, still he is spoken of only with reference to the injured part as wounded; and such, too, is the method of the Spirit here: therefore he says, that they as to their outward being are condemned, but inwardly, as respects the spirit, are preserved in life.

But how does that, where He says that they live, agree with that which he subjoins, that they are dead? I will explain it according to my understanding, yet not so as to limit the Holy Ghost in that he calls the unbelieving dead. For I cannot accept the sense that to those that are dead and perished, the Gospel has been preached. This, then, would be what St. Peter means, that the Gospel has been freely published and universally spread abroad, concealed neither from dead nor living—neither from angels nor yet from devils, and preached not secretly in a corner, but so publicly that all creatures might hear it that have ears to hear, as Christ gave command in the last of

Mark: "Go ye forth and preach the Gospel to all creatures." If, therefore, it is preached in such a manner, there will those be found who are condemned after the flesh, but live after the spirit.

V. 7. *But the end of all things is at hand.* This is also a remarkable passage, for already nearly 1500 years are passed since then. St. Peter preached that the time is neither near nor brief, yet he says, *that the end of all things is at hand;* as John also declares in his first epistle, chap, ii., "It is the last hour." If it were not the Apostle's language, we might say it was contradictory: but by this we must firmly abide, that the Apostle has truth with him. Yet what he means here he shall explain himself in the second epistle, where he tells us why the time is said to be near, and says: "One day is with the Lord as a thousand years, and a thousand years as one day;" of which I have spoken above. So that we must explain it in this manner, that it shall not be as long hereafter to the end of the world as it has been from the beginning to the present time. And it is not to be expected that one should live two or three thousand years after the birth of Christ, so that the end shall come before we look for it. Wherefore he further adds:

V. 7, 8. *Be ye therefore sober, and watch unto prayer. And above all things have fervent charity among yourselves: for charity shall cover the multitude of sins.*

Here you perceive the reason why we are to watch and be sober; namely, that we may be prepared to pray for ourselves and our neighbors. Since charity cannot be fervent unless you keep the body in subjection, that charity may have place within you. Here St. Peter has quoted a passage from the book of Proverbs, ch. x. 12. *Hate stirreth up strife, but love covereth the multitude of sins.* And this is what St. Peter means: Subdue your flesh and lusts: unless you do it, you will easily offend one another, and yet not easily be able to forgive one another. Take care, therefore, that you subdue the wicked lusts, so you shall be able to show charity one to another, and to forgive, for charity covereth sins.

This passage has been explained to the prejudice of faith, inasmuch as they tell us: "You say that faith alone makes us righteous, and that no one through works may be free from sin. Why then do Solomon and Peter, as in this passage, say, *love covers sins?*" Answer. Whoever has hatred toward another, says Solomon, ceases not to stir up strife and bitterness. But where there is love, it covers sins and cheerfully forgives. Where there is wrath, or in other words, where there is an intractable man, reconciliation is not permitted; he remains full of wrath and hate. On the other hand, a man who is full of love is he whom one cannot enrage, however much injury may be done him; he perceives it all, but does as though he saw it not. So that the *covering* is spoken of as regards our neighbor, and not as it respects God. Nothing shall cover up sin before God for you, except faith. But my love covers the sin of my neighbor; and just as God with His love covers my sins, if I believe, so too should I cover my neighbor's sins. Therefore He says, Ye should have charity one to another, that one may cover the other's sins. And love covers not only one, two, or three sins, but the multitude of sins; cannot suffer and do too much; covers up all. So St. Paul also speaks and teaches in accordance with this passage, I. Cor. xiii. 7. *Charity beareth all things, believeth all things, hopeth all things, endureth all things.* It has respect to the best good of all, can suffer all, and take for the best whatever shall be imposed upon it. There follows, further:

V. 9. *Be hospitable one to another without grudging, and minister one to another, as every one has received the gift.* He is said to be hospitable who cheerfully acts the host. When the Apostles went abroad one with another and preached, and sent their younger brethren here and there, it was necessary that one should lodge the other. How well would it be, even now, that men should preach from one place to another, from city to city, from house to house,—and without remaining too long in one place, might see to it that where one was weak he should be helped, and where one had fallen down he should be lifted up, and things of that sort. St. Peter directs that this should take place without murmuring; that no one should suffer it to seem too much for him. This is also a work of love, as it follows immediately afterward, that we should minister to one another! Wherewith? With the gifts of God which every one has received. The gospel directs that every one be the servant of the other, and beside, see to it that he abide in the gift which he has received, which God has bestowed upon him; that is, the state, whatever it be, whereunto he has been called.

God's will is not that a lord should serve his servant, that the maid be as the mistress, and a prince serve the beggar;—for he will not break down magistracy. But his meaning is, that men should serve one another spiritually, with their hearts: although you are a high and great lord, yet should you employ your power to this end, that you may therewith serve your neighbor. Thus should every one hold himself for a servant; the lord may still remain a lord, and yet hold himself, in his own esteem, no better than the servant: so that he even cheerfully would become a servant if it were God's ordering; and the same is applicable to other conditions.

V. 10. *As good stewards of the manifold grace of God.* God has not bestowed upon us all like grace; therefore should every one inquire to what he has been appointed, and what kind of gift has been bestowed upon him. When he discovers this, let him use it for the service of his neighbor, as St. Peter further explains, and says:

V. 11. *If any man speak, let him speak as the word of God.* That is, if any one has the grace that enables him to preach and teach, let him teach and preach. As St. Paul says, also, Rom. xii. 3: "That no one think more of himself than he ought to think, but every man according as God has dealt to him the measure of faith. For as we have many members in one body and all members have not the same office, so we, being many, are one body in Christ, and every one members one of another; and have many gifts, differing according to the grace that has been given unto us." And then follows, "Has any one a prophecy, let it be in accordance with faith; Has any one a ministry, let him wait on his ministering: Does any one teach, let him wait on his teaching." He teaches the same doctrine also elsewhere, in his Epistles to the Corinthians and Ephesians.

For this reason has God distributed various gifts among men which should be employed to this intent alone, that one should minister therewith to another, especially those who are in authority, be it in preaching, or some other ministry.

Now St. Peter says, here, *If any one speak, let him speak as the word of God.* This point is worthy of special remark, that no one is to preach anything but what he is sure is the word of God. There St. Peter has shut up the Pope's mouth, and lo! he will be St. Peter's successor, so cunningly has he managed it. Further:

V. 11. *If any one ministers, let him do it as of the ability which God giveth.* That is, whoever rules in the christian church and has an office or ministry for the care of souls, he is not to proceed as he may choose, and say, "I am sovereign lord, I must be obeyed; what I do shall remain established." God requires that we should do no otherwise than as he directs. So that since it is God's work and ordinance, let a bishop do nothing except he be sure that God sanctions it, that it is either God's word or work.

And besides, inasmuch as God will not permit that we should regard as a matter of sport what we do with the christian church, we must stand in such an assurance as this, that God speaks and works through us, and that our faith may also say, "That which I have spoken and done, God also has spoken and done; on this I will even die."

And yet if I am not certain of the matter, then my faith will rest upon the sand when the devil assaults me. Thus here it is emphatically forbidden us to receive the command of any bishop, unless it is also the case, that he is certain that he does what God does, and can say, "I have God's word and command for it." Where that is wanting, we must hold him for a liar.

For God has prescribed that our conscience must rest on the bare rock. This is said also of government in general, that no one might follow his own darkness, and that nothing might be done of which he was not sure that God would sanction it. Whence you perceive how St. Peter so long ago thrust down to the ground the government of Popes and bishops, as we have it at the present day. Now follows:

V. 11. *That God in all things may be glorified through our Lord Jesus Christ, to whom be praise and dominion for ever and ever; Amen.* For this reason it is, you are to be so confident, (he means), that God speaks and does all that you speak and do. For if you perform a work of which you are not sure that God has done it, you cannot praise and give thanks. But where a man is certain of it, in that case he may praise and thank Him for His word and works' sake, though he should be belied and held up for derision. Therefore it is a shameful and ruinous thing that in Christendom any one should govern in opposition to the word and works of God. Therefore, from necessity, has St. Peter subjoined that in which he instructs how government should be ordered among christian people. Then follows, further:

V. 12. *Beloved, be not surprised at the fiery trial which is to try you, as though some strange thing happened unto you.* That is a mode of speech not common in our language. But St. Peter uses this very phraseology, in order to remind us of that concerning which the Holy Scripture speaks. For the Scripture is accustomed to speak of suffering as though it were a furnace full of fire and heat. St. Peter has spoken in the same manner, above, in the first chapter: "That the trial of your faith be found far more precious than the perishing gold that is tried by fire." We may also read in the prophet Isaiah, chap. xlviii., God says: "I have tried thee in the furnace of affliction;" and Ps. xvi., "With fire hast thou tried me;" and Ps. xxv., "Lord, thou wilt consume and destroy my nerves and my heart;" also, Ps. lxv., "We have passed through fire and water." Thus the Scriptures are accustomed to illustrate what we call suffering, by burning or trial by fire. This is St. Peter's conclusion, that we should not suffer ourselves to be surprised, or to think it strange and wonderful that the heat or fire should meet us, whereby we are tried, just as gold is when it is melted in the fire.

When faith begins, God does not neglect it; He lays the cross upon our back in order to strengthen us and make our faith mighty. The Gospel is a powerful word, but it cannot enter upon its work without opposition, and no one can be sure that it possesses such power, but he who has experienced it. Where there is suffering and the cross, there its power may be shown and exercised. It is a *living* word, and therefore it must exercise all its energy upon the dead. But if there is no such thing as death and corruption, there is nothing for it to do, and none can be certain that it possesses such virtue, and is stronger than sin and death. Therefore, he says, *are you tried;* that is, God appoints for you no flame or heat (in other words, cross and suffering, which make you glow as in a furnace), except to try you, whether you rely upon His word. Thus it is written, Wisdom x., of Jacob, "God appointed for him a severe conflict, that he might learn by experience that divine wisdom is the strongest of all things." That is the reason why God imposes the cross on all believers, that they may taste and prove the power of God which through faith they have possessed.

V. 13. *But be ye partakers of the sufferings of Christ.* St. Peter does not say that we should feel the sufferings of Christ, that thereby we should be partakers with Him through faith, but would say this: just as Christ has suffered, so are you to expect to suffer and be tried. If you do thus suffer, then do you therein have fellowship with the Lord Christ. If we would live with Him, we must also die with Him. If I wish to sit with Him in His kingdom, I must also suffer with Him, as Paul also says, repeatedly.

V. 13. *Rejoice, that in the time of the revelation of His glory, ye may be glad with exceeding joy.* Though you should be brought to torture and the flames, you would still be happy. For though there be pain as to the body, there shall yet be a spiritual joy, inasmuch as you are to be happy forever. For this joy springs here from suffering, and is everlasting. Yet whoever cannot bear his sufferings cheerfully, and is dissatisfied, and chooses to contend with God, he shall endure, both here and hereafter, eternal torment and suffering. Thus we read of holy martyrs, that they have submitted cheerfully to torture, thus opening the way to eternal enjoyment; as for instance, of St. Agatha, that she went as joyfully to prison as though it had been to a dance. And the Apostles went also with joy, and thanked God "that they were counted worthy to suffer for Christ's sake."

In the time of the revelation of His glory. Christ does not permit Himself as yet to be seen as a Lord, but is still a sharer with us in our labors. So far as He is

Himself concerned, He is truly such, but we who are His members, are not Lords as yet. Still we shall yet be Lords, when His glory at the last day shall be revealed before all men, brighter than the sun.

V. 14. *If ye be reproached for the name of Christ, happy are you.* Christ is a hateful name with the world; whoever preaches of Him must endure to have the most esteemed on earth slander and revile his name. But this in our times is more strange and unseemly, that they who persecute us bear also the name of Christ; they say they are Christians and baptized, yet in fact renounce and persecute Christ. This is indeed a sad strife. They hold the same name as tenaciously as we do, against us. For this reason we greatly need consolation,—although the most discreet and pious follow after us,—that we may abide firmly and remain cheerful. But how?

V. 14. *For the Spirit of glory and of God resteth upon you. On their part He is evil spoken of, but on your part He is glorified.* Ye (he says) have within you a Spirit, that is, the Spirit of God and of glory, such as makes you glorious. But this does not take place on earth, but it shall take place when the glory of Christ shall be revealed at the last day. Besides, He is not only a Spirit that makes us glorious, but one which we also regard as glorious in Himself. For it belongs peculiarly to the Holy Spirit to purify and glorify, even as He has made Christ pure and glorious. Now the same Spirit (he says) rests upon you; and forasmuch as ye bear the name of Christ, it is slandered by them. For He must endure to be reviled and slandered, to the highest degree. Therefore it is not you who receive the reviling; it belongs to the Spirit, which is a Spirit of glory: be not anxious; He will regard it and raise you to honor. This is the consolation which we as Christians have, that we may say, That word is not mine, this faith is not mine, they are all the work of God: whoever reviles me reviles God, as Christ says in Matthew x., "Whoever receiveth you receiveth me;" and on the other hand, "Whoever reviles you reviles me." St. Peter, therefore, would say, Know that the Spirit which you have is strong enough easily to punish His enemies; as God says also in Ex. xxiii., If thou wilt hearken to my commandments, I will be the enemy of thine enemies. And the Scripture often repeats it, that the enemies of the saints are the enemies of God. If we only have experience that we are Christians, and believe, we shall not be ashamed, but the reviling is directed more especially against God Himself. Therefore, he says, be ye cheerful and happy, for that opposition is to the Spirit, which is not yours, but God's. Now he adds an admonition:

V. 15, 16. *But let no one suffer as a murderer, or a thief, or an evil-doer, or a busy-body in other men's matters; but if any man suffer as a Christian, let him not be ashamed, but let him glorify God on this behalf.* He would say, now, You have heard how you are to suffer, and conduct yourselves under it, but beware that it do not come upon you because you have deserved it on account of your evil deeds, but for Christ's sake. Yet this is not now the case with us, for we must suffer, notwithstanding the fact that those who persecute us bear also the name of Christ, so that no one can die because he is a Christian, but only as an enemy of Christ, and even they who persecute him say they are real Christians, and say, too, that he is blessed who dies for Christ's sake. Here the Spirit alone must determine, since you must know that you are a Christian in the sight of God. God's tribunal is a secret one, and when He has uncovered the matter, He will judge no more according to the name, since at that time the name of the most exalted must vanish away.

Now, St. Peter says, If ye suffer in this manner, *be ye not ashamed, but glorify God.* Here he makes the suffering and anguish the more welcome, because it is great, insomuch that we praise God through it, and because we are not worthy of it. Yet now all will shrink therefrom. Of what advantage is it to embrace the cross in monasteries? The cross of Christ does not save me. I must, indeed, believe in His cross, but I must myself bear my own cross. His suffering must I experience inwardly, if I would possess the true treasure. Let St. Peter's bones be holy, yet how does it help you? You and your bones should be holy, too, which can take place only when you suffer for Christ's sake.

V. 17. *For the time is come that judgment must begin at the house of God; and if it first begin at us, what shall the end be of them that obey not the Gospel of God?* He here brings two passages from the prophets together in one. As to the first, Jeremiah says, xxv.: "Behold, I send my judgments upon the city which is called by my name; and if first of all I afflict my dearly beloved children who believe on me, who first of all must suffer and past through the fire, do ye who are my enemies, ye who do not believe, suppose that ye shall escape punishment?" So in chap. xlix. he says: "They whose judgment was not to drink the cup, have assuredly drunken, and thinkest thou that thou art he that shall not drink?" That is, I strike my beloved, that you may see how I shall treat my enemies. Observe here the force of the words: if God holds his saints in such esteem, yet has been willing to have them judged and exposed with such severity, what will then be done with the others?

So also Ezekiel, chap. ix., saw armed men with their swords, who were to slay all, to whom God said, begin at my sanctuary. That is what St. Peter means in this place. Therefore he says, the time is come, as the prophets have foretold, when judgment must begin with us. When the Gospel is preached, God arrests and punishes sin, since it is He that kills and makes alive. The pious he gently strokes, and first of all is the rod of kind correction: but what then will be done with those that do not believe? As though he had said, if He proceeds with such severity toward His own children, you may infer what must be the punishment of those who do not believe.

V. 18. *And if the righteous scarcely be saved, where shall the ungodly and the sinner appear?* This passage is also taken from the book of Proverbs, chap. ii. 31.: "If the righteous be recompensed in the earth, where shall the godless abide?" The same thing also is said here by St. Peter. The righteous can hardly be saved and only just escapes. The righteous is he who believes, yet in his faith, even, *he* has trouble and labor in order to persevere and be saved, for he must pass through the fire. Where then will *he* be found who has not faith? If God gives thus to faith a shock that makes it tremble, how can *he* abide steadfast who is without faith? whence he concludes:

V. 19. *Wherefore let them that suffer according to the will of God, commit their souls to Him as a faithful creator, in well-doing.* That is, they to whom God appoints suffering, that they have not themselves sought out and invited, should commit their souls to his charge. These are they that do good, abide in good works, fall not away because of suffering, commit themselves to their Creator, who is faithful. This is to us a great consolation. God created thy soul without thy care or coöperation, while as yet thou wast not; so is he also able to preserve it. Therefore commit thyself to Him, yet in such a way that it be joined with good works. Not that you are to think,—now I will not be afraid to die; you must see to it that you are a true Christian and prove your faith by your works. But if you go on so venturously, it will be wise to examine how it will go with you. This is the last admonition which St. Peter gives to those that suffer for Christ's sake. We pass now to

CHAPTER V.

V. 1-4. *The elders which are among you I exhort, who am also an elder, and a witness of the sufferings of Christ, and partaker of the glory which shall be revealed. Feed the flock of Christ which is among you, and take the oversight of it, not by constraint, but willingly, not for the love of vile gain, but of a ready mind, not as Lords over the heritage, but be ye examples for the flock. Thus when the Chief Shepherd shall appear, ye shall receive the enduring crown.*

There St. Peter gives a direction for the behaviour of such as are to preside over the people in the spiritual government. He has already said in the last chapter, that no one should teach or preach anything, unless he be sure that it is the word of God, so that our conscience may stand on the firm rock. For this is imperative on us as Christians, that we must be assured what is well-pleasing to God, or not. Where this is wanting none can be a Christian. Afterward he taught us, that whatever work or office any one might have, he should discharge it as though God wrought in it. But the present passage refers particularly to the bishops or pastors as to what their fitness and conduct should be. But here you must pause and learn the meaning of the words. The expression presbyter or priest is a Greek word, rendered in Dutch an elder, just as in Latin these were called senators; that is, a number of aged, careful men of much experience. So Christ also has called his officers and his council, who bear spiritual rule; that is, who are to preach and provide for some christian church. Therefore you must not mistake, though they are called at the present day by a different title, priests. For of those who are now called priests, Scripture knows nothing. Put the real state of things as it now comes to pass out of sight, and apprehend the matter thus: that St. Peter and the other Apostles, when they arrived at a city where there were faithful people or Christians, have selected there some few aged men of honorable standing, having wife and children, and being well-grounded in the Scriptures. These were called presbyters. After this Peter and Paul call them *Episcopos*, that is, bishop. So that priest and bishop are one and the same thing. Of this we have a fine example in the legend of St. Martyn, where an individual, with several companions, arrives in Africa at a certain place, and perceives a man lying there in a hovel, whom they took for a husbandman, though they knew not who he was. Afterwards, when the people had come together at that place, this very man arose and preached, when they perceived that it was their pastor or bishop; for at that time they were not distinguished from other people by their peculiar kind of clothing and attendance.

Those elders, says St. Peter, who are to care for and to oversee the people, do I admonish, who am also one. Hence you clearly perceive that they whom he calls *elders*, have been in the ministry and have preached, since he speaks of himself also as an elder. And here St. Peter humbles himself—does not say that he was a Lord, although he might have had authority for it since he was an Apostle of Christ, and speaks of himself not only as a fellow-elder, but also as a witness of the sufferings that were in Christ. As though he had said, I do not merely preach, but am a partaker with Christians, even suffering Christians. Thereby he shows that wherever Christians are they must suffer and be persecuted. Such is a genuine Apostle. If such a Pope or a bishop were to be found among these men that bear the title at the present day, we would gladly kiss his feet.

And partaker of the glory which shall be revealed. This is something still more exalted, and evidently a bishop must not lightly say it. For here St. Peter claims to be a saint. He was certain that he should be saved, for he had strong assurance, as when Christ said, "I have chosen you"—yet it had cost much pains ere the Apostles attained it. They must first be humbled and wickedly derided. Now, although he knew that he was a partaker of salvation, still he is not proud, neither does he exalt himself, although he is a saint. But what were the elders therefore to do? It follows:

V. 2. *Feed the flock of Christ which is among you.* Christ is the chief Shepherd, and has many shepherds under Him,—as also many herds of sheep which He has committed to His shepherds, here and there, as St. Peter writes in this place, in many lands. What are these shepherds to do? They are to feed the flock of Christ. This the Pope has arrogated to himself, and thus claims that he is sovereign lord, and will dispose of the sheep as he chooses. We know very well what feeding is,—namely, that the shepherd should distribute provision and set food before the sheep, that they may thrive. Besides, they are to guard lest the wolves come and rend the sheep,—that is, that they may not assault and worry them.

Now St. Peter says, particularly, the *flock of Christ*, as though he should say: Do not imagine that the flock is yours, ye are only servants. But our bishops speak with all confidence the reverse of this. They say, you are *my* sheep. But we are Christ's sheep; for so he said above, "Ye are now returned to the Shepherd and Bishop of your souls." The bishops are Christ's servants, and their business is to guard Christ's sheep, and feed them. Therefore to feed them is nothing else but to preach the Gospel, whereby souls are nourished, made fat and fruitful,—since the sheep thrive upon the Gospel and the word of God. This is alone the office of a bishop. So Christ says also to Peter,

"Feed my sheep,"—that is, the sheep which you are to feed, are not yours, but mine. Yet from this they have inferred the doctrine that the Pope has external power over all Christendom, and yet none of them preaches to you one word out of the Gospel; and I fear that since St. Peter's times there has been no Pope that has preached the Gospel. There has certainly been none who has written and left anything behind him in which the Gospel was contained. Saint Gregory, the Pope, was certainly a holy man, but his sermons are not worth a farthing; so that it would seem that the See of Rome has been under the special curse of God. It is very possible that some Popes may have endured martyrdom for the Gospel's sake; but nothing has been written of them to show that it was the Gospel. And yet they go on and preach that they must feed the flock; and yet they do nothing but bind and destroy the conscience, by laws of their own, while they preach not a word of Christ.

It is probable, indeed, that among all Christians many might be found, both men and women, as able to preach as those who are thus employed. But certainly among all these multitudes there are many people who have not this ability. And therefore some one must be selected to strengthen them, so that the wolves shall not come and tear the sheep. For a preacher must not only feed the sheep, so as to instruct them how they are to be good Christians, but, besides this, must guard against the wolves, lest they attack the sheep and lead them astray with false doctrine, and introduce error such as the devil would not find fault with. But there are many people to be found at the present day, quite ready to tolerate our preaching of the Gospel, if we would not cry out against the wolves and preach against the prelates.

But though I were to preach the simple truth, and feed the sheep and give them good instruction, still it is not enough unless the sheep be guarded and protected, so that the wolves do not come and carry them off. For what is it that is built, if I throw out one stone and see another thrown into its place? The wolf can very readily endure to have the sheep well fed; he had rather have it so, that they may be fat. But this he cannot endure, the hostile bark of the dogs. Therefore is it a most important matter, if well considered, that we should truly feed the flock, as God has commanded it.

The flock, he says, *which is among you*,—that is, which is with you, not that they are to lie at your feet. And *oversee them not by constraint, but willingly, not out of love for vile gain*. There he has expressed, in a single word, what the prophet Ezekiel writes, chap. xxxiv., of shepherds or bishops. And this is the meaning: you are not only to feed them, but also pay attention and be carefully faithful where it is called for and there is need. And here he uses a Greek word, *Episcopountes*,—that is, *being bishops*, and it comes from the word *Episcopos*,—

that is, rendered in Dutch, *an overseer, a guardian*, who is on the watch or lookout, and takes notice of what every one around him wants. Observe, then, how a bishop and an elder are one and the same thing. So that *that* is false which they now say, that the bishop's office is a dignity, and that *he* is a bishop who wears a pointed hat on his head. It is not a dignity, but a ministry; so that he who has it should oversee and provide for us, and be our guardian, so as to know what is generally needed; that when one is weak and has a troubled conscience, he should then give help and comfort; when one falls, that he should raise him up, and things of this sort; so that the people of Christ may sufficiently be cared for, both in soul and body. For this reason, I have often said, that if a proper form of government was to be now established, there must in such a case be in one city as many as three or four bishops, who should have the oversight and care of the Church, providing for the general wants.

And here St. Peter touches on two points which might well appall any one from taking the charge over a people. In the first place, there are some to be found who are truly devoted, yet yield reluctantly to becoming preachers; for it is a wearisome office for any one to have the general oversight,—how the sheep live, so as to direct and help them,—since there must be oversight and watchfulness night and day, that the wolf do not break in; so that body and life must be devoted to it. Therefore he says, *you are not to do it of constraint*. True it is, that no one should force himself uncalled into the ministry; but if he is called and required for it, he should enter it willingly, and discharge what his office demands. For they who do it from constraint, and who have no appetite and love for it, will not properly discharge it.

But there are others, worse than these, who stand up before the people and thereby seek their own gain, so as to feed their own belly. These men are anxious for the wool and milk of the sheep; they ask no questions about the food,—just the course of our bishops now,—a thing that has become almost everywhere a scandal and a shame, for in a bishop it is especially scandalous. For this reason both the apostles Peter and Paul, as well as the prophets also, have repeatedly spoken of it. So Moses says, "You know that I have coveted no man's cattle." The prophet Samuel, also, "You know that I have taken of you no man's ass or ox." For if he whose duty it is to feed the flock is anxious merely for wealth and gain, he will in a short time become a wolf himself.

V. 2. *But of a ready mind.* That is, that a bishop have an appetite and inclination thereto. This is the character of those who willingly minister, and do not seek the wool of the sheep. Thus we have two kinds of false shepherds: the one, those who serve unwillingly; the other, those who do it gladly, but for the sake of avarice.—Further, he says:

V. 3. *Not as lords over the heritage.* This is the character of those who rule willingly enough for honor's sake, in order that they may rise high, and become powerful tyrants. Therefore he admonishes them that they should not act as though the people was subject to them, so that they might be gentlemen, and might do as they chose. For we have a Master, who is Christ, who rules over our spirits. The bishops are to do no more than feed the sheep. Here St. Peter has broken down and condemned all that rule which the Pope now maintains, and clearly determines that they have not power to give one word of additional command, but that they are to be only servants, and say, "Thus saith Christ thy Master, therefore you are to do it." So Christ also speaks: "The kings of this world have dominion, and men call them who are in authority their gracious lords; but you are not to be like them." Now the Pope speaks the reverse,—"Ye shall rule and have authority."

V. 3-4. *But be ye an example for the flock; so shall ye, when the Chief Shepherd shall appear, receive the enduring crown.* That is, see to it that you go before them at their head, and exhibit such a conduct that your life may be an example to the people, and they may follow after you. But our bishops say to the people, "Go there and do so and so;" and they sit on cushions and play the gentleman, imposing burdens on us which they will not bear themselves, while they will not preach a word, and call others to account if they have not done it for them. But if it should be required of them, they would soon be weary of their dignity.

Therefore St. Peter does not appoint any temporal reward for bishops. As though he would say, "Your office is so great that it never can be rewarded here, but ye shall receive an eternal crown, which shall follow it, if ye truly feed the sheep of Christ." This is the admonition which St. Peter gives to those who are to care for souls, from whence you may confidently infer and clearly prove, that the Pope, along with his bishops, is Antichrist, or an enemy of Christ, since he does nothing of that which St. Peter here requires, and neither teaches nor practices it himself, but even acts the counterpart, and will not only not feed the sheep or let them be fed, but is himself a wolf and tears them, and yet makes it his boast that he is the vicar of the Lord Christ. He certainly is that, for since Christ is not there, he, like the devil, sits and rules in Christ's place.

Whence it is necessary carefully to remember these plain texts and others like them, and to hold them up against the Pope's government, so that when any one asks or questions you, you may be able to answer and say, "Christ said and practised so and so; the Pope teaches and practices directly the opposite. Since they are opposed to one another one of them must be false; but certainly Christ is not. Whence I conclude that the Pope is a liar and the real Antichrist."

In this way must you be prepared with Scripture, so that you can not only challenge the Pope as Antichrist, but know how to prove it clearly, so that you could die secure of it, and withstand the devil even in death.—It follows, further:

V. 5. *Likewise, ye younger, submit yourselves unto the elders.* We have now the last admonition in this chapter. St. Peter would have such order in the christian church, that the young should follow the old, so that all may go on harmoniously; those beneath submissive to those above them. If this were now to be enforced, we should not need many laws. He would strictly have it so that the younger shall be directed according to the understanding of the older, as these shall best judge that it shall be for the praise of God. But St. Peter presumes that such elders are to be instructed and established in the Holy Ghost. For should it happen that they are themselves fools, and without understanding, no good government could originate with them; but if they are persons of good understanding, then it is well that they should rule the youth. But St. Peter is not speaking here of civil, but of church government, that the elders should rule those that are spiritually younger, whether they be priests or even old men.

Be ye all of you subject one to another, and therein manifest humility. Here he turns and modifies his command, directing each to be subject one to another. But how is that consistent, that the elders should rule, and yet all should be subject one to the other? Are we then to overturn what has been said? Some one perhaps would give such a gloss as this, that St. Peter spoke above of the elders,—here he speaks of the younger. But we shall let the words stand, granting that they are spoken generally; as Paul also says in Rom. xii., "That each in honor prefer one another." The younger should be subject to the old, yet in such a manner that the latter shall not regard themselves as masters, but even should submit and follow, where a younger is more judicious and learned; just as God in the Old Testament often selected young men, provided they were more wise than the old.

So Christ also teaches, in Luke xiv.: "When thou art bidden, sit not down in the highest place, lest a more honorable than thou be bidden, and then he that bade thee and him come and say to thee, give this man place; and thou begin with shame to take the lower place; but when thou art bidden, go and sit down in the lowest place, that when he that bade thee cometh, he may say unto thee: Friend, go up higher;" and then he introduces the passage as it is found in many places: "He who exalteth himself shall be humbled, and he that humbleth himself shall be exalted."

Therefore should the younger be subject to the elder, and yet the elder on the other hand should be so disposed that each one in his heart shall hold himself as the least. Were this done we should have delightful peace, and all would go well on earth. This, therefore, says he, should we do, *exhibit humility*.

For God resisteth the proud but giveth grace to the humble. That is, those who will not give place God casts down; and on the other hand, he exalts those who humble themselves. It is a common expression—would to God he lived like common folks.

V. 6. *Humble yourselves therefore under the mighty hand of God.* Since God requires that each should be subject to the other; if it is done willingly and cheerfully, he will exalt you. But if you will not do it willingly, you shall do it from constraint. He will cast you down.

That He may exalt you in his own time. It seems, when God suffers his own children to be cast down, as though he would at length desert them. Therefore he says: Do not mistake on this account, and suffer yourself to be blinded, but be confident, since you have a sure promise that it is God's hand and will. Therefore should you not regard the time, however long it be, that you are brought low; for though He has cast you down, He will yet lift you up. Hence it follows:

V. 7. *Cast all your cares upon Him, for He careth for you.* You have such a promise as this, whereby you may rest secure that God doth not forsake you, *but careth for you*. Therefore let all your cares go, and cast your burden on Him. These words are exceedingly precious; how could He have made them more sweet or tender? Why does He employ so great allurement? It is in order that no one might easily despond and give up his purpose. Therefore He gives us such consolation as this: that God not only looks upon us, but cares also for us, and has a heartfelt regard for our lot. He further says:

V. 8. *Be sober, be vigilant, for your adversary the devil goeth about as a roaring lion, seeking whom he may devour.* Here he gives us a warning, and would open our eyes, and it would be well worthy that the text should be written in golden letters. Here you perceive what this life is, and how it is described, so that we might well be ever wishing that we were dead. We are here in the devil's kingdom, just as in case a pilgrim should arrive at an inn, where he knew that all in the house were robbers; if he must enter there he will yet arm himself in the best way he can devise, and will sleep but little: so are we now on earth, where the prince is an evil spirit, and has the hearts of men in his power, doing by them as he will. It is a fearful thought if we properly regard it. Therefore St. Peter would warn us to take heed to ourselves, and act the part of a faithful servant, who knows the state of things here. For this reason he says: be sober, for they who indulge themselves here in eating and drinking, and are like fat swine, are such as can be fitted for nothing useful. Therefore must we have ever by us such a talisman as this.

And be vigilant (he says), not only as to the spirit but also as to the body. For a vitiated body, prone to sleep when it eats and drinks itself full, will give the devil no opposition, though it belong even to those swine who have a faith and spirit.

Wherefore should we then be sober and vigilant? *Because your enemy the devil goeth about as a roaring lion, seeking whom he may devour.* The evil spirit, sleeps not—is cunning and wicked. He has purposed with himself that he will assault us, and he knows the right trick therefor; goes about like a lion that is hungry, and roars as though he would gladly devour all. Here St. Peter gives us an important admonition, and forewarns us of our enemy, that we may protect ourselves against him; as Paul also says, "we are not ignorant of the devices of the wicked spirit." That "going about" tends to make us heedless, and thereupon follow wrath, hatred, pride, lust, contempt of God.

And here observe especially, that he says *the devil goeth about*. He does not pass before your eyes, when you are armed against him, but looks out before and behind you, within and without, where he may attack you. If he now meets you here, he will quickly return there, and attack you in another place; he changes from one side to the other, and employs every kind of cunning and art that he may bring you to fall; and if you are well prepared in one place, he will quickly fall in upon another; and if he cannot overthrow you there, then he assaults you somewhere else, and so never gives it up, but goes round and round, and leaves no rest to any one. If we then are fools and do not regard it, but go on and take no heed, then has he as good as seized upon us.

Let every one now look to this; surely each shall trace something of this in his own experience. He that has examined knows it well. Therefore it is so sad for us that we go about so heedlessly. If we rightly regard it, we should cry out, *death rather than life.* Job has spoken thus: "Man's life on earth is nothing but an encampment, a mere conflict and strife." Why then does God thus leave us in life and misery? In order that faith may be exercised and grow, and that hastening out of this life, we may have a desire of death, and an anxiety to depart.

V. 9. *Whom withstand, firm in the faith.* Sober you should be, and vigilant, but to this end,—the body must be in a proper frame. Yet with all this, the devil is not routed; this only suffices to afford the body less occasion for sin. The true sword is this, that ye be strong and firm in the faith. If you in heart grasp hold of the word of God and maintain your hold by faith, then the devil cannot gain the advantage, but will be compelled to fly. If you can say, "This has my God said—on this I stand," then shall ye see that he will quickly depart, and ill-humor, evil lusts, wrath, avarice, melancholy and doubt, will all vanish. But the devil is artful, and does not readily permit you to come to this, and so assaults you in order to take the sword out of your hand; if he can make you full, so that your body is unguarded and inclined to wantonness, then will he quickly wrench the sword from your grasp. Thus He served Eve: she had God's word; if she had continued to depend on it she would not have fallen, but when the devil saw that she held the word so loosely, he tore it from her heart, so that she let it go and he triumphed.

Thus St. Peter has sufficiently instructed us how to contend with the devil. It requires not much running hither and thither; is besides a work that you can do, yet no longer than you depend through faith on the word of God. If he comes and would drive you into despondency because of sin, only seize hold of the word of God that speaks of the forgiveness of sin, and venture yourself thereon; then will he be compelled quickly to let you alone. St. Peter says, moreover:

Knowing that the same afflictions are accomplished in your brethren that are in the world. That is, be not surprised that you must meet opposition from the devil; but comfort yourselves, inasmuch as ye are not alone, but there are others besides you who must endure such suffering, and reflect that you have your brethren to share with you in the strife.

There now you have the Epistle in which you have sufficiently heard a truly christian doctrine; in what a masterly manner he has described faith, love, and the Holy Cross; and how he instructs and warns us as to how we should contend with the devil. Whoever comprehends this Epistle, has doubtless enough, so that he needs nothing more but that God teach him richly from that which likewise overflows in the other books. But that is besides nothing different from this; for here the Apostle has forgotten nothing which it is necessary for a Christian to know.

Finally, he does what every faithful preacher should do, in that he not only takes care to feed the sheep, but also cares and prays for them; and concludes with a prayer that God may give them grace and strength, that they may understand and retain the word.

V. 10. *But the God of all grace who hath called us unto His Eternal glory by Christ Jesus, after that ye have suffered a while, make you perfect, establish, strengthen, settle you.* That is the wish wherewith he commits them to God—God, who alone bestows grace, and not a single grace, but all grace richly in one, who has called you through Christ that ye might have Eternal glory, not through any desert of your own, but for Christ's sake; if ye have Him, ye have through faith, without merit of yours, Eternal glory and salvation, which will prepare you, that you may be strong, grow, and stand, and that ye may be able to accomplish much; and to this end He will strengthen and establish you, that ye may be able to bear and suffer all.

V. 11. *To him be praise and power for ever and ever, Amen.* Praise is the sacrifice that we as Christians should offer up to God. He only adds, in conclusion:

V. 12. *By your faithful brother Silvanus, (as I suppose), have I written briefly, to admonish and manifest that this is the true grace of God wherein ye stand.* Although I well know (he would say) that you have heard this before and know it well, so that you do not need that I should teach it unto you, yet have I written this to you (as those that are truly Apostles should do), that I might also admonish you that you abide therein, since you are tried and exercised; and you are not to imagine that I preach any otherwise than as you have already heard.

V. 13. *The Church that is at Babylon greets you.* Such was the practice of writing in the Epistles the farewell. *The Church at Babylon,* says he, *greets you.* I suppose, but am not fully confident, that he here meant Rome, for it has been generally supposed that the Epistle was written from Rome. Still, there were two Babylons,—one in Chaldea, the other in Egypt, which is now Al Cair. But Rome is not called Babylon, except figuratively, in the sense, as was said above, of thronging corruption. Thus, Babel means, in the Hebrew, a confusion. So, perhaps, he has called Rome a confusion, or Babel, since *there* was also such disorderly conduct, and a confused multitude of all kinds of shameful practices and vices; and whatever in the whole world was scandalous had flown together there. In this same, he says, is a church gathered of such as are Christians, who greet you. But I will readily leave every one to hold it as he will, for no importance attaches to it.

My son, Marcus, also. Some say that he here means Mark, the Evangelist, and calls him his son, not literally, but spiritually,—as Paul calls Timothy and Titus his sons, and says to the Corinthians that he has begotten them in Christ.

V. 14. *Greet ye one another with a kiss of charity.* This custom has now passed away. In the Gospel we read distinctly that Christ received his disciples with a kiss, and such was then a practice in those lands. Of this kiss, St. Paul often speaks, also.

Peace be with you all that are in Christ Jesus. Amen. That is, who believe in Christ. This is the adieu wherewith he commits them to God.—Thus we have concluded this first Epistle. God grant His grace, that we may hold and keep it. Amen.

THE SECOND EPISTLE GENERAL OF ST. PETER

PREFACE.

St. Peter wrote this Epistle because he saw how the true, pure doctrine of faith had become falsified, darkened and suppressed. And he has wished to meet a two-fold error, springing from a wrong understanding of the doctrine of faith, and guard against it in both directions; namely, that we should not ascribe to works the power of making us righteous and acceptable before God, though these works belong to faith; and, on the other hand, that no one should think that there may be faith without good works. For if any one preaches concerning faith, that it justifies us without any addition of works, the people say, "One need do no works," as we see it in our daily experience; and, on the other hand, when they fall on works and exalt them, faith must be prostrated, so that the middle way is one to be retained with difficulty, where there are not preachers of the right kind.

Now, we have ever taught this doctrine, that to faith we are to ascribe all things, one as well as another; that it alone makes us just and holy in the sight of God. Moreover, that if faith is present, out of it good works must and should proceed, since it is even impossible that we should pass this our life quite indolent, and do no works. Thus St. Peter in this Epistle would also teach us, and thus meet those who perhaps out of the former Epistle might have received the wrong apprehension that it sufficed for faith, though we should at the same time do no work. And against this the first chapter especially aims, wherein he teaches that believers should try themselves by good works, and become assured of their faith.

The second chapter is against those who exalt works merely, and depreciate faith. Therefore he admonishes them against the false teachers who should come, who, through the teachings of men, should destroy faith entirely. For he clearly saw what a cruel trial there would yet be in the world, as had even then already begun; as St. Paul says, II. Thes. ii., "The mystery of iniquity already works."

Thus is this Epistle written as a warning for us, that we prove our faith by our good works, and yet that we trust not to our works.

CHAPTER I.

V. 1. *Simon Peter, a servant and Apostle of Jesus Christ, to those who have attained like faith with us, in the righteousness which our God gives, and our Saviour, Jesus Christ.* Such is the subscription and the superscription of this Epistle, that we may know who writes it, and to whom he writes it, even to those who have heard the word of God and abide in the faith. But what sort of a faith is this? In the righteousness (says he) which God gives. Thus he grants justification to faith alone,—as St. Paul, also, in Rom. i. In the Gospel is that righteousness revealed which avails with God, which comes from faith; as it stands written: "The just shall live by faith." Thus St. Peter would admonish them that they should be armed, and not let the doctrine of faith be torn away, which they have now apprehended and thoroughly known.

And to this end he adjoins, *in the righteousness which God gives*, that he may separate from it all human righteousness. For by faith alone are we righteous before God; wherefore faith is called a righteousness of God, for with the world it is of no account; yea, it is even condemned.

V. 2. *Grace and peace be multiplied among you, through the knowledge of God and Jesus Christ our Lord.* This is the greeting usually prefixed to the Epistles; and it amounts to this: I wish you, in place of my service for you, to increase in grace and peace, and grow ever richer and richer in the grace which comes from the knowledge of God and the Lord Christ,—that is, which none can have but he who has the knowledge of God and Jesus Christ.

The Apostles, and the prophets also, in the Scripture, are ever setting forth the knowledge of God. As Isaiah, xi: "They shall not injure or destroy in my whole mountain, for the land is filled with the knowledge of God, as the land is covered with the water." That is, so overflowingly shall the knowledge of God break forth, as when a mass of water gushes up and rushes forth and swallows up a whole land.

Thence shall such peace then follow, that no one shall wrong another, or make him suffer.

But this is not to know God, that you should believe as the Turks, Jews, and devils believe, that God has created all things, or even that Christ was born of a virgin, suffered, died, and rose again; but this is the true knowledge, whereby you hold and know that God is thy God and Christ is thy Christ, which the devil and the false christians could not believe. So that this knowledge is nothing else but a true christian faith; for if you thus know God and Christ, you will then confide in them with your whole heart, and trust them in good and ill, in life and death. Such trust evil consciences cannot possess. For they know no more of God, except that He is a God of St. Peter and all the saints in heaven. But as their own God they know Him not, but hold Him as their task-master and angry judge. To have God, is to have all grace, all mercy, and all that man can well receive; to have Christ, is to have the Saviour and Mediator, who has brought us to say that God is ours, and has obtained all grace for us with Him. This also must be implied, that Christ is yours and you are His, then have you a true knowledge. A woman that lives unmarried can well say that a man is a husband, but this can she not say, that he is her husband. So may we all well say, this is *a* God, but this we cannot say all of us, that He is *our* God, for we cannot all trust upon Him nor comfort ourselves as His. To this knowledge belongs also that which the Scripture calls *faciem et vultum domini*, the face of the Lord, whereof the prophets speak much; who ever sees not the face of the Lord knows Him not, but sees only His back,—that is, an angry and ungracious God.

And here you perceive, that St. Peter does not set himself particularly to write of faith, since he had already done that sufficiently in the First Epistle, but would admonish believers that they should prove their faith by good works; for he would not have a faith without good works, nor works without faith, but faith first and good works on and from faith. Therefore, he says, now, also:

V. 3. *According as His divine power (whatever serves for life and godliness) is abundantly given us.* This is the first point, where Peter essays to describe what sort of blessings we have received through faith from God, even that to us (since we have known God by faith) there is given every kind of divine power. But what sort of power is it? It is such power as serves us toward life and godliness; that is, when we believe, then we attain this much, that God gives us the fullness of His power, which is so with and in us, that what we speak and work, it is not we that do it, but God Himself does it. He is strong, powerful, and almighty in us, though we even suffer and die, and are weak in the eyes of the world. So that there is no power nor ability in us if we have not this power of God.

But this power of God which is in us, St. Peter would not have so explained, as that we might make heaven and earth, and should work such miracles as God does; for how would we be advantaged by it? But we have the power of God within us so far as it is useful and necessary to us. Therefore, the Apostle adjoins, and says, *whatever serves for life and godliness;* that is, we have such power of God that by it we are eminently favored with grace to do good and to live forever.

Through the knowledge of Him who hath called us. Such power of God, and such rich grace, come from no other source but from this knowledge of God; for if you count Him for a God, He will deal also with you in all things as a God. So Paul also says, I. Cor. i., "Ye are in all points enriched in every kind of word and knowledge, even as the preaching of Christ is made powerful in you, so that ye have henceforth no want." This is now the greatest thing of all, the noblest and most needful that God can give us,—so that we are not to receive all that is in heaven and on earth; for what would it help you, though you were able to go through fire and water, and do all kinds of wonderful works, and had not this? Many people who perform such miracles shall be condemned. But this is wonderful above all things else, that God gives us such power, that thereby all our sins are forgiven and blotted out, death, the devil and hell, subdued and vanquished; so that we have an unharassed conscience and a happy heart, and fear for nothing.

Through His glory and virtue. How does that call come, whereby we are called of God? Thus: God has permitted the holy Gospel to go forth into the world and be made known, though no man had ever before striven for it, or sought or prayed for it, of Him. But ere man had ever thought of it, He has offered, bestowed, and beyond all measure richly shed forth such grace, so that He alone has the glory and the praise; and we ascribe to Him alone the virtue and the power, for it is not our work, but His only. Wherefore, since the calling is not of us, we should not exalt ourselves as though we had done it, but render to Him praise and thanksgiving, because He has given us the Gospel, and thereby granted us power and might against the devil, death, and all evil.

V. 4. *Whereby are given unto us exceeding precious and great promises.* St. Peter adjoins this, that he may explain the nature and method of faith. If we know Him as God, then do we have through faith that eternal life and divine power wherewith we subdue death and the devil. Though we see and grasp it not, yet is it promised to us. We really have it all, though it does not yet appear, but at the last day we shall see it present before us. Here it begins in faith; though we have it not in its fullness, we have yet the assurance that we live here in the power of God, and shall afterward be saved forever.

Whoever has this faith has the promise; whoever does not believe possesses it not, and must be lost forever. How great and precious a thing this is, Peter explains further, and says:

So that ye by the same might become partakers of the divine nature, while ye flee from the corrupting lusts of the world. This we have, he says, through the power of faith, that we should be partakers and have association or communion with the divine nature. This is such a passage that the like of it does not stand in the New or Old Testament, although it is a small matter with the unbelieving that we should have communion with the divine nature itself. But what is the divine nature? It is eternal truth, righteousness, wisdom; eternal life, peace, joy, happiness, and whatever good one can name. Whoever then becomes partaker of the divine nature, attains all this,—that he is to live forever, and have eternal peace, delight and joy, and is to be perfectly pure, just, and triumphant over the devil, sin and death. Therefore St. Peter would say this much: As little as any one can take away from God, that He should not be eternal life and eternal truth, just as little shall any one take it away from you. Whatever one does to you he must do to Him, for whoever would crush a Christian must crush God.

All this, that word, the divine nature, implies, and he also used it to this end, that he might include it all; and it is truly a great thing where it is believed. But, as I said above, this is merely instruction, in which he does not lay down a ground of faith, but sets forth what great, rich blessings we receive through faith; wherefore he says, that ye shall have all if ye so live as to prove your faith, whereby ye flee worldly lusts. So he speaks, now, further:

V. 5. *Give then all your diligence, and add to your faith, virtue.* Here St. Peter takes up the admonition, that they should prove their faith by good works. Since such great blessing is bestowed upon you through faith (he would say), that ye really have all that God is, do this besides: be diligent, and not sluggish; add to your faith, virtue; that is, let your faith break out before the world, so as to be zealous, busy, powerful, and active, and to do many works; let it not remain idle and unfruitful. Ye have a good inheritance and a good field, but see to it that ye do not let thistles and weeds grow upon it.

And to virtue, discrimination. Discrimination or knowledge is, in the first place, that one should manifest an outward conduct, and the virtue of faith, in accordance with reason. For we should so far bridle and check the body, that we may be sober, vigorous, and fitted for good works; not that we should torture and mortify ourselves as some famous saints have done. For though God is likewise opposed to the sins that remain in the flesh, yet does He not require that for this reason you should destroy the body. Its viciousness and caprice you should guard against, but yet you are not to ruin or injure it, but give it its food and refreshment that it may remain sound and in living vigor.

In the second place, discrimination means that one should lead a life carefully exact, and act with discretion in regard to outward things, as food and things of that sort,—that one should not act in these things unreasonably, and that he should give his neighbor no provocation.

V. 6. *And to discrimination, temperance.* Temperance is not only in eating and drinking, but it is regularity in the whole life and conduct, words, works, manners; that we should not live too expensively, and should avoid excess in ornament and clothing; that none come out too proudly, and make too lofty a show. But in regard to this St. Peter will not fix any rule, measure, or limit, as the Orders have prescribed for themselves, who have wished to do all by rule, and have framed statutes which must be exactly observed. It is a thing not to be tolerated in Christendom, that men should require by laws that there be a common rule on *temperance;* for people are unlike one to another; one is of a strong, another is of a weaker nature; and no one in all things is at all times situated as another. Therefore every one should see to himself how he is situated, and what he can bear.

And to temperance, patience. Thus would St. Peter say: though ye lead a temperate and discreet life, ye are not to think that ye shall live without conflict and persecution. For if ye believe, and lead a fair christian life, the world will not let it alone; it must persecute and hate you, in which you must show patience, which is a fruit of faith.

And to patience, godliness. That is, that we in all our outward life, whatever we do or suffer, should so conduct ourselves that we may serve God therein, not seeking our own honor and gain, but that God alone may be glorified thereby; and that we should so demean ourselves that men may take knowledge that we do all for God's sake.

V. 7. *And to godliness, brotherly love.* In this St. Peter obliges us all to extend a helping hand one to another, like brethren, so that one should protect another, and none hate nor despise nor injure another. This is also an evident proof of faith, whereby we show that we have the godliness of which he has spoken.

And to brotherly love (charity), common love. Common love extends to both friend and enemy, even to those who do not show themselves friendly and brotherly towards us. Thus St. Peter has here comprehended in few words whatever pertains to the christian life, and whatever are the works and fruits of faith, discretion, temperance, patience, a God-fearing life, brotherly love, and kindness to every one.

V. 8. *For if such dwell richly in you, it will not permit you to be idle or unfruitful in the knowledge of our Lord Jesus Christ.* That is, if ye do such works, then are ye on the right path, then do ye have a real faith, and the knowledge of Christ becomes active and fruitful in you. Therefore see to it that ye be not such as beat the air. Restrain your body, and act toward your neighbor even in such a manner as ye know that Christ has done toward you.

V. 9. *But to whomsoever such is wanting, he is blind, gropes with the hand, and has forgotten the purifying of his former sins.* Whoever has not such a preparation of the fruits of faith, gropes like a blind man here and there, rests in such a life that he knows not what his state is, has not real faith, and has of the knowledge of Christ nothing more than that he can say he has heard it. Therefore he goes along and gropes like a blind man on the way, in an unconscious life, and has forgotten that he was baptized and his sins were forgiven him, and is unthankful, and is an idle, negligent man, who suffers nothing to go to his heart, and neither feels nor tastes such great grace and blessing.

This is the admonition which St. Peter gives to us who believe, to urge and enforce those works by which we shall evidence that the true faith is in us. And, besides, this ever remains true, that faith alone justifies; where this then is present, there works must follow.—What follows further, now, is meant to strengthen us.

V. 10. *Wherefore, dear brethren, give so much the more diligence to make your calling and election sure.* The election and eternal foreknowledge of God is indeed in itself sure enough, so that man does not need to make that sure. The calling is also effectual and sure. For whoever hears the Gospel, and believes thereon, and is baptized, he is called and saved. Since we then are also thereunto called, we should apply so much diligence (says Peter), that our calling and election may be assured with us also, and not only with God. This is now such a mode of scriptural expression as St. Paul uses, Eph. ii., "Ye were strangers to the covenant of promise, so that ye had no hope and were without God in the world." For although there is no man, neither bad nor good, over whom God does not reign, since all creatures are His, yet Paul says he has no God who does not know, love, and trust Him, although he had his being in God

Himself. So here, also; although the calling and election are effectual enough in themselves, yet with you it is not yet effectual and assured, since you are not yet certain that it includes you. Therefore St. Peter would have us make such calling and election sure, by good works.

Thus you see what this Apostle attributes to the fruits of faith. Although they are due to our neighbor, that he may be benefited by them, still the fruit is not to be wanting, that faith may thereby become stronger, and do more and more of good works. Besides, this is quite another kind of power from that of the body, for that grows weary and wastes away if it is used and urged somewhat too far: but as to this spiritual power, the more it is used and urged, the stronger it becomes; and it suffers injury if it is not exercised. For this reason did God introduce Christianity at the first in such a manner as He did, driven and tried by the wrestling of faith, in shame, death, and bloodshed, that it might become truly strong and mighty, and that the more it was oppressed the more it might rise above it. This is St. Peter's meaning in this place, that we should not let faith rust and lie still, since it is so ordained that it is ever made more and more strong by trial and exercise, until it is assured of its calling and election, and cannot fail.

And here is also a bound set as to how we should proceed with reference to election. There are many light-minded persons who have not felt much of the power of faith, who fall in this matter, stumbling upon it; and they trouble themselves at first with it, and by reason would satisfy themselves whether they are elected, so that they may be assured whereon they stand. But desist from this, at once; it is a thing that cannot be apprehended (grasped). But if you will be assured, you must reach it by the way which St. Peter here strikes out for you. If you choose another for yourself, you have failed already, and your own experience must teach you so. If faith is properly exercised and tried, then are you at last assured of the fact that you cannot fail, as now further follows:

For if ye do these things ye shall never fall. That is, ye are to stand fast, not stumble nor sin, but go onward thoroughly upright and active, and all shall go well with you. But if you would set it right by your reasonings, the devil will soon throw you into despair and hatred of God.

V. 11. *And so shall an entrance be ministered unto you abundantly, into the everlasting kingdom of our Lord and Saviour Jesus Christ.* This is the way by which we enter the kingdom of heaven. Therefore, no one should propose, by such dreams and reasonings concerning faith as he has invented in his heart, to enter therein. There must be a living, active, tried faith. God help us! How have our deceivers written, taught and spoken against this text, yet whoever has even the least measure and only a spark of faith, shall be saved when he comes to die.

If you would pry into this matter, and in this way attain such faith quickly and suddenly, you will then have waited too long. Yet you are to understand well, that they who are strong have enough to do, although we are not to despair even of such as are weak, for it may indeed well happen that they shall endure, though it will be sorely and hardly, and will cost much striving; but whoever carefully sees to it in his life, that faith is invigorated and made strong by good works, he shall have an abundant entrance, and with calm spirit and confidence go into that life to come, so that he shall die comfortably, and despise this life, and even triumphantly go on, and with gladness hasten to that. But those, who would come in otherwise, shall not enter thus with joy; the door shall not stand open to them so wide; they shall, moreover, not have such an abundant entrance, but it shall be, narrow and a hard one, so that they tremble, and would rather their life-day should be in weakness, than that they should die.

V. 12. *Wherefore I will not be negligent to remind you always of such things, although ye know them, and are established in this present truth.* That is the same that we also have often said, although God has now let such a great light go forth through the revelation of the Gospel, so that we know what true christian life and doctrine is, and see how all Scripture insists upon it, yet this (light) we are not to neglect but use daily, not for doctrine, but for the sake of remembrance. For there is a twofold office in the christian church, as St. Paul says, Rom. xii.: "If any one teaches, let him wait on teaching; if any one admonishes, let him wait on admonition." To teach, is when any one lays down the ground of faith, and sets it forth to those who have no knowledge of it. But to admonish, or as Peter here says, *to remind*, is to preach to those who know and have heard the matter already, so that they are seized hold of and awakened, in order that they should not be heedless, but go onward and prosper. We are all beladen with the old sluggard load, with our flesh and blood, that chooses for ever the byroad, and keeps us ever subject to its load, so that the soul easily falls asleep. Therefore we are ever to urge and shake it, as a master urges his servants, lest they become sluggish, although they know very well what they should do; for while we must pursue this course for our temporal support, far more must we do it in this case in spiritual matters.

V. 13. *For I count it proper, so long as I am in this tabernacle, to awaken and remind you.* Here St. Peter calls his body a tabernacle wherein the soul dwells; and it is a phrase like that where in the first Epistle he speaks of the body as a vessel or an instrument. So St. Paul also speaks, II. Cor. v.: "We know that if our earthly house of this tabernacle were broken down, that we have a house built by God, a house not made with hands, eternal in heaven, and for the same we long earnestly, for our dwelling which is from heaven. For as long as we are in this tabernacle we earnestly long," &c. Also, "but yet we are consoled and know that while we are at home in the body we are absent from the Lord, but we have far greater desire to be out of the body and to be at home with the Lord." There the Apostle Paul speaks also of the body as a house, and makes two homes, and two sojournings. So Peter speaks here of the body as a tabernacle wherein the soul rests, and he makes it mean enough; he will not call it a house, but a hut or pent-house, such as shepherds have. Great is the treasure, but small is the house in which it lies and dwells.

V. 14, 15. *For I know that I must soon lay off my tabernacle, even as the Lord Christ hath showed me. But I will take care that ye by all means, after my departure, may keep such things in your remembrance.* Here Peter testifies of himself that he has become assured of eternal life, and to him God had shown beforehand when he should die; but this took place for our and our faith's sake, for there must have been some such persons as knew assuredly that they were elected, who should lay down and settle faith, that we might know that they preached not the doctrine of men, but the word of God. But ere they have come to such an assurance, God has thoroughly proved them first, and purified them. Thus Peter now says, I will not only remind you with the living voice, but set such things also in writing, and charge you, through others, that ye ever hold them in remembrance, through my life and after my death, and not let them go. There see how great anxiety the Apostle had for souls; yet, alas! it has helped nothing.

V. 16-18. *For we have not followed cunningly devised fables, when we have made known unto you the power and coming of our Lord Jesus Christ, for we have been witnesses of His majesty, when He received from God the Father honor and praise, by a voice which came to Him from the excellent glory, this is my well-beloved Son, in whom I am well pleased; and this voice, which came from heaven, we heard, when we were with Him on the holy mount.* There St. Peter touches upon the history written in the Gospel, Matt. xvii., how Jesus took to Himself three of his disciples, Peter, James and John, and led them aside up a high mountain, and was glorified before them, and His face shone like the sun, and His clothing was white as the light, and there appeared to Him Moses and Elias, who spoke with Him, while a light cloud overshadowed them, and a voice out of the cloud said, This is my beloved Son, in whom I am well pleased; hear ye Him. When the disciples heard that, they fell on their faces, and were very much afraid. But Jesus went to them, roused them up, and said, stand up, be not afraid; then they lifted up their eyes, and saw no one but Jesus only, and when they went down from the mountain He charged them that they should tell no one of this sight till He arose from the dead.

So St. Peter would now say, that which I preach to you of Christ and of His coming, this Gospel that we preach, we have not devised or yet imagined, nor taken it from cunning fabulists who know how to speak brilliantly of all things (such as at that very time the Greeks were), for it is mere fable, and fancy, and idle babbling that they cunningly give forth, and wherein they would be wise,—such we have not listened to, nor have we followed them; that is, we preach not what is from the hands of men, but are sure that it is of God, and have become so through our eyes and ears;—that is to say, When we were with Christ upon the mountain, and saw and heard His glory; for His glory was this, that His face shone like the sun, and His clothing was as white as snow; besides, we heard a voice from the highest Majesty, "This is my beloved Son; hear ye Him."

So confident should every preacher be, and not be in doubt thereon, that he has God's word, that he could even die for it, since it is worth our life. Now there is no man so holy that he must needs die for the doctrine which he has taught of himself; wherefore it is inferred here that the Apostles have had assurance from God that their Gospel was God's word. And here it is also shown that the Gospel is nothing else than the preaching of Christ. Therefore we should hear no other preaching, for the Father will have no other. "That is my dear Son," He says; "hear Him." He is your Teacher—as though He had said, "When ye hear Him, then ye have heard me." Wherefore Peter now says, we have preached Christ and made Him known to you, that He is Lord, and rules over all things, and all power is His; and that whosoever believes on Him has likewise such power. Such things we have not ourselves devised, but have seen and heard them through God's revelation, by which He has charged us that we should hear Christ.

But why does Paul separate from one another the power and the coming of Christ? The power consists, as we have heard above, in that He is mighty over all things; that all must lie at His feet; and this shall continue as long as the world stands. While we are flesh and blood, and live upon the earth, so long shall Christ's kingdom flourish, even to the last day. Then shall come another period, when He shall give up the kingdom to God the Father, whereof St. Paul speaks, I. Cor. xv.: "Christ the first fruits; afterwards those that belong to Christ, who are His at His coming. Afterward is the end, when He shall answer for the kingdom to God and the Father." Also: "But when all shall be subject to Him, then shall the Son also be subject to Him who subdued all for Him."

How? Is then the kingdom not God the Father's now? Is not all subject to Him? Answer:—St. Paul explains himself in the same place, and says: "So that God may be all in all;" that is, whatsoever any one shall need or should have, that God will be; as St. Peter has told us above, that we should be partakers of the Divine nature. Wherefore we shall also have all that God has, and all that is needful for us we shall have in Him,—wisdom, righteousness, strength and life,—a truth which we now believe, hearing it merely, and having it in the word of God. But then shall the word cease, when our souls shall be enlarged and see and feel it all as a present thing. This is what St. Paul means, and St. Peter also: that the power of Christ's kingdom now proceeds; now He gives the word, and thereby, through His humanity, reigns over the devil, sin, death, and all things. But at the last day this shall be made clear. Therefore, although God ever rules, still it is not yet manifest to us. He clearly beholds us, but we behold Him not. Therefore must Christ surrender up to Him the kingdom, so that we also shall see it, while we then shall be Christ's brethren and God's children. Thus Christ received from God honor and glory (St. Peter here says) when the Father made all things subject to Him, and made Him Lord, and glorified Him by this voice, in which He says, "This is my well-beloved Son, in whom I am well pleased."

By this St. Peter would confirm his doctrine and preaching, that it might be known whence it came. But this experience was no more than that he had heard this, and was able to preach of it. But the Holy Spirit must also come and strengthen him, that he may believe in it, and preach and confess it cheerfully. The former thing belongs only to the office of the preacher, not to the soul; but this belongs to the Spirit.

V. 19. *We have also a sure word of Prophecy, and ye do well in that ye give heed to it, as to a light that shines in a dark place, till the day break and the morning star rise in your hearts.* There St. Peter grasps right hold upon the matter, and would say this much: all that I preach is to subserve this end, that your conscience may be assured, and your heart may stand firm on this, and not let itself be torn therefrom, and that thus both I and you may be certain that we have God's word. For it is an important matter as respects the Gospel that we should receive and hold it clean and pure, without addition and false doctrine. Therefore Peter begins henceforth to write against human doctrines.

But why does he say we have a sure word of prophecy? Answer: I hold, indeed, that we shall have no more prophets, such as the Jews had in former times in the Old Testament. But a prophet eminently should he be who preaches of Jesus Christ. Therefore, although many prophets in the Old Testament have foretold concerning things to come, yet they came and were sent by God, for this reason especially, that they should foretell Christ. Those, then, who believe on Christ are all prophets, for they have the true head-article that the prophets should have, although they have not the gift of making known things to come; for as we, through the faith of our Master, are Christ's brethren, are kings and priests, so are we prophets also, all of us through Christ. For we can all say what belongs to salvation and God's honor and a christian life, besides of future things, so much as this is necessarily known to us, viz., that the Last Day shall come, and that we shall rise from the dead; besides, we understand the whole substance of Scripture. Whereof Paul also says, I. Cor. xiv.: "Ye can all prophecy, one after another."

This now, is, what Peter says: we have such a word of prophecy as is sure in itself; see to it only that it be sure to you; and ye do well in paying heed to it:—as though he should say: It will be a thing of necessity to you to hold firmly by it; for it is in regard to the Gospel as though one were imprisoned in the house, in the midst of the night, when it was stock dark. Then it were a matter of necessity that one should kindle a light, till the day came when he could see. Eminently such is the Gospel in the midst of the night and darkness, for all human reason is mere error and blindness, while the world is even nothing else but a kingdom of darkness. In this darkness has God now kindled a light, even the Gospel, whereby we may see and walk, while we are on the earth, till the morning dawn comes and the day breaks.

Thus this text is also strongly against all human doctrine; for since the word of God is the light in a dark and gloomy place, it follows that all besides is darkness. For if there were another light besides the word, St. Peter would not have spoken as he has. Therefore look not to this, how gifted those men are with reason who teach any other doctrine, however grandly they put it forth; if you cannot trace God's word in it, then be in no doubt as to its being mere darkness. And let it not disturb you at all that they say they have the Holy Spirit. How can they have God's Spirit if they do not have His word? Wherefore they do nothing else but call darkness light and make the light darkness, as Isaiah says, chap. v.

This is God's word—even the Gospel—that we are ransomed by Christ from death, sin and hell: whoever hears that, he has this light and has kindled this lamp in his heart, even that by which we may see the one that enlightens us, and teaches us whatever we should know. But where this is not, there we rush on, and by matters and works of our own device would find out the way to heaven. Whereof, by your light, you can judge and see that it is darkness. Wherefore since they have not the light, neither would receive it, they must remain in darkness and blindness. For the light teaches us all that which we ought to know and what is necessary to salvation—a thing which the world by wisdom and reason knows not. And this light we must still have and depend upon, even to the last day. Then shall we have no more need of the word, just as we put out the lamp when the day breaks.

V. 20, 21. *And this ye should know first of all, that no prophecy of the Scripture is of any private interpretation; for prophecy came not aforetime by the will of man, but holy men of God spake as they were moved by the Holy Spirit.* Here Peter falls upon the matter of false doctrine: since ye know this, he says, that we have the word of God, abide thereon, and suffer yourselves not to be drawn from it by others that teach falsely, though they come and give forth that they have the Holy Spirit. For this ye should know first of all (the second matter he would speak of afterward), that no prophecy of the Scripture is of any private interpretation; by this be directed, and do not think that ye shall explain the Scripture by your own reason and wisdom.

In this the private interpretation of Scripture by all the fathers is thrown down and rejected, and it is forbidden to build on such interpretation. Though Jerome, or Augustine, or any one of the fathers have explained it of himself, yet would not we have it from him. Peter has forbidden you to explain it of yourself at all. The Holy Spirit will explain it Himself, or it shall remain unexplained. If now any one of the holy fathers can prove that he has his explanation from the Scriptures, which give assurance that it should be so explained, then it is right; where this is not the case, I for one shall not believe him. Thus Peter lays hold on the boldest and best teachers; wherefore we should rest assured that none is to be believed who sets the Scripture forth where he of himself opens and explains it. For there can be no true sense obtained by private interpretation. Here have all the teachers and fathers who have explained the Scripture stumbled, so far as they are extant to us. As when they refer the passage of Christ, Matt. xvi.: *Thou art Peter, and on this rock will I build my church,* to the Pope. That is a human, self-invented explanation; therefore, no one is to believe them, for they cannot prove out of the Scripture that Peter is ever spoken of as Pope. But this we can prove, that the rock is Christ and faith, as Paul says. This explanation is the right one; for of this we are sure, it has not been invented by men, but drawn from God's word. Now what is found written and foretold in the prophets, says Peter, that men have not searched out nor invented; but holy and pious men have spoken it from the Holy Spirit.

Thus this is the first chapter, wherein St. Peter has first of all taught us what those really good works are whereby we must give proof of our faith. In the second place, that no man in Christendom should preach anything but God's word alone. The reason why it should be so is no other, as we have said, except that men should preach that word which shall remain forever, whereby souls may be won, and eternal life. Now there follows a just admonition, which Christ and Paul and all the Apostles have also given, that each should look out for himself and guard against false teachers.

It is especially necessary for us to observe it carefully, so that we shall not suffer that right and authority which all Christians have, to be torn from us, to judge and decide on all doctrines; and shall not let it come to this, that we first wait till the Councils determine what we are to believe, and then follow that. This we are now to look at.

CHAPTER II.

V. 1. *But there were false teachers also among the people, as also among you there shall be false teachers.* This is what St. Peter would say: All prophecy must proceed from the Holy Spirit, even to the end of the world, just as it has gone forth from the beginning of the world, so that nothing shall be preached but what is God's word. Yet it has ever so happened, that close upon the true prophets and word of God, there have been false teachers, and so also it shall continue. Therefore, since ye have God's word, ye should take heed to yourselves that ye do not have false teachers besides. This is a sufficient admonition, and it cannot fail where the true word of God is preached; that close upon it false teachers also should rise up. The reason is this,—not every one lays hold on the word, and believes thereon, although it is preached to all. They who believe thereon, follow it, and hold it fast; but the greater part, they who do not believe, receive a false sense therefrom, whence they become false teachers. This matter we have not seriously considered, nor have we attended to this warning; but we have gone astray, and whatever has been preached that we have done. Thereon we have stumbled and fallen, and been led away by delusion, as though the Pope, with his priests and monks, could not err. Thus those that should have been on their guard against such things, have been the first that have urged them upon us. So that we are not free from blame, though we have a wrong belief, and follow after false teachers: it shall be of no help to us, that we have not known, since we were warned beforehand. Besides, God has bidden us that we should each determine what this or that one preaches, and give account thereof; if we do not, then are we lost; wherefore it concerns every one's own soul's salvation to know what God's word is, and what false doctrines are.

Such warnings against false teachers are, besides, very frequent, here and there, throughout the Scripture. St. Paul, Acts xx., gives just such an admonition in his preaching, when he blesses those of Ephesus and gives them his farewell; and he speaks in this manner: "I know that after my departure there shall come in among you grievous wolves, who shall not spare the flock; yea, there shall even of your own selves arise men who shall teach corrupt doctrine, who shall draw disciples after them." Christ proclaims it also in Matt. xx.: "If anyone shall say to you (he says), lo! here is Christ, or lo! there, then are ye not to believe it; for there shall arise false Christs and false prophets, and great signs and wonders shall they do, that shall lead into error, if it were possible, even the elect." And again, Paul, I. Tim., iv.: "The Spirit speaks expressly that in the last times some shall depart from the faith, and cleave to erring spirits and doctrines of the devil by which they speak lies in hypocrisy." As forcefully as such admonition has gone forth, so careful should we have been; yet it has been of no avail. The admonition has been kept silent, and thus we have still wandered, and suffered ourselves to be led astray.

Now let us see who those false teachers may be, of whom Peter here speaks. I think that God has ordained by special counsel that our teachers should have been called doctors, that it might be seen whom Peter means. For he as much as uses the word here; false doctors,—that is, false teachers, he says,—not false prophets or false apostles. In this he fairly hits the high schools, where such a class of men is made, and whence all the preachers have come forth into the world; so that there is not even a city under the Popedom, which does not have such teachers made in the high schools. For all the world thinks that they are the fountain, the streams of which are to teach the people. This is a desperate error, since no more cruel thing has ever come upon the earth than has come forth from the high schools. Therefore Peter says, that such vain, false teachers are to be; but what shall they do? This follows further:

Who shall privily introduce damnable heresies. He calls them damnable heresies (sects), or states and orders, because whosoever is persuaded into them is already lost. These shall they secretly bring in, he says, not that they shall preach that the Gospel and the Holy Scriptures are false, for that would have worked quite against them,—but these names, God, Christ, faith, church, baptism, sacrament, they shall still hold, and suffer to continue. But under these names they bring forward and set up something of another sort. For there is a great difference, whether I say this man preaches against this doctrine or in accordance with it. When I preach thus, that Christ is the Son of God and truly man, and whoever believes on Him shall be saved,—that is right preaching and the true Gospel. But if one preaches that Christ is not the Son of God, nor truly man, moreover that faith does not save, it is said in plain contradiction to it. Whence St. Peter speaks not (for this is what our high schools, priests and monks do not attempt), except of those associate doctrines which they introduce through the true doctrine. As when they speak after this manner,—it is true that Christ was God, and is man; that He died for our sins, and no one can be saved who does not believe upon Him. But that belongs only to the common estate (of Christians); but we will set up a more complete one, in which men shall vow chastity, poverty, and obedience, as well as fast, endow institutions, &c. Whoever does this shall go full tide up to heaven. Where now men preach and hear such things as that there is nothing better and more saving than virginity and obedience, and that the monk and the priest are in a higher and more perfect estate than mankind in general, there is nothing said against the pure christian doctrine directly, nor are faith and baptism denied, nor that Christ is the Saviour. But yet there is such doctrine brought in with them, leading men away from the right path, that they build upon their own life and works, and hold nothing more in regard to Christ, but just these words: we believe that Christ is the Son of God, and man; that He died and rose again; that He is the Saviour of the world, &c. But they repose no faith in Him, for if they did that, they would not rest an hour upon their life.

Thus they have also preached and said among the people: "Ye are Christians already, but that is not enough; ye must also do such and such works, build churches and cloisters, found masses and vigils," &c.

The great multitude has tumbled into this notion, and thought it was right. Hereby Christendom is divided and separated into as many sects, almost, as there are states and people.

But this is what men should have preached and taught: Ye are Christians indeed, and, just as well as those a hundred miles away, ye have all of you one Christ, one baptism, one faith, one spirit, one word, one God; so that no work that man can do helps to make a Christian. Thus, were men included in a common faith, there would be no difference before God, but one would be as another. This unity have they rent asunder, in that they say, "You are a Christian, but you must do works in order that you may be saved;" and thus they lead us away from faith to works. Therefore St. Peter says, if we will explain it right, nothing but this: there shall come high schools, doctors, priests and monks, and all classes of men, who shall bring in ruinous sects and orders, and shall lead the world astray by false doctrines. Such are those whom he means here, for they all hold to the notion that their state and Order saves them, and they cause men to build and trust thereon; for where men do not hold to this view, they carefully keep clear of entering them.

And shall deny the Lord who bought them. "Oh," say they, "we do not deny the Lord at all!" But if any one says, "Since you are ransomed by Christ, and His blood blots out your sin, what will you blot out by your mode of life?" Then they say, "Ah! faith does not do it alone, works must also aid towards it." Thus they confess the Lord Christ indeed with their mouth, but with their hearts they quite deny him. See how admirably St. Peter expresses it. They deny the Master, he says, who has bought them: they should be under Him as under a master whose own they were. But now, though they believe indeed that He is their master and has purchased the whole world by His blood, yet they do not believe that they are bought, and that He is their master; and they say "He has indeed bought and ransomed them, but then this is not enough,—we must first by our works expiate the sin and make satisfaction for it." But we say, if you yourself take away and blot out your sin, what has Christ then done? You certainly cannot make two Christs who take away sin.

He should and must be the only one that puts away sin. If that be true, then I cannot understand how I am myself to cancel my own sin. If I do it, I can neither say nor believe that He takes it away. And it is the same thing with denying Christ; for although they hold Christ to be their master, they deny that He has bought them. They believe, indeed, that He sits above in heaven and is Lord; but that which is His peculiar office, to take away sin, this they take from Him, and ascribe it to their own works. Thus they leave to Him nothing more than the name and title; but His work, His power, and His office, they will have themselves. So that Christ has truly said, "Many shall come in my name, and say, I am Christ, and shall seduce many." For they are this preëminently, not who say, "I am called Christ," but "I am He;" for they seize to themselves the office that belongs to Christ, thrust Him from His throne, and seat themselves thereon. This we see before our eyes, insomuch that no one can deny it. Therefore St. Peter calls them damnable or ruinous heresies, for they run all of them straight to hell; so that I suppose that among a thousand, hardly one is saved. For whoever shall be saved therein must say this much: "My obedience, my chastity, &c., do not save me; my works do not take away any sin from me." But how many there are who have these views, and remain in such a damnable state!

And shall bring upon themselves quick damnation. That is, their condemnation shall quickly overtake them; although it is plain that God forbears long, yet He will come soon enough. But it is not a thing that respects the body, that we should be able to see it with our eyes, but just as the fifty-fourth Psalm says, "They shall not live out half their day;" that is, death shall seize upon them ere they themselves suspect, so that they shall say, like Hezekiah, Is. xxxviii., "I have said in the midst of my life, I must go down into the grave;" as though they should say, "O Lord God, is death already here?" For those men who do not live by faith, who are never more and more weary of life, the longer they live the longer they would live, and the holier they seem the more terrible will death be to them, especially to those who have scrupulous consciences and cruelly urge and vex themselves by works, for it is not possible to vanquish death by human powers. Where faith is wanting, the conscience must tremble and despair. Where faith is strong, death comes too slow; while, on the other hand, he comes to the unbelieving always too soon, for there is no end to the thirst and love of life.

This is what Peter means here: these people who set up such sects, and so deny Christ, must come to die with the greatest unwillingness, trembling and desponding; for they can have no other thought but this, "Who knows whether God will be gracious to me and will forgive my sins?" and they remain forever in such doubt, "who knows it,—who knows it?" and their conscience is never at peace. The longer they thus continue, the more terrible is death to them; for death cannot first be subdued, till sin and an evil conscience have been taken away. So will their condemnation come upon them hastily, so that they must abide in eternal death.

V. 2. *And many shall follow their destruction.* It may be seen before our eyes, that it has come to pass just as St. Peter first declared. There has been not a father or mother who has not wished to have a priest, monk, or nun, from among their children. Thus one fool has made another; for when people have seen the misfortune and misery that are found in the marriage state, and have not known that it is a safe estate, they have wished to do the best for their children, to help them to a happy life and freedom from wretchedness. So that St. Peter has foretold here nothing else but just that the world should become full of priests, monks, and nuns. Thus youth, and the best that are in the world, have run with the multitude to the devil. St. Peter says it, alas! only too truly, that many should follow them to this destruction.

By whom the way of truth shall be blasphemed. This, too, is a thing that may be seen before our eyes. To blaspheme is to libel, damn, and curse; as when one condemns the christian estate as error and heresy. If one now should preach and say that their course is against the Gospel, because they lead men away from faith to works, then they go about and cry, "Thou art cursed, thou leadest the world astray." And they blaspheme even yet more, in perverting what Christ has said, and saying no! to it. As when they, out of that which Christ has bidden, make nothing but a story, so that they forbid what Christ would have left free, and make that sin which He makes none, besides condemning and burning whoever preaches against it. The way of truth is a well-ordered life and walk, in which there is no fraud nor hypocrisy, such as that faith is in which all Christians walk. This they cannot bear; they blaspheme and condemn it, so as to praise and sustain their Order and sect.

V. 3. *And through avarice, with feigned words shall they make merchandise of you.* This is specially the way of all false teachers, that they preach from avarice, that they may fill their belly, just as we see that not one of them has held a mass or vigil *gratis*. So, too, there is never a cloister or monastery built, whereto there must not fall a full measure of tribute. So, too, there is not a cloister in the world that serves the world for God's sake. It is all of it done merely for gold. But if any one really preaches faith, *that* does not bring in much gold; for then, all pilgrimages, indulgences, cloisters, and monasteries, to which more than half the wealth of the world has been devoted and given, must cease; whereof none has any use but the priests and monks only.

But how do they act to get the gold into their own hands? *With feigned words*, says Peter, *shall they make merchandise of you.* For they have selected the word by which they make money of the people, for this very purpose, as when they say, "If you give the dear Virgin, or this or that saint so many hundred florins, you do a most excellent good work, and merit so much indulgence and forgiving of sin, and ransom as many souls from purgatory."

This and the like are just carefully feigned words, to the end that they may shave us of our gold; for in all this there is really no desert, nor grace, nor blotting out of sin. Still they explain the noble words of Scripture all of them in such a way, that they may traffic with them for gold. So, also, there has come of the holy, gracious Sacrament, nothing else but a traffic, for they do nothing with it but smear the people's mouth, and scrape their gold from them. Observe, then, whether St. Peter has not drawn and painted our clergy to the life.

Whose judgment now of a long time lingereth not, and their damnation slumbereth not. They shall not drive this on at length, nor carry it out, (he would say); for when they urge it most strongly, their sentence and condemnation shall fall upon them. Even now it goes forth; they shall not escape it,—as St. Paul also says, II. Tim. iii.: "Their folly shall be revealed to all, so that they shall be put to shame;" God grant that they may be converted and come out from their dangerous state, when they hear and understand it, for though there are some who have not been seduced into this state, yet is it in itself nothing but a mere pernicious sect.

Thus St. Peter has attempted to describe the shameful, godless life that should succeed to the genuine doctrines of the Gospel, which the Apostles preached. Now he goes further, and sets before us three terrible examples—of the angels, of the whole world, and of Sodom, how God condemned them,—and speaks thus:

V. 4. *For if God spared not the angels that sinned, but has thrust them down to hell in chains of darkness, and given them over to be reserved for judgment.* By these words St. Peter terrifies those who live so gay and secure as we see those do who cleave to that which the Pope has enacted, in that they are so confident and shameless that they would tread every one under foot. Therefore he would say this much: Is it not great presumption on their part that they go on so eagerly, and would bring every thing to pass by their own head, as though God should yield to them, and spare them, who yet spared not the angels? As though he had said, these examples should justly terrify even the saints, when they see such a severe sentence in that God has not spared those high spirits and noble beings who are far more learned and wise than we, but has thrust them into chains of darkness;—such is the severe sentence and condemnation whereto He has ordained them, in which they are held bound and imprisoned, so that they cannot flee away out of the hands of God, since they have been cast into outer darkness, as Christ says in the Gospel.

And here St. Peter shows that the devils have not yet their final punishment, but still go about in a hardened, desperate state, and look every moment for their judgment, just as a man that is condemned to death is perfectly desperate, hardened, and more and more wicked. But their punishment has not yet overtaken them, but they are now only bound and reserved for it. This is the first example.—Now follows the second:

V. 5. *And spared not the old world, but saved Noah, the eighth person, a preacher of righteousness, and brought the flood upon the world of the ungodly.* This is, moreover, a fearful example, such indeed that there is not a more bitter one in the Scripture. One might almost despair in view of it, who was even strong in faith. For when such language and such a sentence go to a man's heart, and he thinks of it, that so he too ought to die, he must tremble and despond, if he is not well prepared, since among so many in the whole world, no one but these eight only were saved. But how have they deserved it, that God by such a severe sentence should have drowned all, one with another, in one mass, husband and wife, master and servant, young and old, beast and bird? Because they led such a wicked life. Noah was a pious man and a preacher of righteousness, and had already lived five hundred years, before the flood, when God commanded him to build an ark,—on which he wrought a hundred years thereafter; and he led throughout a uniformly godly life. Whence you may judge what a cross he had to bear, and in what care and anxiety the pious man stood, when he must needs show, by words and works, that he was a Christian. For it cannot be allowed that faith should conceal itself, and not break out before men by words and well-doing. So this man, alone, perhaps, long before God bade him build the ark, exercised the preacher's office, and spread the word of God not in one place, but, beyond doubt, through many lands. So that he must thus have suffered much and great persecution even, inasmuch as he is specially (as Peter says) sustained and kept by God, or he would soon have been overwhelmed and slain; for he must thus needs bear upon himself much envy and hate, and make even many high, wise and holy people his enemies. Had the matter not been helped, then the world would have despised the word of God, and been ever growing more wicked. When they had now driven on their wickedness to great length, God said, "My Spirit shall not always strive with men, since they are flesh; yet will I give them the term of an hundred and twenty years." Besides, "I will destroy from the earth the men whom I have created, from man even to the reptile, (I will destroy them)." These words he preached and enforced daily, and began to build the ark as had been commanded him; and he labors on it a hundred years. But the people laughed at him, and were only so much the more obstinate and foolish. But what the sin was for which God destroyed the world, the text of Gen. vi. tells us, that the children of God,— that is, those who came of holy parents, and were instructed and brought up in the faith and in the knowledge of God, sought after the daughters of men, since they were fair, and took for their wives whom they would. Thereafter they came from this to be powerful tyrants, who did everything that they chose after their own caprice; wherefore God punished the world and destroyed it by the flood.

V. 6. *And reduced the cities of Sodom and Gomorrah to ashes, overthrowing and condemning them.* This is the third example drawn from the destruction of those five cities, Gen. xix. Whereof also the prophet Ezekiel speaks, in chap. xvi., addressing the city of Jerusalem: "this was the sin of Sodom thy sister,— pride, fullness of bread, luxury and idleness, and that to the poor they did not reach out the hand, and have lifted themselves up, and have wrought such shameful cruelty before me that I have even destroyed them." For Sodom was a land, like the garden of the Lord, as Moses says, and a rich mine of costly oil and wine and all things, so that every one would think, here dwells God. For this they were secure, and led such a shameful life as Moses has written of. Such sin breaks out only where there is an assurance that they have enough to eat and drink and to spare, and idleness is joined therewith; just as we still see, the richer cities are the more shamefully do men live in them; but where there is hunger and cumber there the sins are so much the fewer. Therefore God permits, in regard to those that are His, that their education should be severe, that they may remain pure.

These are the three fearful examples whereby St. Peter threatens those that are godless. And as he insists upon it so, we must hold that this is its import. And it is spoken especially of the spiritual order—pope, cardinals, bishops, priests, monks and nuns, and all who hang upon them. These are, as it were, angels in the Apostles' stead, appointed to this very end, that they should preach and make known God's word; for an angel is a messenger, or one sent, who discharges his message by word of mouth, for which reason preachers are called in Scripture angels,—that is, messengers of God. Such angels should our clergy be. But as these angels of old fell off from God, and set themselves above God, and wished to be their own masters, so these do also, and have nothing but just the name of messengers, as those have the name alone of angels. So these also, as they have gone off from God, shall be held in chains of darkness and reserved to condemnation; as he has said above, that their sentence does not linger, nor their damnation slumber, although punishment has not as yet overtaken them.

Beside, they are like that former world, who, although they heard the prophets and the word of God, yet blasphemed and reviled them; and as Moses writes, took to themselves wives according to their pleasure, whomsoever they would, and became great and powerful tyrants. Observe, then, whether all that which Moses wrote of those is not now taking place. These are the great scamps that live in revelry, oppress the world by their tyranny, and no one must ask of them why they play the fool. Whomsoever they will they take for wife or daughter, in spite of any one's complaining; for if any one finds fault with it they are themselves judges, and there is no one who can win their cause of them. Therefore whatever they can devise to bring into their hands by oppression or fines, that also they execute. And if any one should seize upon it, they then say, "it is the spiritual possession of the churches; it is exempt, and no one must lay hands on it." And as to those who preach God's word, they punish them to the taking away their life, and declare God's sentence on those that laugh at them; they will not hear the word, and they persecute the very preachers of righteousness, and, remaining great and mighty lords, would retain their title, so that they may be called spiritual, like those that are God's children, yet rule with full power in all obstinacy; but they must at last be subdued and destroyed. But the others who preach God's word shall be kept and sustained.

Thirdly: as the land where the cities of Sodom and Gomorrah were was a mine of fat, and all had enough of what the earth could bear, thereby the people became indolent, glutted themselves with food and drink, and to none of the poor did they reach out the hand. Such is the case also with our Spiritual Estate, who possess generally the best land, the best castles and cities, and the greatest rents and tribute, while they have enough also to eat and drink. Besides, there is not a more indolent class of people on earth, that lives without anything of care or labor, and is fed by the sweat of the poor. But what indolence brings along we may see before our eyes. The Pope forbids them to take a married wife, so that if they then keep their concubines and have children they must give gold to the bishop for every child, whereby they will smooth the thing over and cancel the sin. I will not here speak of other secret sins which one dare not lightly stir up.

Finally, you here see that St. Peter accounts of the Spiritual Estate no otherwise than as of Sodom and Gomorrah, for they are all such people as no one can be benefited by who lend none a helping hand, but seize to themselves all they can, under the pretence, which they put forth, that what is given to them is given to God, and they let no one be helped though he suffer want. Wherefore just as those were overthrown and turned to ashes, so shall these also be destroyed at the last day.

V. 7. *And rescued righteous Lot who was troubled greatly by the libertine course of the wicked.* Was it not a great aggravation that they not only rushed publicly and shamelessly into whoredom and adultery, but into such sins as may not be mentioned,—insomuch that they did not even spare the angels who came to Lot, and they rushed on thus in their course, both young and old, in all the corners of the city! Against this, righteous Lot had daily preached and warned them, but all in vain, except that he is vexed by them, since he must stand still yet cannot smooth over the evil, just as is the case with us now, for there is no more hope to reform or help this grievous course of life that the world leads.

V. 8. *For while that righteous man dwelt among them, since he must see and hear it all, they vexed his righteous soul from day to day, by their ungodly deeds.* Here Peter describes the cross which this holy man must have borne, while he preached to the people and brought up his daughters in faith; and so it is accounted toward him by God. Now St. Peter decides how the godless shall be kept for punishment at the last day.

V. 9, 10. *The Lord knoweth how to deliver the godly out of temptation, but to reserve the unjust to the day of judgment to be punished, but especially those that walk after the flesh in the lust of uncleanness.* This is certainly deep passion and earnestness in the Apostle. If God spared not (says he) the young new world, how much more severely and fearfully will he now punish those to whom the Gospel has been revealed and preached, and before which no such great light has arisen; as Christ also declares, Matt. xi., "Woe to thee, Capernaum, who art exalted even to heaven! thou shalt be thrust down to hell; for if the deeds that have been done in thee had been done in Sodom, it had been standing at this day; for I say unto you, it shall be more tolerable for Sodom in that day than for you." But such threatening is in vain. The godless do not turn themselves for it.

To live in the lust of uncleanness is to live just like an unreasoning beast—according to mere sense and every kind of lust. So everything is ordered by the Pope, ordered as it has pleased him, and all must subserve their wilfulness and tyranny; and they have warped and explained all just as it has pleased them, and thereupon said, "the holy See at Rome cannot err," while there is not one who has preached anything of faith or love; but they have taught nothing except what they have themselves imagined.

V. 10, 11. *And those who despise governments, presumptuous, self-conceited, tremble not to revile dignities, whereas the angels, who are greater in power and might, bring not a railing accusation against them before the Lord.* He calls kings, princes and lords, and all civil magistracy, governments; and not the Pope and bishops, for these are not to be lords at all; since Christ, in the New Testament, is represented only as a servant—so that one Christian is to serve another, and hold him in honor. Wherefore *this* is St. Peter's meaning: that they should be subject and obedient to civil magistracy; as the sword is introduced by God's ordinance, stand thou in fear. Yet they do the very reverse of this. They have excepted themselves, and say they are not subject to the civil magistracy; yea, they have not only excepted themselves, but have even subjected those to themselves, and trampled on them with their feet, and permit themselves shamelessly to be called lords, even by kings and princes, just as the Pope writes of himself that he is a lord of heaven and earth, and has in his hand both the civil and spiritual sword, and that every one must fall at his feet.

Besides, St. Peter says that they do not tremble to blaspheme dignities; for it has become to the Pope a small and slight thing to put kings and princes under ban, to curse them, and depose them, and moreover excite mischief among them, and stir them up one against another. And as to those who have opposed themselves, these he has quickly overthrown and trodden on, not because they have done anything against faith or love, but only because they have not been willing to be subject to the Romish See, or kiss the Pope's foot, because, forsooth, his power was as much greater than that of secular princes as the sun is than the moon, or as the heaven is high above the earth; so they lyingly blasphemed, while yet they are bound to be subject and obedient to them, and should bless them and pray for them, as Christ our Lord subjected Himself to Pilate, and gave to the Emperor the penny tribute. They ought, therefore, to tremble at reviling against dignities; yet are they unaffrighted and presumptuous in regard to it, and they revile with all zeal and recklessness, while yet if even the strongest angels cannot endure judgment against themselves from the Lord, and besides are struck dumb from cursing and reviling the very One from whom they cannot escape, how then will these wretched people endure it?

V. 12, 13. *But these are like unreasoning brutes, that are born, in accordance with their nature, to be taken and destroyed; they speak evil of that which they do not know, and in their own ruin shall they perish, and receive therefrom the reward of their unrighteousness.* Unreasonable brutes, Peter calls them, as though they had within them not a spark of anything that smacked of spirit, performed no spiritual duty that they should do, but lived like the fool, and became effeminate through a carnal life. But in that he says they are naturally born to be taken and destroyed, it may be understood in a two-fold manner: first, as of those that take and destroy, such as the wolf, lion, bear, the sparrow-hawk and eagle,—so these grasp to themselves, and tear away from others all they can, goods and honor. Secondly, of those that shall be taken, crushed and destroyed at the judgment of the last day.

They count temporal enjoyment as the fullness of pleasure. See how indignant St. Peter is! I must not chide the young gentlemen so grievously. They think if they only live well, and have good times, then they have enough of all things, and are right well off; this one can easily trace in their spiritual claim, when they say that whoever touches them as to their property or their belly, is of the devil. They themselves cannot deny this, that their whole system is framed to this end, that they may have lazy and idle times, and all that can suffice them. They will lade themselves with no trouble or labor, but every one must make and devote enough for them. They must go to the choir and pray. God has commanded all men that they should eat their bread by the sweat of their brow, and He has imposed trial and anxiety upon all. Meanwhile, these young masters would slip their heads out of this noose, and busy themselves with kisses. But this is the greatest blindness, that they are so dumb, and therefore hold that such a shameful life is right and lovely.

Spots are they, and blemishes. They know not but that they adorn Christianity, as the sun and moon do heaven, and are the noblest and most precious jewels, like gold and precious stones; yet St. Peter calls them spots of shame and blemishes. The true christian life develops from faith, serves every one in love, bears the holy cross, which is the true badge, ornament, jewel and honor of the Christian Church;—but these have, in place of the cross, lust and luxury; instead of love to their neighbor, they seek their own interest, snatch all to themselves, and let nothing go from themselves to another for his advantage. Thus they know of faith just nothing at all. For they are nothing but the spots and stains which Christianity must have as its shame and derision. That is chiding enough, certainly, for our spiritual lords.

They lead an effeminate life through your charity, feast richly on your goods. What was given at first out of christian love, to procure a common fund for widows and worthy persons, and also for the poor, so that no one among the Christians need suffer want or beg,—property of this kind is now all devoted to monasteries and cloisters, from which our ecclesiastics fill their bellies, living upon it most luxuriously, and revelling in it; and to this end they say it belongs to them, and no one shall restrain them for it. The Holy Spirit will not permit that the servants of the church should lead an effeminate life from other people's labor; but to the laboring class, and to man, woman and child generally, was it properly devoted of old.

V. 14. *They have eyes full of adultery.* Such must always follow when the body is crammed with food and drink, and loiters indolent, as was said above. Wherefore does St. Peter say,—not, they are adulterers,—but, *they have eyes full of adultery?* It is as much as though he should say, They think ever on nothing but fornication, and can never restrain their roguery, nor be satisfied and quiet. This is the cause of their continual gluttony and revel, so far as they can push it, and thus they are suffered to live at large and unpunished, just as they like,—as follows:

Their sin is not to be interfered with. The Pope has forbidden any prince or secular magistrate to punish ecclesiastics, and where they maintain their own authority he puts them under bann. But this matter is committed to the bishops; yet, since they are knaves themselves, they look through their fingers. Thus they have excepted themselves from subjection to civil government and the sword, so that no one shall dare to restrain them in their caprice, and they all live according to their own lusts, like those of old before the deluge.

They allure to themselves light-minded souls. With such great show as they exhibit in their knavish life, as going through with mass, begging, singing, &c., do they allure and draw light-minded and unstable souls, who are without faith, to imagine that everything is spiritual; and all is shaped to this end, that men may think that in that estate every one shall have enough, and good times besides, and, moreover, that he shall reach heaven; and yet it is all done only to this end, that they may fill their bellies and their dirt-bag.

They have a heart penetrated with covetousness. This vice is so gross and open among the ecclesiastics, that even the common people have complained of it. Yet he says not, they are covetous, but, they have a heart penetrated with covetousness, and especially exercised therein. This may be seen in the fact that they have invented so many swindling and cunning stories that it is impossible to count them, by which they bring all the world's wealth to themselves.

All that this class practices and pursues is simple, pure covetousness, and must all be worth money enough. They show it also most plainly of all, as they are equipped and prepared on all sides to call on men for their gold; so that St. Peter was certainly not a liar.

They are children of cursing. That is, in the Hebrew, as much as to say, they are cursed children, subject to the curse of God, so that before God they have no favor or salvation, and only become more wicked from day to day, and continually, also, greater blasphemers of God; so that they surely lade themselves full enough with the wrath and terrible judgment of God. That is surely spoken severely and fearfully enough; while it is high time that whoever can flee and run, should flee and run forth from this cursed state. Should we bear such a *title, that* is certainly pitiful; but if the High Majesty also arraigns, curses, and condemns,—who will endure it?

V. 15. *They have forsaken the right way, and gone in error.* They should have taught the right way,—how we must cleave to Christ, and come to God by faith, and through love to our neighbor; and thereafter bear the holy cross, and endure whatever meets us therefor. But they preach no more than this, "go hither and thither,—be monk and priest,—found churches, masses, &c., &c.;" and they lead away the people from faith to their own works, which yet are such as are of no use to their neighbor.

V. 15, 16. *And have followed the way of Balaam, the son of Bosor, who loved the reward of unrighteousness, but had a rebuke for his transgression, the dumb beast of burden speaking with man's voice and reproving the folly of the prophet.* Here he brings in an illustration from the fourth book of Moses, xxii.-xxiv. When the children of Israel had journeyed out of Egypt and had come into the land of the Moabites, king Balak sent to a prophet in Syria, by the name of Balaam, and besought him that he would come and curse the Jewish people, that they might become weak and that he might slay them. Then God appeared to Balaam, and forbade him to curse the people; therefore the prophet declines to comply with Balak. Thereupon the king sent to him once more, and promised to give him large wealth. Then God permits him to go to him, yet he shall say nothing but what He shall direct him to say.

Upon this, he rose up and mounted upon an ass. The angel of God came and walked in the way, and stood before him with a drawn sword. The ass saw it, and turned aside out of the way, at which the prophet struck her, that she should go in the way. Then the angel went to a narrow place where the ass could not turn aside, and when she presses herself against the wall and bruises the prophet's foot, she is forced to fall under him upon her knee, while he is angered so as in his rage to strike the ass with his staff. Then God opens the mouth of the beast to speak with the voice of a man, and she said, "What have I done to you that you should strike me so?" And he said, "Ah! if I had now a sword in my hand, I would slay you." Then the ass answered and said, "Am I yet the ass upon which thou hast ridden continually even to this day, and have I done it for no more than this?" Then were the eyes of the prophet opened, so that he saw the angel with the drawn sword, at which he was affrighted and would have turned back; but the angel of the Lord bade him go on, but thereupon forbade him to speak anything else than what He should say to him.

When now the prophet was come to the king, he takes him up to a height from which he could see the whole people of Israel. Then the prophet bade him erect seven altars, and on each offer a sacrifice; and then went aside and asked the Lord what he should say. And God gave him his word in his mouth. And he rose up to bless and glorify the people of Israel with fair words; and this he did three times, one after another. Then was the king filled with wrath, and said, "Did I not call thee that thou shouldst curse mine enemies? and yet thou hast blest them now these three times. I had thought that I should have honored thee, but the Lord hath turned thee away from honor." Balaam answered and said, "Yet I told thee at first, that though thou shouldst give me thine house full of silver and gold, still I could speak nothing else but what God should say to me."

Yet did the prophet afterward give the king counsel how he should manage with the people, although he might not curse them and overcome them by power,—so that they sinned against God. Then the king sets up an idol, by name Baal-Peor, and causes that the Moabite women, daughters of lords and princes, should ensnare the people to themselves to sacrifice to their gods; and when they had brought them to themselves, they made supplication to the idol with meats and drinks, and committed sin with the women. Then was God angry, and commanded the chief of the people to be hung upon the gallows, and permitted four and twenty thousand men to be overcome in one day. Such was this prophet Balaam's advice, for the sake of gold.

Of this St. Peter here speaks, and would say that our ecclesiastics are specially Balaam's children and scholars; for just as he gave evil counsel to set up an idol so that the children of Israel should be brought to sin and provoke God that they should be slain, so have our bishops also set up an idol, in God's name,—to wit, their human doctrine of their own works; and they let faith go, and they lure to themselves christian souls whom they injure, and thereby provoke God to anger, so that he has punished the world with blindness and stupidity. For all this we may thank our spiritual masters.

Thus Peter compares especially these false teachers to the prophet Balaam, since they even, like Balaam, purely for the sake of gold, set up such idolatry and ruin souls.

Besides, he mentions his right name, for Bileaam or Balaam is he called in Hebrew, a swallower or swiller, like one who gapes his throat open, and swallows and devours all. This shameful name must he bear, because he has brought so many people into sin, insomuch that they are destroyed and overcome.

Such Balaamites are our bishops and ecclesiastics, who are the throat of the devil, by which he draws so many souls to himself, and swallows them down. But the surname of this prophet is, the son of Bosor,—that is to say, flesh,—or, as Moses says, son of Beor, that is, of a fool. A fool is his father. So are these, also, blind, dull and foolish people, who must yet needs rule; such a people as the flesh bears, for the spirit makes men of another stamp. So God has given these in the Scripture their own name, and therein they are so painted to the life, that we may know in what account they are to be held.

Now the dumb beast of burden, the ass, signifies the people that lets itself be bridled and ridden, and goes as it is led, like the ass, who was forced and beaten cruelly when he went out of the way into the ditch, and must neither give place before the angel in the way so long as it could help, nor turn aside, and so must fall down. For in the same way have these seducers also urged on the people, until these last have become sensible that it is a thing not to be endured, and that they deal unfairly with them, and have wished to turn them aside from the way. But the harshness has been so gross whereby they have troubled the people, that at length God has opened our lips and given words into our mouths, so that even the children speak of it; whereby their folly is made plain, so that they must be ashamed. In this way we ought to meet them when they go about, and give out that it belongs not to the laity to read the Scripture, and therefore say, we must hear what the Councils determine. For then you may answer, Has not God spoken even by an ass? Be content with our knowing that ye, in times past, preached the word of God; but now ye have become fools, and are possessed by avarice, what wonder is it that now the common people have been roused and impelled by God to speak the truth, though it has been so burdened and oppressed like a dumb beast of burden. This is their likeness, taken from the prophet Balaam. Now St. Peter says further of these false teachers:

V. 17. *They are wells without water, and clouds driven about by the whirlwind.* In like manner Solomon presents us a comparison, in Prov. xxv., and says, "As when a great cloud and strong wind go forth, and yet no rain follows, so is a man who makes high boastings of himself, and does not make good his words."

So Peter says here, also, *they are wells without water, and clouds driven about by the whirlwind;* that is, they make great show, and have nothing beside. They are like the dry, false and exhausted wells, although they have the fame and title of being true wells. For Scripture calls those who teach, wells, as the ones from whom should flow that wholesome doctrine by which souls are to be quickened. To this office are they anointed and set apart. But what do they do? Nothing, as a general thing; for they have nothing else but just the bare name, just as they are called shepherds, and yet are wolves.

Besides, they are the clouds which the wind drives about—not like the thick, black and lowering clouds which are wont to give us rain, but like those fleecy ones which move about and fly in the air, and are very light, which the wind drives wherever it will, after which no rain can follow. So our teachers also sweep about and move high in Christendom, like the clouds in heaven, but let themselves be driven about wherever the devil chooses, to whom they are ready to yield in all kinds of lusts. But yet they preach not a word of God, like true teachers and preachers, who are called clouds in Scripture (as Is. v.),—as also by all that gives forth water, preachers are typified in Scripture.

For whom is reserved the blackness of darkness forever. They live now at their ease, and things go with them just as they themselves would have them. But there shall come an eternal darkness upon them, although they do not believe nor apprehend it.

V. 18. *For they speak in swelling words, which have nothing back of them.* If you ask how they may be called wells without water, and clouds without rain, while they yet preach throughout the whole world, St. Peter answers: they rain and preach, alas! altogether too much; but they are only vain, swollen and puffed-up words, by which they blow the poor people's ears full, so that men think it is something fine; and yet it is nothing but show. Just as the monks, with high, bold words, set forth their obedience, poverty and chastity, so that men think they are a holy people, while yet it is nothing but mere trickery, and certainly no faith nor love can be found among it. Like this, also, is their pretence that the estate of bishops is a more perfect estate, while these yet do nothing else but ride about pompously on their fine horses, and now and then consecrate churches and altars, and baptise bells. Such puffed-up and swollen words are the whole spiritual law of the Pope, throughout.

And they allure, through guile, to the lust of the flesh, those who had well-nigh escaped, and now they walk in error. This is what these wells and teachers do, so that they who were almost escaped must fall into the snare of wickedness, and for the first time be truly captured. A child that has been baptised, rescued from all sins, snatched from the devil and set out from Adam into Christ, when he comes to reason is soon entangled and led away into error. Men should be taught of faith, and love, and the holy cross, while our clergy go their own way, throw up their work whereby these persons fall back again into error, even though they had escaped it. But how does this come to pass? Thus: in that by guile they allure the people to the lust of the flesh. Their strongest persuasion is in their saying that priests, monks and nuns should not be married, and should bind themselves to maintain chastity, by which they do no more than allure to unchastity, forasmuch as the wretched people must perish in their wicked lusts, and there is nothing to help them.

But here you clearly see that Peter speaks of none other than teachers who bear rule in Christendom, where men are baptised and believers,—for among the Turks and heathen, no one has so escaped; it is only among Christians, where they have the chance to lead souls astray, and bring them into the snare of the devil.

V. 19. *And they promise them freedom, while they themselves are the servants of corruption, for of whom any one is overcome, his servant has he become.* They set up Orders by which a man is to be saved,—as Thomas, the monk preacher, has shamelessly written, that when a man shall enter into one of these Orders, be it as vile as it may, it is as though he had but just come forth from his baptism; and then they promise him freedom and forgiving of sins by works of his own. Such blasphemy must we hear, while they set their human fancies and ludicrous conceits, destitute of faith, on a level with faith and baptism which God has established, and which are peculiarly his work. Who is to endure this and still keep silent? Such stories have the monks gotten up, and they cram them into the young; and such teachers as these men have set up for saints. But the other saints, truly such, they have burnt to ashes.

V. 20. *For if they have escaped the pollution of the world through the knowledge of the Lord and Saviour Jesus Christ, but shall be again entangled and overcome in the same, their last end is worse for them than the first.* There Peter shows why they are the servant of corruption. To confess Christ is to know what he is, even our Saviour, who forgives us our sins from pure grace. By this confession we escape the vice and come out from the pollution of the world. But though they should already have been delivered from sin in baptism, they shall afterwards be plunged therein, for that they have again gone from faith to their own works. For where there is no faith, the Spirit is absent; but where the Spirit is absent, there is nothing but flesh, so that there can be nothing at all that is pure. So has it come to pass hitherto in regard to Christianity. Rome first heard the pure Gospel, but afterward went back and fell away to human doctrines, until even upon herself all abominations have come up; so that her last end has become worse than her first, in that she is now far more hopeless in her heathenism than she ever was before she heard the word of God.

V. 21. *For it had been far better for them that they had never known the way of righteousness, than that they should know it, and turn themselves away from the holy command that has been given them. For it has happened to them according to the proverb, The dog turns to his own vomit again, and the sow after her washing wallows in the mire.* This proverb St. Peter has taken out of the book of Prov. xxvi., where Solomon says, "A man who repeats his folly is like the dog who turns again to his vomit." By baptism they have thrown off unbelief, and have been washed from their polluted life, and have entered upon a pure life of faith and love, while they fall off from it again to unbelief and their own works, and defile themselves again in the dirt. So that we are not to make this proverb bear on works; for little is accomplished by one's saying and directing at confession, "Thou shalt henceforth be chaste, meek, and patient," &c. But if you will be pious, pray God that he will give you a real faith, and see to it that you forsake your unbelief. When you shall then have attained faith, good works shall afterwards take care of themselves, so that you will live purely and chastely, even though you should secure yourself by no other means; and though, again, you might awhile conceal the mischief in your heart, yet at last it comes out.

This is the second chapter of this Epistle, wherein Peter speaks specially of our teachers, how shamefully we have been treated by them. We have indeed had warning enough, but we have not minded it, so that the fault is ours that we have not laid hold on the Gospel, and that we have by our lives deserved such anger of God. We hear it generally, all of us, with gladness, when some one assaults and upbraids the Pope along with his priests and monks; but yet, no one will draw advantage to himself from it. It is not such a trifling matter of sport that one must laugh at it, but of such seriousness that the heart should fear and tremble on account of it. Therefore should we lay hold upon it with seriousness, and pray that God would turn away from us his anger and such plagues. For this calamity has not come upon us unforeseen, but it is sent upon us by God as a punishment,—as Paul says, II. Thes. ii.: "Since they have not received the love of the truth, that they might be saved, therefore shall God send upon them strong delusion so that they shall believe a lie," &c., &c. For had the punishment gone but so far that the false teachers only were lost, it would have been yet a little thing against the fact that they have had the rule, and carried all the world with them to hell. Therefore, in regard to the evil, we are to take no counsel except to apprehend the matter in Godly fear and humility, confess our guilt, and pray God to turn away the punishment from us. By prayer must one contend against the false teachers, although the devil do not let him win.—Now follows, next:

CHAPTER III.

V. 1, 2. *This is the second Epistle which I write to you, beloved, in which I stir up your pure minds to remembrance, that ye may think upon the word which was said to you before by the holy prophets, and upon our command, who are Apostles of the Lord and Saviour.* Here St. Peter comes to us again, and warns us in this chapter to be prepared, and look every moment for the last day. And so he says in the first of it, that he has written this Epistle, not in order to lay down a ground of faith, which he had done before, but to awaken, remind, arrest, and urge them not to forget the same, and to abide in the clear view and understanding which they have of a true christian life. For it is the preacher's office, as we have said often, not only to teach, but also continually to admonish and restrain. For since our flesh and blood ever clings to us, God's word must be stronger in us, that we may not give room to the flesh, but strive against it, and gain the upper hand of it.

V. 3, 4. *And know, first of all, that in the last days there shall come scoffers who walk after their own lusts, and say, Where is the promise of his coming? for since the fathers fell asleep, all things remain as from the beginning of creation.* Yet are men swayed hither and thither by a book concerning Antichrist, wherein it is written that the people before the last day shall fall into such error that they shall say, there is no God, and shall scoff at all that is preached of Christ and the last day. That is true, whencesoever it has been taken. But we are not so to understand it as that the whole world shall say and hold such things, but the greater part. For that time is even now at hand, and shall prevail yet more when the Gospel shall come down among the people, when the proud ones shall lift themselves up, and the secrets of many hearts break forth, which are now hidden and unknown. There have even already been many who have altogether rejected the idea of the coming of the last day.

Of such scoffers St. Peter here warns us, and tells us of them beforehand, that they must come, and rush into this hazard and live as they list. At Rome and in Italy this word is now at length fulfilled, and they who come thence, bring such errors also forth with them; for just as they have a long time perplexed themselves therein, so, also, must they perplex the people by the same means. And even though the last day were now before the door, such people must come abroad. So shall be fulfilled that which Christ says, Mat. xxiv.: "Just as it was in the time of Noah, so shall it also be at the coming of the Son of Man; for as they were in the days before the deluge, they ate, they drank, they married and were given in marriage, even to the day when Noah entered into the ark, and they knew it not till the flood came and swallowed them all; so, also, shall the coming of the Son of Man be." Also, "The Son of Man shall come at an hour when ye think not." Also, Luke xxi.: "This day shall come as a snare, upon all that dwell upon the earth." And once more, Luke xvii.: "As the lightning lightens over us from heaven, and shines upon all that is under the heaven, so shall the Son of Man be in His day,"—that is, so quick and unforeseen and sudden shall He break in upon it, while the world shall be living above all, for itself first, and shall throw God's word to the winds.

Therefore this shall be a sign of the last day that it is near, when the people shall live as they list, according to all their lusts, and such talk goes about among them as this: "Where is the promise of his coming? the world has stood so long and continued to abide, is it now for the first time to be otherwise?" Thus Peter warns us that we should not be surprised, and that we have a sure sign that the day will soon come.—It follows, further:

V. 5, 6. *But this in their obstinacy they will not know, that the heavens of old, besides the earth standing out of the water and in the water, were (made) by God's word, yet through the same, was the world in its time destroyed by the flood.* Such people they are, he says, as show not so much diligence as to read the Scripture, but obstinately refuse to think and be aware that so also it was of old, when Noah built the ark; the world which stood and was made through the water and in the water, was destroyed by water, and the people were yet so safe and secure that they thought, surely there is no danger,—yet they were all alike destroyed by water. As though he should say,—if God has for once destroyed the world by water, and shown by an example that he can sink it, how much more will he do it now that he has promised to do it.

But here St. Peter speaks somewhat particularly of the creation. The heaven and the earth stood fast aforetime; they were made of water and stood in the water, by the word of God. Heaven and earth have a beginning; they have not been forever; the heaven was made from the water, and there was water above and beneath,—but the earth is made and stands in the water, as Moses writes, whom St. Peter here quotes. All is sustained by God's word, as it also was made by the same, for it is not their nature so to stand. Therefore if God did not sustain it, it must all soon fall down and sink into the water. For God spoke a word of power when he said, "let the waters under the heavens gather themselves into a separate place, that the dry land may be seen;" that is, let the water put itself aside and give room for the earth to come forth, whereon man might dwell,—yet naturally the waters should spread themselves over the earth. Therefore this is, at the present day, one of the greatest miracles that God works.

Now St. Peter would say this: so obstinate and stupid are these scoffers, that they will not do honor to the Holy Spirit, though they read how God holds up the earth in the water, whence they should be convinced that all stands in the hands of God. Therefore, since God at that time drowned the earth, so he will deal with us even yet again. For that example should certainly convince us that, as in that very case he has not lied, so again he will not lie.

V. 7. *But the heaven which yet is, and the earth, are by his word sustained, that they be reserved for fire in the day of Judgment and condemnation of ungodly men.* At that time, when God destroyed the world by a flood, the water pressed down from above, up from beneath and from all sides, so that nothing could be seen but water only; because the earth, as its nature was, must be swallowed up in the water. But now he has promised, and given the rainbow for a sign in heaven, that he will no more destroy the world by water. Therefore he will destroy it and let it perish by fire, so that here it shall be fire only, as there it was water only. Of which St. Paul, II. Thes. i., says: "When now the Lord Jesus shall be revealed from heaven, together with the angels of his power, and with flaming fire," etc. So I. Cor. iii.: "Every one's work shall be revealed; the day of the Lord shall make it clear, which shall be revealed with fire." So when the last day breaks and bursts in on the world, it will in a moment be fire only; what is in heaven and in earth shall be turned to dust and ashes, and all things must be changed by fire, as that change took place by water. This shall be a sign that God will not lie so long as He has left that for a sign.

V. 8-10. *But of this one thing, beloved, be ye not ignorant; that one day with the Lord is as a thousand years, and a thousand years as one day. The Lord is not slack concerning his promise as some men count slackness, but he is long-suffering toward you, and wills not that any one should perish, but that all should come to repentance; but the Day of the Lord shall come as a thief in the night, in which the heavens shall pass away with a great noise, but the elements shall be melted with fervent heat, and the earth and the works that are therein shall be burned up.* With these words St. Peter meets those of whom he has just spoken, who say: "The Apostles have said much about the Last Day coming quickly,—and yet so long a time is past, and still all continues as heretofore." And he has quoted this passage from Moses, in the lxxxix. Ps., where he says: "A thousand years are in thine eyes as yesterday, when it is past." This is the scope of it.

There are two ways of viewing things,—one for God, the other for the world. So also this present life and that to come, are twofold. This life cannot be that, since none can reach that but by death,—that is, by ceasing from *this* life. This life is just to eat, drink, sleep, endure, bring up children, etc., in which all moves on successively, hours, day, year, one after another: if you wish now to apprehend that life, you must banish out of your mind the course of this present life; you must not think that you can so apprehend it, where it will all be one day, one hour, one moment.

Since then in God's sight there is no reckoning of time, a thousand years must be before him, as it were, a day. Therefore the first man, Adam, is just as near to him as he who shall be last born before the last day. For God sees not time lengthwise but obliquely, just as when you look at right-angles to a long tree which lies before you, you can fix in your view both place and parts at once,—a thing you cannot do if you only look at it lengthwise. We can, by our reason, look at time only according to its duration; we must begin to count from Adam, one year after another, even to the last day. But before God it is all in one heap; what is long with us is short with him,—and again, here there is neither measure nor number. So when man dies, the body is buried and wastes away, lies in the earth and knows nothing; but when the first man rises up at the last day, he will think he has lain there scarcely an hour, while he will look about himself and become assured that so many people were born of him and have come after him, of whom he had no knowledge at all.

This, then, is St. Peter's meaning: the Lord does not delay his promise as some scoffers let themselves imagine, but is long-suffering; therefore should ye be prepared for the last day,—for it will come soon enough to every one after his death, in that he will say, "lo! I have but just now died!" But it comes upon the world all too soon: when the people shall say, "there is peace, no danger threatens," it shall break forth and come upon them, as St. Paul says, I. Thess. v. And with so great a noise shall the day tear its way and burst forth like a great storm, that in a moment must all be wasted.

V. 11, 12. *Since then all this must pass away, how careful should ye be in all holy conduct and a Godly life, that ye wait for and hasten to the coming of the day of the Lord.* Since ye know this, that all must pass away, both heaven and earth,—think how ye shall be prepared to meet this day, by a holy and godly life and conversation. For Peter describes this day as one that is to come even now, so that men should be prepared for it, to hope for it with joy, and even hasten to run to meet it, as that which sets us free from death, sin and hell.

V. 12, 13. *In which the heavens shall pass away by fire, and the elements shall be melted with fervent heat; but we look for a new heaven and a new earth, according to his promise, in which dwelleth righteousness.* God has promised by the prophets, here and there, that he would create a new heaven and a new earth,—as in Is. lxv., "Behold, I will create a new heaven and a new earth, wherein ye shall be happy, and shout and leap for joy." So in xxx. "The appearance of the moon shall be as the light of the sun, and the splendor of the sun shall be seven times as bright, as though seven days were joined one into another;" and Christ says, Matt. xiii., "The righteous shall shine like the sun, in their Father's kingdom." How that is to pass away we cannot know, except that the promise is, that such a heaven and earth are to be, wherein no sin, but righteousness only, and the children of God shall dwell; as also St. Paul says, Rom. viii., there shall be pure love, pure joy, and nothing but God's kingdom.

Here some may disquiet themselves as to whether the saints shall have their station in heaven or on earth. The text seems to imply that man shall dwell upon the earth,—yet so that all heaven and earth shall be a paradise wherein God dwells, for God dwells not alone in heaven, but in all places, wherefore the elect shall be also even where He is.

V. 14. *Therefore, my beloved, since ye look for such things, be diligent, that ye may be found of him without spot, and blameless, in peace.* Since ye have escaped, he says, such misery, and come to so great joy, ye should suffer yourselves to be persuaded to despise willingly all that is upon the earth, and suffer cheerfully whatever duty requires. Therefore should ye be diligent, that ye may live a peaceful and blameless life.

V. 15. *And the long-suffering of our Lord Jesus Christ account for your salvation.* In that He so spares, and delays, and does not come to speedy judgment, take account of this as designed for your benefit. He had good reason to be angry and to punish, yet out of His grace He does it not.

V. 15, 16. *As also our beloved brother Paul, according to the wisdom that has been given unto him has written, as he also in all his letters speaks thereof, in which are some things hard to be understood, which the unlearned and unstable wrest, as they also do other Scriptures, to their own destruction.* There St. Peter bears testimony for the Apostle Paul in respect to his doctrine, which shows plainly enough that this Epistle was written long after St. Paul's Epistles. And this is one of the passages which might be adduced to maintain that this Epistle is not St. Peter's, as also there was one before this in this chapter—namely, where he says, "the Lord wills not that any should be lost, but that every one should give himself to repentance." For it falls some little below the Apostolic spirit; still it is credible that it is none the less the Apostle's, for since herein, he is writing not of faith but of love, he lets himself down somewhat, as the manner of love is, inasmuch as it humbles itself toward its neighbor, just as faith rises above itself.

But he has yet seen that many unstable spirits wrested and perverted St. Paul in his words and doctrines, inasmuch as some things in his Epistles are hard to be understood,—as when he speaks in this way, "that no one is justified by works, but by faith alone;" so, too, "the law is given to make sin more gross;" so, too, "where sin abounded, there grace much more abounds," and more passages of the same sort. For when men hear such, then they say, if that is true, we will go on indolently, and do no good work, and so be righteous, as men even now say, that we forbid good works; for if one so perverts St. Paul's own words, what wonder is it that they should, in like manner, pervert ours?

V. 17, 18. *But ye, my beloved, since ye know this beforehand, beware for yourselves that ye be not led away by the error of the wicked likewise, and fall from your own steadfastness. But grow in grace, and in knowledge of our Lord and Saviour Jesus Christ, to whom be praise, now and forever. Amen.* Since ye know, he says, all that has been said above, and see that many false teachers must come, who lead the world astray, and such scoffers as pervert the Scripture and will not understand it, take care of yourselves; guard against them with diligence, that ye fall not from the faith by doctrines of error; and grow, so as to become stronger from day to day by the steadfast practice and preaching of the word of God. Here observe how great care the Apostle shows for those who have come to believe, which urged him even to write these two Epistles, wherein is richly comprehended what a Christian should know, besides also that which is yet to come. May God give his grace, that we also may seize hold upon and retain it. Amen.

THE EPISTLE OF
SAINT JUDE

V. 1, 2. *Jude, a servant of Jesus Christ, but a brother of James, to those that are called to be holy in God the Father, and preserved in Jesus Christ, mercy unto you and peace and love be multiplied.* This Epistle is ascribed to the holy Apostle, St. Jude, brother of the two Apostles, James the Less and Simon, by the sister of the mother of Christ, who is called Mary (wife) of James or Cleopas, as we read in Mark vi. But this Epistle cannot be looked upon as being that of one who was truly an Apostle, for the author speaks in it of the Apostles, as being much their junior. It has even nothing peculiar about it, except that it refers to the second Epistle of St. Peter, from which it has taken nearly all its words, and is scarcely anything else than an Epistle against our clergy, bishops, priests and monks.*

> * It is well known that at an early period the book of Jude was reckoned among the *antilegomena*. This was mainly in consequence of its references to the Apocryphal books of Enoch and of the Ascension of Christ. Yet De Wette, than whom none would be more disposed to sift it thoroughly, says, "no important objection to the genuineness of the Epistle can be made good; neither the use of the Apocryphal book of Enoch, nor the resemblance of v. 24 to Rom. xvi. 25, nor a style of writing which betrays a certain familiarity with the Greek tongue. The Epistle is less open to suspicion, as the author does not distinctly claim to be an Apostle, nor can a pretext for forgery be discovered." Again, he says: "they who regard the Son of Alpheus and the brother of the Lord as one and the same person, are quite consistent in regarding our Jude likewise as an Apostle." To this view De Wette himself does not accede, and thus agrees substantially with Luther.

V. 3. *Beloved, since I gave all diligence to write unto you of the common salvation, I am necessitated to write to you, and admonish you, that ye should contend earnestly for the faith which was once delivered to the saints.* That is as much as to say,—I am necessitated to write to you, so that I may remind and admonish you how ye should go forward and persevere in the faith which has already, before this, been once preached to you; or as though he should say, It is necessary that I should admonish you that ye be on your guard and remain in the right way; but as to why this is needed, he gives the reason, and says:

V. 4. For there are some men who have secretly come in, who were ordained of old to this condemnation. For this cause will I remind you that ye should abide in the faith which ye have heard, because there is even now a wavering, and already there have come preachers, who set up other doctrines besides faith, by which people are led away gently and unsuspectingly from the true way. So St. Peter also said, in his Epistle, "there shall be false teachers among you, who shall secretly bring in destructive heresies, &c." These, he says, "are long ago appointed to such a sentence of condemnation." This we now well understand, since we know that no one is righteous and justified by works of his own, but only through faith in Christ, insomuch that he must rely on the work of Christ as his chief good. Then where there is faith, whatever is done as works is all done for the good of our neighbor, and thus we guard ourselves against all works which are not performed with the intent that they shall be of service to our neighbor, as is now the estate of priests and monks. Therefore wherever any one now secretly introduces anything else than this doctrine of faith, in regard to such orders and works, he leads the people astray, so that they shall be condemned along with him.

Who are godless, and turn the grace of God into wantonness. That Gospel which is given us concerning the grace of God, and which sets Christ before us, as he is offered to and bestowed upon us, with all that he has, that we may be freed from sin, death and all evil, such grace and blessing offered to us by the Gospel, they use merely to indulge their wantonness,—that is, they call themselves Christians, indeed, and praise the Gospel, but they bring in such an order, as therein to work their own caprice, in eating and drinking and wanton life, while they make their boast and say we are not in a secular but a spiritual estate, and under such names and pretence they have grasped all enjoyment, honor and pleasure. This, already, says Jude, begins. For we read that it had already begun a thousand years ago; that the bishops then wished to be Lords and to be more highly exalted than common christians, as we also see in St. Jerome's Epistles.

And they deny God, that he alone is Lord, and our Lord Jesus Christ. This is what St. Peter said also in his Epistle; but this they deny (as we have heard). It is not done by their *mouth*, for with this they confess that God is one Lord, but they deny that Christ is Lord in fact, and by their works; they hold, not Him, but themselves as their Lord,—for while they preach that fasts, pilgrimages, church ordinances, chastity, obedience, poverty, etc., are the way to salvation, they lead the people astray to their own works, and yet are silent about Christ; and it is just as much as if they said, Christ is of no avail to you, His works noway help you, but you must by your own works merit salvation. Thus they deny the Lord who has bought us with his blood, as Peter says.

V. 5, 6, 7. *I will therefore remind you that ye once knew this, that the Lord, when he saved the people out of Egypt, afterward destroyed those that believed not. Also, the angels, who kept not their first estate, but left their own habitation, he has reserved to the judgment of the great day, in everlasting chains, under darkness. As also Sodom and Gomorrah, and the cities lying about them, which in like manner as these, rioted in fornication, and went after strange flesh, are set forth for an example, and bear the pain of eternal fire.* Here he adduces, also, three examples, as St. Peter does in his Epistle; but the first which he presents is to this effect: that God permitted the children of Israel whom he had brought out of Egypt by many wonderful works, when they did not believe, to be overthrown and defeated, so that of them all not more than two survived, when there were numbered, of all that went forth from twenty years of age and above, more than six hundred thousand men. This example he sets forth as a warning and a terror; as though he should say, those who are now called Christians, and under this name turn the grace of God into wantonness, are to beware to themselves that it do not come to pass with them as it came to pass with those. And true enough, these are the times when the Popedom is exalted and the Gospel kept secret through the whole world; when, too, there comes continually one plague after another, by which God has punished the unbelieving and thrown them into the throat of the Devil.

V. 8. *Like them also are these dreamers, who defile the flesh.* These teachers he calls dreamers; for just as when a man lies in a dream he deals with images, and thinks he has something real, but when he wakes up it is nothing at all,—but he sees then that it was a dream, and counts it of no importance,—so, too, what these say is nothing else than a mere dream; for when once their eyes shall be opened, they shall see that it is nothing at all. As when they go about pretending that their tonsure and cowl, obedience, poverty and chastity are well-pleasing to God, they have this before their eyes; yet, in God's sight it is nothing but a mere dream. So he has given them a truly fitting name, inasmuch as they deal with dreams, by which they cheat themselves and the world.

But especially do the Apostles ascribe to the clerical order the vice of leading an unchaste life; and God long ago foretold that they should have no wives. Now it is scarcely possible that God should work as many miracles as there are persons in the order, so that it cannot be that they are chaste. So, likewise, has the prophet Daniel spoken, chap. xi., of the Pope's rule: "He shall not regard women (in marriage)." This is the external characteristic, as the inward is that they are dreamers.

Who despise government, and speak evil of dignities. Their third characteristic is, that they will not be subject to civil authority. Yet we have been taught, while we live on earth, that we are all under obligation; that we are to be subject and obedient to the sovereignty; for the Christian faith does not do away with civil rule,—therefore no one can except himself from it, because the Pope's decree concerning the Church's freedom is a mere devil's law.

V. 9. *But Michael the archangel, when he contended with the devil, and disputed about the body of Moses, durst not let drop against him a railing accusation, but said, The Lord rebuke thee.* This is one of the reasons why this Epistle was formerly rejected, because here an example is adduced which is not found in Scripture, to the effect that the angel Michael and the devil contended with one another about the body of Moses. But this should have been found there, since so much is written about Moses in the last of Deuteronomy, of God's burial of him, and yet no one knew his grave. Besides, Scripture testifies in regard to him, that no other prophet has arisen in Israel like Moses, whom the Lord knew face to face, &c. But it has been said, in reference to the same text also, that his body was left concealed, so that the Jews might not regard it with idolatrous veneration, and for this reason the angel Michael must needs oppose the devil, who wished that the body should be discovered, that the Jews might pray to it; and although Michael was an archangel (says Jude), yet was he not so bold as to curse even the devil,—and yet these scoffers trample under foot the authority that has been ordained of God; they curse in seven, eight and nine ways, though they are men merely; while this archangel dared not curse the worst devil that was ever condemned, but said no more than, the Lord restrain and punish thee.

V. 10. *But these scoff at what they know nothing of, for what they know naturally as brute beasts, in those things they corrupt themselves.* Such scoffers are they, that they can do nothing else but anathematize and curse, and give over to the devil for his own not only kings and dignities, but God also and the saints, as may be seen in the bull, *Coena Domini.* They know not that our salvation stands on the foundation of faith and love; they cannot endure that their works should be rejected and condemned, and that it should be preached that Christ alone must help us by His works. Therefore they curse and scoff at all Christian doctrine which they are ignorant of. But what they know, through natural perception,—as the founding of masses and the like,—will bring in gold and treasures; to this they devote themselves with energy, and thereby corrupt themselves and every one else.

V. 11. *Woe unto them, for they have gone in the way of Cain.* Cain struck his brother dead, simply because he was more pious than himself. For his brother's offering was acceptable before God, but his own was not. So now the way of Cain is, to rely on one's own works, and scoff at those works which are good and true, and circumvent and slay those who go in the right way, just as these very ones also are doing.

And have hurried for reward into the error of Balaam. They should be fixed inwardly in the hope of Divine grace; yet they go forth and put their trust in various outward works, of this kind and that, and they do them only for the sake of gold, that they may fill their bellies, like the prophet Balaam, as we have heard in Peter's Epistle.

And perished in the rebellion of Korah. Of the rebellion of Korah, and how he was destroyed, with his house, we have an account in the fourth book of Moses, xvi. Moses was summoned and called for this purpose, that he should lead the people out of Egypt; and his brother Aaron likewise was appointed of God as High Priest. Now Korah was also of the same tribe, and their friendship should have been enduring, and something more than common: yet he attaches to himself two hundred and fifty men of the foremost and most distinguished among the people, and excites such a commotion and tumult, that Moses and Aaron are forced to flee. And Moses fell upon his face, and prayed that God might not accept their sacrifice; and he bade the congregation of the people draw back from them, and said to them: "Hereby shall ye surely know if the Lord hath sent me; if these men die and disappear as all men disappear, then the Lord hath not sent me; but if the Lord shall do some new thing, so that the earth shall open her mouth and swallow them up, and they go down alive into hell, then shall ye know that these men have reviled the Lord." When he had spoken these words, the earth quaked and opened, and swallowed up Korah, together with the other leaders of the rebellion, with all that they had, so that they went down alive into hell; and the fire consumed the other two hundred and fifty men who had joined themselves to him.

This example Jude sets forth for these scoffers who blame us for making a commotion, while we preach against them, for they are the real ones who make all the trouble. For Christ is our Aaron and chief-priest, whom we should allow to rule alone; but this the Pope and bishops have been unwilling to endure. They have set themselves up, and have wished to have the power to rule along with the authority, and so have arrayed themselves against Christ; but God has punished them, in that the earth has swallowed them up and covered them, since they are absorbed and swallowed up in an earthly life and pleasure, and are nothing but pure worldliness.

V. 12, 13. *These live on your charities, and are vileness itself, while they feast with you, feeding themselves without fear; clouds they are without water, driven about by the wind; barren, fruitless trees, twice dead and plucked up by the roots; wild waves of the sea, which foam out their own shame; wandering stars, for whom is reserved the blackness of darkness forever.* Of this we have heard enough in St. Peter's Epistle. All the world have brought up their children to be ecclesiastics, and to have an easy life of it, and not to support themselves by their own hands and labor; nor must they even preach, but only live without care in their luxury, and keep up good spirits by feeding on the wealth that poor people earn by their sweat. So men think they must be the best part, and the jewel, as it were, of Christendom, while they are merely shame-spots and an abomination, and live well, as we say, on the wealth that belongs to them as priests. They are without care or fear; they think the devil may not overthrow them; they feed not the sheep, but are themselves the wolves that devour the sheep; they are clouds that hang over us in the air, sit up high in the churches, as those that should preach, and yet they do not preach at all, but let themselves be driven by the devil this way and the other.

So, too, he says, they are leafless, fruitless trees, like the trees of autumn; they have neither fruit nor leaf; they stand there only like other trees; let themselves be looked upon as Christian bishops, but there is with them neither word nor work, but all is dead to the root. Moreover, they are like wild waves of the sea; that is, as the wind tosses and throws up waves and billows upon the water, so these, too, go just as the devil leads them. And they foam out their own shame; like a heated pot, they are so full of pollution that they run over, and cannot retain command of themselves, but all must out. They are wandering stars, planets as they are called, that go backward, and not in a steady, straight course, so that they make no true progress; their life and doctrine is mere error, in which they lead themselves astray, and all that follow after them. Therefore for them is reserved the blackness of darkness forever.

Thus Jude has appraised and painted our spiritual masters, who, under the name of Christ and Christianity, introduce all sorts of profligacy, and snatch to themselves all the wealth of the world, and authoritatively subject all men to themselves.

There follows now, further:

V. 14. *Enoch, also, the seventh from Adam, prophesied of such, and said, Behold, the Lord cometh with ten thousand of His saints, to execute judgment upon all.* This language of Enoch is nowhere to be found in Scripture. For this reason some of the Fathers did not receive this Epistle, although there is not a sufficient reason for rejecting a book on this account. For St. Paul, also, in II. Tim. iii., makes mention of two that opposed Moses, Jannes and Jambres, names that are not even to be found in the Scriptures. But be this as it will, we let it pass. Still this is true, that God, from the beginning of the world, has left it to some to make His word known (the word that promises His favor and salvation to believers, but threatens the unbelieving with judgment and condemnation), even till Christ's coming down from heaven, when it is openly preached to the whole world. But before the birth of Christ God took to Himself for this purpose only a single line, from Adam to Abraham, and thence to David, down to Mary the mother of Christ, who possessed His word. Thus the Gospel has always been preached in the world, but never so generally as now in these last times.

Thus, also, this father, Enoch, insisted on that word of God which he received from his father, Adam, and which he had of the Holy Spirit. For the Scripture says also of him, Gen. v., that he led a godly life, and therefore he was taken of God, so that he was seen no more. Hence, also, has been derived the notion that He will come again before the last day; but it is not to be supposed that men would understand it of a spiritual advent, as that his preaching was based upon the last day, as this passage is, wherein that day is spoken of with as much assurance as though it were in full view. *The Lord is coming already*, he says, *with many thousand saints;* that is, with such a multitude as cannot be numbered. For this can only be said of the last day, on which He will come with all His saints, to execute judgment. For before this, He has not come with many thousand saints, but alone, into the world; and this, not to judge, but to bestow grace.

V. 15. *And to punish all the ungodly among them, for all their godless life, wherein they have been ungodly.* This passage Jude does not inappropriately quote, inasmuch as he is speaking of false teachers, who are to come before the last day; and the conclusion is thence to be drawn, that the Lord by his coming will overthrow the Pope and his government; since there is no other help for it; for as long as the world stands, there will be no (voluntary) ending or reformation of it. The passage, moreover, cannot be understood of any others, but of our clergy, who have shamefully led all the world astray. Their system cannot be worse, and even though it were worse, it must yet hold on to the name of Christ, and under the same introduce all kinds of mischiefs.

Thus he refers this passage to the last judgment, and names those who shall suffer judgment. Whence we infer what our young clerical gentlemen shall expect at the last day, be the time long or short.

And for all the hard speeches which Godless sinners have uttered against Him. There he at once strikes upon their life and preaching, and would say this much:— They speak fiercely and harshly against the Lord who is to come; they are shameless and proud; they deride and revile him, as St. Peter has said. He speaks not of their sinful, shameful life, but of their godless state. But the godless is he who lives without faith, although he leads a passable life outwardly. Outwardly wicked works are indeed the fruits of unbelief, but we speak more particularly of that as a godless state, where the heart is full of unbelief. These very godless ones the Lord will punish, he says, because their preaching is shameless and presumptuous, for they stick ever to their own wilfulness; do not permit themselves to be swayed at all, and are as hard as an anvil, to condemn and revile continually. Thus has Enoch struck in this passage at the very estate which before the last day should be in the world, as we now see it before our eyes. Jude says, further:

V. 16. *There are murmurers and complainers who walk after their own lusts, and their mouth speaketh swelling words.* When men will not let their own circumstances be fair and favorable, then there is nothing but murmuring and complaining. So when one does not give a Bishop the title he claims, then they cry out against disobedience. Besides, they are such a class of people as we cannot guard against, for they give out that they have a right over soul and body; they have grasped in their own hands both the civil and spiritual sword, so that they cannot be controlled, since no one must preach against them; they have got rid of all tax, tribute, and rent, so that no one dares to touch their wealth, besides, none dares preach a word without first asking them about it. And even though one should attack them with Scripture, yet they say that none but they only must be suffered to explain Scripture. Thus they live in all respects as they will, according to their lusts. For they cannot explain that to us, as they would be glad to, since we have subjected ourselves both to the Gospel and to the civil sword, but they would be free and uncontrolled of both. And, moreover, their whole law and claim is nothing but the fullness of mere high, proud, puffed-up words, which have nothing to back them.

And they hold themselves up for respect, for advantage sake. This is their way of judging all, according to the person; in all the Pope's laws, through and through, you do not once find that a bishop is to humble himself below a priest, or aim at anything, as the fruit of a christian walk,—but all is merely of this sort: the curate is to be subject to the priest, the priest subject to the bishop, the bishop to the archbishop, but he to the patriarch, the patriarch to the Pope, and after this, how each is to wear the robe, the tonsure and the cowl, possess so many churches and benefices.

Thus they have reduced it all to an outward matter, and such is the child's play and fool's work, they are driving at; and they have accounted it gross sin, if any one does not hold to such views. So that Jude says well, that they put a mask upon everything, and have this only before their eyes. Thus no one knows anything of faith, of love, nor of the Cross; whence the people generally are content to eat and play the fool, and devote all their property in the manner they do, as if to the true service of God; it is thus that they hold themselves up to respect for advantage sake.

V. 17, 18. *But, my beloved, remember ye the words that were said before by the Apostles of our Lord Jesus Christ, when they said to you that in the last times there should come scoffers who should walk after their own lusts, in a godless state.* This passage shows also clearly, that this epistle is not by St. Jude the Apostle, for he does not count nor reckon himself among the other Apostles, but speaks of them as of those who preached long before him; so that it is reasonable to suppose that another pious man wrote the epistle, one who had read St. Peter's epistles and had drawn this from that source. Who these scoffers are, we have said above: they walk, moreover, after their own lusts,—not merely their fleshly lusts, but those of that godless life which they lead, and they shape all as it pleases them; they care neither for worldly authority, nor the word of God; they are neither under external nor internal government, whether divine or human; they float about between heaven and earth in their lust, just as the devil leads them.

V. 19. *These are they who make sects, sensual, who have not the Spirit.* There he has touched on what Peter speaks of, their secretly bringing in of pestilent sects, for these are they that have separated themselves; they divide the unity that is in faith, will not let the ordinary estate of a Christian answer,—namely, that wherein one serves another,—but they set up other estates, and pretend to serve God by these. Besides they are sensual or brutish men, who have no more understanding and spirit than an ox or an ass; they walk according to their natural reason and fleshly mind. They have no God's-word by which they judge themselves, or by which they can live.

V. 20, 21. *But, ye beloved, build yourselves up on your most holy faith, through the Holy Spirit, and pray, and keep yourselves in the love of God.* There he defines, in few words, that in which a thoroughly Christian life consists. Faith is laid for the foundation on which we are to build; but to build is to grow from day to day in the knowledge of God and of Jesus Christ, and this takes place through the working of the Holy Spirit. When we are thus built up, we shall do no work to merit anything or to be saved by it, but all to the service of our neighbor. Thus we are to watch, that we abide in love, and not fall from it, like these fools who set up particular works and a peculiar life, and so draw people away from love.

And look for the mercy of our Lord Jesus Christ unto eternal life. That is the hope, toward which the Holy Cross moves. Therefore should our life be so shaped as to be nothing else than a steady longing and waiting for that life to come; yet so that that waiting be grounded on the mercy of Christ, so that we shall call upon Him with such an understanding as that he is to help us from this to that life out of pure mercy, and not for any work or merit of ours.

V. 22, 23. *And of these take pity, and distinguish them; but as to those, save them and draw them out of the fire.* That is not well expressed in Dutch, but Jude would say this much: on some take pity, some save; that is, let your life be so shaped that it shall allow you to have compassion on these who are wretched, blind and dumb; have no joy or pleasure over them, but let them go, keep from them and have nothing to do with them. But as to those others, whom ye can draw forth, save them by fear,—deal kindly and gently with them, as God has dealt with you; treat them not harshly or rudely, but feel toward them as toward those that lie in the fire, whom you are to draw forth and rescue with all care, consideration and diligence; if they will not suffer themselves to be drawn out, we should let them go and weep over them,—but not like the Pope and his inquisitors, burn and destroy them by fire.

And hate the garment spotted by the flesh. We have indeed received the Holy Spirit by faith, and have been made clean; but as long as we live here, the old garment of our flesh and blood clings to us still and will not relax its hold. This is the spotted garment that we should lay off and draw away from as long as we live.

V. 24, 25. *Now unto Him that is able to keep you from stumbling, and present you faultless before the presence of His glory with joy; to God who alone is wise, our Saviour, be glory and majesty, dominion and power, now and forever. Amen.* This is the close of this Epistle. Thus the Apostles do when they have written, taught, admonished and prophesied; thus they pray, express their wishes, and give thanks. Thus we have seen in the Epistles both what is true christian and false unchristian doctrine, as well as life.